Uncharted Waters

Dedicated to my very best sweetie, Bill Vossler

Copyright © February 2024 Nikki Rajala

Book Cover Design by 100 Covers
Photograph by Jenni Grandfield at Fort William Historical Park in Thunder Bay, Ontario, Canada.

ISBN 979-8-9854355-0-4

All rights reserved.

No part of this book may be reproduced or transmitted in any form or by any means, electronic or mechanical, including photocopying, recording or by any information storage and retrieval system, without permission in writing from the author.

Uncharted Waters

Book 3
The Chronicles of an
Unlikely voyageur

by
Nikki Rajala

Map of the route André and his crew traveled:

1. Lachine
2. Chaudière Falls
3. Grand Calumet
4. Baptism Point
5. Lake Nipissing, French River
6. British Fort St. Joseph
7. Green Bay

More accurate maps of the route are available on my website at nikkirajala.com under Resources.

CHAPTER 1

André, sweating and exhausted, hefted a chunk of wood to the chopping block, balanced it, eyed it and swung his ax.

Chonk. The wood split and fell to the ground.

"*Deux cents cinquante-six, deux cents cinquante-sept,*" he puffed after tossing them onto the pile: 256 and 257.

It's nearly midsummer—I should be steering one of Antoine's new birch bark canoes. Three weeks ago I should have left with his brigade for the rendezvous, but here I am, at home, missing adventure. If only I could have clerked in the fur trades. But after Mama took ill and Papa fell on his bad shoulder, what else could I do but stay to help them recover? My chance to be a voyageur is over. I'll be a villager forever. Or worse—in France under Denis' thumb. There's nothing like a big brother who does everything right and expects me to follow his footsteps.

Despite being surrounded by birdsong, the fully-leaved trees, an occasional butterfly or rabbit, the scent of cut wood—all which might have cheered him—André felt discouraged. He couldn't show it—his foster father, Joseph, was in the cottage not a hundred yards away, coaxing Berthe, his foster mother, to take her medicine.

Gritting his teeth, he balanced another chunk of wood, swung at it and sliced it evenly. Chonk. "*Deux cents cinquante-huit, deux cents cinquante-neuf,*" he grunted: 258 and 259. He glanced at the growing pile of split firewood. With one hand André wiped his sweaty forehead and with the other reached for another piece of wood as he tried once more to lose himself in the task. And added another dozen or two chunks of firewood to the pile.

Deux cents quatre-vingts. Deux cents quatre-vingt-un. Deux cents quatre-vingt-deux. Deux cents quatre-vingt-trois: 280, 281, 282, 283.

The gate near the cottage creaked open. André twisted to stare as three persons entered their yard.

Dread struck. Then confusion.

First marched two British soldiers in fancy uniforms—red wool coats with shiny buttons and light breeches—carrying long muskets. With bayonets! André tried not to panic.

Soldiers of the crown! What could they want? Did I break a law? I try to abide by British laws, even ones that don't make sense.

Following them limped Michel Parrant, a short shabby teen, his eyes darting everywhere but at André.

Michel? He made my life miserable, calling me "Good for Nothing" when I came home from tutoring lessons. What's he doing helping redcoats? Collaborating is dangerous business.

The three intruders ranged themselves in a line. The tall redcoat broke the silence, in English. "Well?"

"*C'est lui,*" Michel said. It's him. He slumped, ashamed.

André quailed, despising Michel. *He's making trouble for me, for us? Probably got paid. I'll act dumb—stall until I know what's going on.*

"Liar," muttered the tall redcoat, in English. "No sash, too young to grow a beard and lives on a substantial farm besides, so he can't be the one. Oh well, we're here. Have him tell us his name."

André did not want them to know he was one of the few French-Canadians who spoke English. He waited tensely, letting them think he was a peasant, a *habitant*.

The short soldier spoke in French, slowly and loudly: "Tell ... the name. ... We want ... to know ... your name ... is. And your age."

André understood the tall man to be the superior officer, the short one his interpreter.

"*Je suis André Didier. Je suis seize,*" he answered in French, hoping to control the flutter in his voice that would give away his anxiety. *Do they know Didier is Joseph's name but not mine, that I am a Quevillon from France? Is Denis in trouble?*

But there was no sign of any interest as the interpreter repeated his name and age to his superior.

"Name's right but that's all. He's too tall, hair's not dark, like the rest of these Frenchy *habitants*, and sixteen ain't old enough to sign on to brigades," the tall soldier snarled, continuing in English. "Ask if he took canoes into the interior. This sour-looking fellow who led us here must be lying—voyageurs are full of themselves. Can't trust any of 'em. It's a wild goose chase to make us look foolish, it is."

The other obeyed. "You are ... er, before now ... the *voyageur*? Into ... far lands?"

"*Je suis un voyageur*," André said. He looked at their haughty faces and straightened his shoulders. In French, he said, "I am a winterer, a Northman, not a pork-eater. Two winters I have lived in the upper country, the *pays d'en haut*, trading with the natives. Four times I have crossed Lake Superior. In the last brigade, I was a steersman—for Antoine Felix."

He waited to see if that name held sway, but they seemed unaware that Antoine was a top brigade guide in the fur trade. Michel glanced at him and quickly averted his eyes.

André lifted his head proudly and gave them look for look while the underling translated. *I won't quiver under their sneers. Though I am nervous about them—they could imprison me for any trumped-up reason. Why are they here?*

His neighbors, all French-Canadian villagers, felt the sting of being deemed inferior by their British overlords. Fearing retribution, they found it difficult to advocate for themselves, especially in English.

The redcoats exchanged a glance as they conferred. The leader said, "Don't like his high-nosed air. And he's still holding his ax. But he sounds capable. Tell him who I am."

"This officer ... he is ... Sergeant Sommers." The tall man's nose went up to show this peasant his importance.

"Tell him he is to see the colonel at headquarters."

"We bring ... summons ... from Colonel Markham ... at the fort in Montreal. ... You will ... follow us."

"*Moi? Pourquoi?*" André squeaked out. Me? Why? He was terrified. His worst fears had materialized—he would be questioned by a British military leader. What had he done?

"Colonel Markham … he is important. He will speak … with you. We leave now."

André started to plead that he must tell his foster parents what was happening, that they would worry.

Sergeant Sommers watched André. "The colonel said now."

The translator jabbed his bayonet at André. "We go. Now. Walk between."

He slumped, submitting to his fate. White-faced and shaken, André set aside his ax, afraid of the the soldiers' bayonets—and what this Colonel Markham might want—and started walking. He didn't dare look back. He didn't see Michel slip away.

Why was I called in? I'm sure I did nothing wrong. Should I have taken the ax, use it to my advantage? No, bad idea—they have bayonets.

Though no one saw him when they paraded through the village, André felt humiliated. *People are hiding behind their curtains, peeking out their windows. What will they think of me? Are villagers ever released from British prisons? Maybe someone will pass a message to Papa and Mama about what's happened. Everyone likes Papa, and many villagers get healing herbs from Mama when they're sick. Will I ever see them again?*

They marched for more than an hour before halting outside a large wooden stockade. From stone guard towers at the corners, soldiers aimed guns in every direction—and at them.

At the gate, two hard-faced guards quickly crossed their muskets to prevent unauthorized entry.

"Halt. State your business."

Sergeant Sommers saluted the guards, reported his errand and was allowed inside. He disappeared while the interpreter stayed with André, puffed up with the importance of capturing what could be an enemy spy.

But guards in red uniforms seemed uninterested in this French-Canadian *habitant*.

After Sergeant Sommers returned, the three of them were passed from sentry to sentry across the bustling compound. André peered at a dozen white-washed buildings, crested with flags and pennants snapping in the light summer breeze. An open grassy yard teemed with platoons of soldiers marching in time to a drumbeat and responding to loud and rapid commands. Several teams manhandled heavy iron cannons. *Will their jail be placed near the edge of the stockade or in the center? What will happen to me now?*

Finally he was escorted to a brick building with a small glass window. The interpreter pointed to the outside wall where André could wait—small comfort under the midday sun. He watched a troop of new soldiers drill, looking uncomfortable in stiff uniforms and clumsy with their muskets.

Grateful for the place to rest, André realized he was thirsty. He looked at his dirty hands and dingy clothes, compared to the soldiers' fine bright uniforms. *How should I conduct myself? What defense can I make? If I'm imprisoned, how will Papa and Mama manage? What will they tell Denis?*

Time droned on. Flies buzzed his ears while he waited and worried. His case was no longer urgent to his guards. First one left and, when he returned, the other disappeared.

Chapter 2

All winter, André had struggled with his contract for employment, starting after New Year's when Antoine announced tumultuous news: after Simon McTavish, the head of the North West Company, had died in July of 1804, the fur trading company had quickly merged with their rival, the XY Company. Suddenly, with less competition, fewer men were needed on the brigades and at fur trade posts serving the interior. So Antoine, as a head trader for the North West Company, would supervise two posts, including the one André had managed a winter ago.

Not being chosen to lead that post disappointed André. *True, my returns were mediocre but my tallies were accurate and my accounts clear. True, I'm untrained and younger than most. But I was sure they'd offer me a position. Or at least compliment my work of taking it over when no one else could.*

Instead, André had signed a five-year contract as a underclerk to go far north. He had imagined crossing icy wild rivers studded with boulders to trade in trackless deep piney forests. That dream had lasted barely a fortnight.

In February, Mama fell ill with lung fever, barely able to breathe. Gasping and too weak to eat, she neared death. She was the village's herbalist—there was no doctor and few others knew which herbs she needed or how to prepare them. Barely a week later Papa had slipped on a patch of ice, injuring his already-scarred shoulder.

They need me, especially now that Papa can't cut firewood or do heavy chores around the cottage. Fair's fair. They immigrated to New France years ago, sacrificing their comfort for my brother and me. With Denis back in France, it's up to me to return their kindness. It's the only honorable thing.

So André had canceled his contract.

But that didn't make him feel honorable. The loss increased his thirst for adventure. His mood had darkened, though he'd hidden it from Papa and Mama.

◈ ◈ ◈

As soon as the spring ice broke on the St. Lawrence, ships came upriver with trade goods and mail. They'd received a letter from Denis, a thick oiled canvas packet tied with string and inside, crisp sheets of parchment, sealed in wax with a fancy design—the family crest. It reminded him of the first letter they'd ever received four years before, when he learned that his real parents had died, that he had a brother Denis, that the two had been sent to New France with Berthe and Joseph Didier who had fostered him for a dozen years.

That first letter opened a whole new life for him. With this one, his hopes plummeted as he felt pressure to live up to his brother's expectations.

André had read aloud Denis' news to his foster parents, who had sent him to be schooled by the priest but had never learned to read themselves.

Denis wrote: "God willing, this year we will welcome our first child. My dear Marie-Thérèse has already lost two babies, but this time she seems strong and healthy. André, do return at Christmastime to France for the baptism. Grandfather is getting on in years and asks to see you."

At that Mama sighed, dreaming of a new baby, of returning to their beloved homeland.

Denis related unsettling information as well. "Napoleon Bonaparte is quite the figure. Building his empire needs an army, so I volunteered as a captain. My troops and I showed ourselves well—until my horse stepped in a rabbit hole and fell. I could not leap away fast enough and was trapped beneath the horse, one of my legs crushed. Months ago, I returned home to recover, but the bones refuse to bind properly. Now that summer approaches, the army will be called again. Could you come here and serve in my stead? Our men would stand behind you—and our estate would receive honor."

Who cares about the French army? We've barely heard of Bonaparte in New France. I know nothing about sword-fighting or armies—I've never ridden a horse. How could I lead as their captain?

"Marie-Thérèse has made a dear friend of Agnes, our neighbor. Her family comes from dukes—so the man she marries will inherit her family estates, which are much larger than ours. It would be an excellent match for us. She is comely."

Denis had scratched out "us" and replaced it with "you."

Marry someone I haven't set eyes on? Never. I won't do it. I don't want to become a soldier or oversee an estate with my brother. He had his chance for adventure—I want mine, to be chosen as a head clerk on the fur brigades. I'll rise in importance and Denis will find someone else to help manage the family estate.

"Berthe's sister and Joseph's nephews ask often about them. We hope they fare well. People here cannot imagine the life of settlers in New France, and it's hard to describe. Their families send fond greetings and deeply yearn to be reunited."

André looked at Papa's glowing face. *They haven't laid eyes on their kin for a dozen years—of course they long to return to France. But to give them the joy of returning, do I have to deny my own dreams?*

Before this difficult winter, André had felt his own destiny calling him. When they both had needed care, the dream dissolved. Wanting a life for himself, wanting to be on a canoe brigade, made André feel selfish for his desire, and unworthy.

But now he awaited a worse future—in a British prison.

Chapter 3

It was another hour before André was brought inside from the hot sun and noisy exercise yard. When his stomach growled, he realized he'd missed his dinner. He was not invited to sit—only men of great importance, high-ranking soldiers and prosperous community merchants were offered that courtesy, not those wearing soiled homespun clothes.

A half-dozen people waited on benches for their turn to enter. One by one, they were admitted to a closed office to speak to the person inside. Others came, and occasionally their turns took priority over everyone else's.

Which oddly relieved André. Without knowing why he was there, each moment surrounded by the members of the British army increased his anxiety, but his case was evidently not pressing.

At last he heard his name called, and the translator prodded him. "Go now. Hurry."

André lurched forward, the translator's elbow still hard in his side.

Sergeant Sommers was already inside, explaining. "Sir, this here's André Didier. Says he knows the route. But these fellows that travel canoe country are too independent by half, if you ask me. If you offered a third of the standard rate, he'd grab it—they have no idea of money."

That scorn made André's blood rise, but he kept his face carefully blank, pretending he didn't understand the English words. Something worse—being interrogated by a British officer—was to come and he needed to be unencumbered by emotion.

"Dismissed, Sergeant."

Surprised, Sergeant Sommers and the translator saluted and they turned on their heels and left.

Now I'm alone. No witnesses. Now what?

Just before they closed the door, a runner darted inside, calling, "Urgent message for the colonel. Urgent." He panted—apparently having run for some distance. The messenger wore rough buckskins, like many of the winterers André knew.

When André dared, he watched as the officer sitting at the desk accepted a packet wrapped in oiled paper and broke open its tie sealed with wax drippings. The officer scanned the letter inside, then sifted through the papers on his desk and extracted one to compare the messages. After releasing the messenger, he read for several minutes.

André examined this important colonel, *Markham, was it*? He appeared to be Joseph's age or older, his hair graying. He wore a new uniform full of gold lace on the collar, heavy epaulets on his shoulders, buff facings on the cuffs. Such finery alarmed André. *And here I am in my oldest clothes, patched and torn. Even my hands are dirty. Why am I here?*

"Do sit," the officer finally said, pausing to verify the name, "André Didier." He indicated a chair facing him. He held himself erect and met André's look with an open gaze.

André sat, surprised. The attempt at hospitality made him nervous. *Why did he ask me to sit? So I don't run away? Because I can't, guarded by all those soldiers.*

"I am Colonel Markham," the officer began, in clear and understandable French. "You look too young to already have had several years' experience in the fur trade. Your age?"

"Sir, I am nearly seventeen," he announced in French. "I first went with the brigades when I was thirteen. I ..." André started to boast, but held back. *This man already knows about me.*

"That squares with what Father Goiffon said. I understand he's tutored you for some years. He described you as honest, loyal and kind, fair, motivated and adaptable, all of which are important to me."

André glowed briefly at Father Goiffon's compliments. Then he stopped short, trembling. *Is this a trick, using kindness, manipulating me into compromising? I'd better be careful.*

"I command soldiers on behalf of His Majesty, the King of England," the colonel continued. "But today I am faced with a dilemma that requires a *voyageur's* assistance. The problem is this —a young child must be transported with all due speed to Fort St. Joseph, a British fort on Lake Huron near Michilimackinac. I cannot assign soldiers to this task—it is not why we train them. Nor do they have the necessary expertise to handle a canoe over the Ottawa River. However, Father Goiffon believes that you might be willing to organize such a venture."

Stunned at the turn-around from what he'd expected, André took a deep breath. Then he spoke, flatly, disappointed. "*Non, c'est impossible.* It cannot be done, so late in the season. The best canoemen left three weeks ago and more, as you must surely know. Nor have I been the leader. *Non, c'est impossible.*"

"True. It's what he said you'd say. Nonetheless I ask you to attempt it—as a British officer, I would have no success in attracting a crew of French-Canadians. Fortunately a child will have little baggage, so such a journey will not require a freight canoe and perhaps only a half-dozen paddlers. Your task, if you will assist me, is to arrange for appropriate crew—which can include yourself. I will see to the canoe, provisions and your other needs. You will be amply compensated. There will be commendations for a job well done and possible further employment, should you wish. Will you undertake it for me?"

André hesitated. The colonel offered the exact thing he desperately wanted—to canoe again into the vast wilderness, the *pays d'en haut*. For a brief second, at the mention of commendations and employment, he imagined important people eager to shake his hand, bowing his head to accept an award, being offered a ceremonial sword for their gratitude, Denis standing in awe.

But ... is there something sinister behind the offer? This Colonel Markham seems straightforward, even sincere. Is that part of a ruse to distract me?

Stalling for time to think. André answered slowly, "*Oui*, perhaps I can learn which able *voyageurs* remain in the hamlets." *How do I go about finding and choosing a crew?*

"Search for the best men available, to be sure, but in gathering this crew, look for qualities beyond the usual bravado, strength and skill. Now, about the canoe, I have already made inquiries—one of a smaller size is already in progress. Inspect it to ensure that it will be sufficient. I shall requisition the standard provisioning, a few trade goods for barter, other needed supplies and advance wages for paddlers. Summer is rapidly approaching and I must settle this—a regiment I command will leave soon. I will hear your report in two days, shall we say?"

Having ended the interview, Colonel Markham looked down again at the papers on his desk, examining the new letter and another that seemed connected.

André waited—and waited.

"Yes, what is it?"

"Am I to be arrested, imprisoned? Am I a collaborator?" André burst out, and then wished he hadn't.

"No, André Didier," the colonel smiled and stood. "Despite what you may have heard, British soldiers are decent and fair. This task—to transport a child—is entirely separate from other military missions and local government enforcement. It is a personal request, not an official one." He extended his hand, to shake André's.

Chapter 4

A different guard escorted André from the office and led him to the compound's entrance gate.

André basked in the compliments of the colonel, and the possibilities of organizing an express canoe he'd been requested to undertake. He envisioned the reunion of the parent and child—a young son sadly waving goodbye to André, who'd become his valued teacher and friend, a grateful father offering his profuse gratitude, or money which André would modestly refuse, a community cheering his canoe full of *voyageurs* as heroes.

What a switch! I expected the worst, and instead this is the best thing that could happen—organize and maybe lead a brigade. If only I had watched the spring leave-taking I'd know who's already gone. But I was too dispirited. Or too proud.

Then he paused—and sighed. *For all the loyalty Father Goiffon spoke of, I forgot to mention my foster parents—how could I leave? Papa still needs help to care for Mama. I'll have to stay here, unless there is an important reason why I must go.*

He was still musing when, a mile beyond the fort's entrance gate, a boy peeked from behind a tree where he was hiding.

"André—wait, wait."

"Michel?" André said, leery. "You led those British soldiers right to our cottage." *He was mean when I needed a friend. And he looks like he sleeps in his clothes.*

"They forced me. I was scared, but I couldn't run away."

André nodded. His community of *habitants* understood the conflicting alternatives when living under another country's rule.

"Thank God they released you." Michel showed genuine concern. "I planned to wait another hour. If you didn't come out, then I'd run back to tell your family."

"*Merci*, Michel," André said. "They would need to know."

"Did they beat you? Threaten you? Force you to confess? Or trick you into spying?"

"*Non.* They need my help."

"Isn't that being a collaborator?" Michel asked.

André suddenly felt unsure. *The colonel didn't ask me to observe things and report back to him.* He wanted to impress Michel. "An important officer asked me to deliver by express canoe a small boy to his father at a British fort near Michilimackinac. I was highly recommended. I am to engage paddlers, approve the canoe, see to the details and numerous tasks in preparation—and probably lead the voyage."

"It doesn't sound like spying."

"*Non.* I'm doing the colonel a personal favor. Returning the boy to his father is something his soldiers can't do."

Both looked away, aware that a favor could be twisted into a different mission. There were many ifs. André's heroic vision of himself faded.

"If all goes well, if we have a quick voyage, I could find a fur post, help them out over the winter and return after the summer *rendezvous*. But first I must locate six or seven good strong *voyageurs*. The best men are gone, but a few paddlers with skill should be around. Papa will help me sort it out."

"Take me," Michel blurted. "I'll go."

André, astounded, turned to face him.

"I always wanted to go with the brigades, such exciting stories the *voyageurs* tell about shooting the rapids, living with the tribes. I dreamed I might live that life. Please, André—let me go with you." His eyes begged.

André debated—Michel had been cruel. He looked gaunt and disheveled. But he was an apprentice, with work.

Michel hung his head. "I know. What right do I have to ask you for kindness? I taunted you and I'm ashamed. But I was envious, André. I wanted schooling like you and it made me feel better to make you feel bad. I regretted being mean but I couldn't say it. I am sorry, truly I am. If you choose me for the brigade, you'll see I'm not that person. You won't regret it."

A memory washed over André of what it had meant to be accepted as a canoeman on his first trip. He shared the same hope. With his own hunger for adventure, his heart softened.

"I need excellent men with experience, trustworthy men. I'll pick the best available, with probably a dozen to choose from, so don't count on it. And you're limping—how can you carry on portages? But you waited for me today—that was kind."

It made no difference to Michel. He looked delighted at this slim ray of hope.

"As the leader, I couldn't show you any favoritism," André went on. "You'd be the greenest one, so the crew will tell you everything you do wrong. They push hard on the new hires."

"Others, they have experience, but me, I learn fast."

"Then again, there's Mama, as sick as she is. First I must talk with them. Maybe I won't even go myself." *She's not well enough for me to leave. What kind of a foster son would desert parents in need?*

"Before you go home, we could leave messages around the village and pass the word to get people talking so you can get the best *voyageurs*."

André was impressed with Michel's suggestion. Michel stood taller and limped less as they visited have a dozen public houses on the way.

So, Michel could be one paddler. Two, with me. I need at least four or five more. If I can find good men, this undertaking could be possible. How ironic that a British colonel has given me another chance at life—and not just to organize, but to lead. It will establish me as a person of worth, so the fur companies will take note of my abilities. It could be my last opportunity.

For the first time in months, André felt hopeful.

CHAPTER 5

After André related his unusual assignment to Papa, then he turned to Mama's health. "The *pays d'en haut*, the upper country, it has been in my mind—I've wanted to return. But you both need me more—I should've told the colonel that I couldn't go. I ... I ... Perhaps I'll only help to organize this brigade."

"André, do you not see?" Papa said. "Each day my Berthe, she grows stronger. This afternoon she walked to her chair outside to sit in the sun. Walked by herself she did, with only her cane. It took her a little longer, to be sure, but last week she had none of that strength. Our neighbor girl, Geneviève, says Berthe needs fewer strengthening herbs. Of course you can go. Between Geneviève and me, we will manage. Of course you must go."

André had forgotten that Geneviève, a young helper, had visited each day. "On our way home Michel and I, we announced it at a few taverns. You remember Michel? He used to tease, but maybe he's not so bad. Anyway, he volunteered, even though he's unlikely to be on my crew. How do I choose paddlers for a single canoe?"

"Gathering a crew is more than placing men in the canoe," Papa mused. "Most brigades aren't like Antoine's, where men simply paddle hard. Oh, *non*, an express voyage, that calls for men who think for you. They see problems you didn't notice, suggest ideas you haven't thought of. Your men must be committed to the task, not just out for their own benefit, especially because they are to carry a child. It helps when they have a stake—not just wages. Even when you make unpopular decisions, they'll be inspired to follow you."

Surprised, André nodded. *Unpopular decisions? They won't simply do what a leader asks? I must inspire them?*

"Tell me again about this Colonel Markham."

"The colonel seems a decent man with a problem that soldiers can't solve. He consulted with Father Goiffon, who recommended me. Is it collaborating or spying if I don't report back?" André needed reassurance.

Papa smoked his pipe in silence for some minutes. "*Non*. But has this colonel thought of how difficult it is, how daunting, to be a lone canoe? Being part of a large brigade means others can help when you have trouble. To be responsible all the time will be exhausting—and a leader must depend on his crew."

André slumped. Depending on others had never been easy for him.

"And the child. He won't be able to sit in a canoe for long hours. How do you keep a small one safe, with many dangers? It will be up to you to protect him—while you are directing the canoemen," Papa said.

"Maybe it's better if the venture doesn't work—for me anyway," André said, overwhelmed by the complexity of the task.

"There are always a few skilled paddlers around. Men like me, men who no longer have their strength, or their knee is lame," Papa pointed out. "Your crew doesn't have to be the strongest men. Instead, good men who have had troubles, they may be better ones to choose."

"Perhaps some signed on but did not paddle with their brigade," Mama said, her voice faint from rarely speaking during her long convalescence.

André was pleased to see her following the conversation, frail as she was.

"Perhaps, my dear," Papa answered, scratching his head thoughtfully. "But that kind of person couldn't be relied on to ferry a child. A man who skips out of his contract thinks of nothing but his own desires. With such a one in your canoe, it would be chancy to carry valuable trade goods and money for wages. You would always have to watch, lest he try to rob you."

"What about that young man Emile, your *devant*? The one who married Geneviève's sister after the last brigade?" Mama said. "He might encourage men to sign on. Don't worry, André. As smart and kind as you are, you will find the right kind of canoemen. Of that I am sure."

Non, André concluded, after they had considered all sides of the problem late into the evening. *There are too many problems. I told the colonel that it wasn't possible. Even with a canoe and good men, how could I be responsible for the welfare of a child? It's too much of a risk. I hoped a door was opening, to let my dream come true. I have to shut it.*

Chapter 6

André sought out Emile Felix, Antoine's younger brother. Once a steersman, now Emile worked on his father-in-law's farm. He no longer sported his colorful sash, but he looked content.

"Marriage suits you," André grinned. "Don't you miss being in a brigade?"

"*Oui*, oh so much. When the canoes left Lachine, I felt lost. But I looked at my lovely Marguerite, and all was well again. You see, in just a few months I will be a father. And a sober crofter—I am building us a house. You must see it."

When André explained his errand, Emile's eyes danced. "Oho, the fast water, it is in your blood!"

"Not only paddle—I might even lead!"

"Being a leader—that's harder than it looks. Alas, it takes more out of Antoine every year. Did you see gray streaks in his beard? But already he is thirty-four. No matter, let us look at this canoe—and then, then we select your crew."

When they arrived at the canoe maker, they learned that a British officer had sent orders—and money to pay for a new canoe. It would be finished in a day or so. André's spirits soared

"Such a little canoe, it'll be easier to paddle on the rivers," Emile said. "On big waters like Lake Huron, though, it will take every bit of your skill to keep this one steady. The Montreal canoes, so long and heavy with the weight of all that cargo and a dozen paddlers, they hold their own. This one, I don't know how it'll fare against those rolling waves on the big lakes."

"Come with us, Emile. To paddle without you, it seems

wrong. Besides, I don't know all the things a *devant* knows—the route, when to tow the canoe at a rapids or when to portage, the best places to camp, so many things you know."

Emile's smile was rueful. "Me—or part of me—I wish it also. What good times we've had, eh, André? But with a little one on the way, I cannot. A son, I am sure, and you must be his godfather. Perhaps he too will be a *voyageur*?"

I so hoped Emile would go.

They stopped by taverns and inns where many old *voyageurs* regaled them with stories of their harrowing adventures, their pranks, their camaraderie.

But Emile's charisma didn't convince them to sign on.

"You feel glum, André, but think—these men, they will tell others and soon everyone will know."

"What of Michel Parrant? I don't know if I trust him, though he apologized sincerely. Michel wants to be a friend."

"That you must decide yourself, André. As the leader, you must feel good about your crew."

"He's thin and he limps. Will he be strong enough?"

"You yourself, André, you once struggled to carry a single pack, much less two."

"Fair enough. On my first trip I was eager, and so is Michel. But I didn't realize how much work canoemen do. You and Pretty Mouse took me under your wing."

"All men as we met today, they boast—they can paddle for hours upon hours, carry extra packs with ease. Perhaps it is true. But Antoine, if he believes they do not have the right kind of heart, he will not hire them."

That I didn't expect. I believe Michel's honest apology reflects the right kind of heart.

"We leave soon. I need strong *voyageurs*."

"Good men, they will come. André, this venture will be a success."

André believed him. He walked lightly, smiling.

Chapter 7

But as he neared home, discouraged at their lack of quick success, André's step became a slow trudge. He pondered Emile's advice.

What if there are no canoemen because everyone is already en route to the rendezvous? Will the colonel abandon the brigade? Or worse—what if the paddlers are all better than I am, so I can't go, or lead? Do I want Michel with me—would I have to teach him? What can he add?

He halted as his eyes lit upon a man walking unsteadily ahead of him. A wave of familiarity hit him. *Could it be ...?*

André ran to catch up to him, and tugged his arm. A battered and scarred face turned toward him.

"Pretty Mouse?" he cried. "Pretty Mouse, it is you. But how is it that you're here? You were supposed to go far north this year!"

Pretty Mouse looked dolefully at his feet.

"Oh, André, Me, I am so ashamed. I wrote my name on a contract, not just the X but my whole name. You know how good that feels? You are wanted, you have a place, and they advance you a few *livres* from your wages to get a new shirt, pay your debts. But you must wait for the starting day. So I found myself in a tavern, telling my friends I will go to Swan River. I was thirsty for high wine. I thought, just one taste, maybe two—but still I was thirsty. Two became three, and more besides. I spent all my advance and still I was thirsty. Then the brigades left—without me. *Oui*, so it was. Now I have no money. I have lost my place. Forever, for I must pay them back or no brigade will ever hire me again. Where will I find the money? And me, I am disgraced." He hung his head, distraught.

"But Pretty Mouse," André cried joyously. "You are just the man I am looking for. I am to lead an express voyage almost to Michilimackinac—and I need a *gouvernail*. I need you! We could be paddling by next week."

"You want me? Do you mean it?" Pretty Mouse looked at André, his plea choked with tears, his eyes huge.

"Or, you could be our guide, figuring out which part of the river we should take, spotting rocks that threaten to rip our canoe. What do you think?" André realized that he'd placed Pretty Mouse in the bow, not the stern where the *gouvernail* steered.

Pretty Mouse straightened as he gazed towards the river, imagining the honor and responsibility of being a steersman. With a grin, he wrapped André in a great bear hug. "You have saved me—twice. Me, I would like nothing better than to paddle with you." He hooked André's arm and swirled him around like a dance partner.

How lucky! André felt like shouting. Here was his old companion from two voyages and two winters, a man he trusted, a man with skill and experience, a man with a kind heart.

When Mama spoke of someone who defaulted on their contract, Papa said that kind of person couldn't be trusted, especially around children. But who could be better than Pretty Mouse? Antoine had already vouched for him.

Good old Pretty Mouse! The nickname was a joke, for his homely face was anything but pretty. Nor was he mouse-like, but bold and talkative. Gladness spread through André.

Mouse's acceptance made the task easier. With four more strong paddlers, he could include Michel. Pretty Mouse would surely lead him to others to complete the crew.

In the rush to the cottage to share his good news, he fairly bounced.

Chapter 8

The whole next day, André waited at home for men to come to him, to ask to paddle with him. To fill the time, he spaded a new kitchen garden for Mama. While he weeded, he puzzled over the details of organizing a voyage, events that must be imagined before they ever put a paddle in the water.

But no *voyageurs* inquired.

In the late afternoon, he added a dozen herbs to the garden. As he watered the new plants, he began to accept that the journey might not take place. *I thought Emile's energy would draw men to our door today. But no one knocked to inquire. If it's only Mouse and me—and Michel—we can't go. I hate to admit that I've failed. I hate to disappoint Colonel Markham.*

By sunset, well after his foster parents had turned in for the night, André had finished weaving a willow fence to keep rabbits out of the new garden. But he was crushed, his plans for naught.

Waiting in the twilight and his personal gloom, he didn't notice a tall figure coming out of the forest.

"André Didier?" said a quiet, echoing voice. "Is this the cottage of André Didier who is going soon to western lands, the *pays d'en haut*?"

André snapped out of his reverie. The man's straight black braids accentuated his native heritage. This man would have plenty of experience in canoes. Relief washed over him.

"I am André, and bound for the British fort, not far from Michilimackinac. Have you knowledge of those parts?"

"Where the waters of the two great lakes meet—that I know. The old fort I also know."

"Where does your tribe live?"

"Seven sleeps past Michilimackinac in the direction of the setting sun, miles inland from Green Bay."

"Excellent! You are Ojibwe? You speak other languages?"

"*Oui.* A little bit, anyway."

"What is your name?"

"I am Reynard."

"Do you steer, or guide?"

"*Non,* I paddle *milieu* and carry."

"Tell me of your experience. Why do you want to go on this voyage?"

Reynard explained he'd grown up paddling, but never as a *voyageur.* His chief had sent him far away to hear the wisdom of two Shawnee leaders, Tecumseh and his prophet-brother. While there, he'd taken ill with a contagion, and only now was he strong enough to make his way back.

"I must return to my tribe—in dreams they call to me. My people need to hear what I have learned."

André paused. *Antoine would like Reynard. He's gone on a distant quest on behalf of his people, a difficult deed—that's the right kind of heart. And they live somewhere around Lake Michigan, so he won't desert before we deliver the boy. Then again, he hasn't paddled the Ottawa River. But he certainly has more skills than he mentioned. He doesn't boast like voyageurs do, but is honest about his ability—and I have confidence in him.*

"I can't say yet if this venture will go—I seek three more strong paddlers," André said truthfully. "But if it does, I'll count you among the crew. Can you come back tomorrow?"

Reynard nodded, took a step back and disappeared into the shadows.

André's shoulders relaxed. Hope surged. He looked up and saw a star twinkling. Suddenly he wanted to sing and shout, he was so happy. Too bad Papa and Mama were already asleep.

Chapter 9

Early the next morning, before Papa and Mama had risen, André left to see Colonel Markham. He dressed carefully in a clean shirt and trousers and his best sash. But that didn't make up for the hard fact of having only three skilled paddlers. Even with Michel, it was not enough to accomplish the colonel's mission. He felt defeated.

If I ask for more time, every day we wait lowers the river—and soon it'll be a month since the last brigades left. The word is out in the village and no one came yesterday. Unfortunately the colonel will have to find another way to send this child.

For these last days, even after being scared about British prisons, I was excited about life. But it's over. When Mama gains enough strength, we'll sail back to France like Denis wants. I'll end up helping to run his farm and join his army and be married to someone they pick for me.

He walked slowly along the river, wishing he had better news to report.

❖ ❖ ❖

Outside a tavern not far from the river path, André was stopped by two older men, shabbily-dressed, their sashes faded. One doffed the knitted *tuque* covering his head—and poked his friend to follow suit.

The first man spoke for them, while the other stood shyly behind, his hair a wild mane with gray strands. They reeked—of high wines and no bath, André guessed.

"You are André, the one who is looking for paddlers?"

André nodded. "That I am."

"How lucky that you, you have come to us so we do not need to find your cottage. Me, I am Jean-Baptiste, but there are so many Jean-Baptistes that I go by Baptiste now. My friend here, he is Gabriel. We are *voyageurs*, just the ones you seek!" Baptiste blustered. "Whatever you want, we can do it. Me, I'm a middleman. Gabriel, he also paddles *milieu*."

They must be forty years old—or more. Are they strong enough? Probably not, but I can at least listen to them. "When were you last on a brigade? And where?"

"Quite some years ago it was. Me, I don't rightly recall the exact year," Baptiste said, narrowing his eyes. "Only once together, we wintered west of Lake Winnipeg."

"What rivers were you on? Who were your *devant* and *gouvernail*?"

Baptiste took a breath, preparing to answer.

"Wait," André said to Baptiste. "Let Gabriel speak. I'd like to hear him too."

Gabriel looked overwhelmed. He kept his eyes down. Finally he said slowly, "Rivers? The Ottawa, that one I remember. The Mattawa, the French, … ."

André grimaced. "Everyone paddles those rivers. After the summer *rendezvous* at Grand Portage, where did you go?"

It took Gabriel several seconds. "Lakes. Big lakes. And little rivers too."

"What post did you winter at?"

Gabriel puzzled for a few moments, shrugged and shook his head apologetically, pointing to his head. "The name, it is gone."

André turned to Baptiste, who answered, "Portage la Prairie. With Pierre and Louis Marier."

"Now tell me of your experience."

Baptiste frowned. "Not a good one, that's for sure. The bitterest winter they'd had in years, and we froze. Because the Cree got sick and couldn't hunt, we all but starved. The beavers were so few we barely filled the canoe to take to the *rendezvous*. Long days of paddling and carrying heavy packs."

"Why do you want to go?"

"We need money," Gabriel blurted, and Baptiste winced.

"*Oui,* wages." André was disappointed. *They'll probably quit as soon as they earn enough for high wines.*

"This trip, it doesn't seem so hard as the fur brigades," Gabriel added. "Me, I can't carry all that cargo."

"One more reason, a small one," Baptiste said. "All my family, they are gone but for one nephew. He is Jean-Baptiste, like me. Named for me and paddled with me on a few brigades. But after a five-year contract or two, he never came back from the *pays d'en haut.* I want to find him. We will ask and maybe we will find him. Or maybe not. This trip, it's the first time, the only time, we could ask."

André had serious qualms about the pair. "What happened to Gabriel?"

Baptiste's bravado wilted. "He fell. 'Twas on our way back that first year—down a rocky portage, hit his head and got knocked silly. After that he wasn't right. Too slow to paddle on the next brigade, or again. A few years later, he needed more help so I stopped paddling too. Now I do odd jobs to feed us."

Not ideal. But they have wintered—that's good. To care for his friend shows his humanity—many old canoemen subsist on only a few livres a year, and Baptiste gave up earning money to be sure his mate survived. That's the kind of heart Antoine would value. They wouldn't be a danger to a child. Do they have enough stamina to paddle for long hours? I feel for them, but I don't see how these two old men can help.

André gazed at Gabriel and then Baptiste, who said nothing. He gently dismissed them. "Sorry, but I'm looking for young men, strong men."

"This late in the season there's not many around who can go," Baptiste said. "Old as we are—we still know a thing or two."

As they shuffled away, Papa's words from an earlier year rang in André's ears, "Think about the choices you skipped over—they may give you a good idea. The impossible is always possible, but it takes longer."

❖ ❖ ❖

André walked slowly to the British fort, wondering what to say to the colonel. He mentally tried placing them in various positions for paddling.

Counting Baptiste and Gabriel makes six. They're old but they could pull, with Michel a shade better. Reynard doesn't want to steer, but he could. Pretty Mouse is the only possible gouvernail. I'll be devant—though guiding from the bow is a lot for me to learn. But sometimes we could swap places. Mouse would flourish with the importance of being in front and I could steer from the stern like before. Still these six are not enough. I wish others had come forth. I'll have to accept it that we're not going.

Chapter 10

At the guard house, the sentinel had no permission for André to enter so he waited. Without fear, he observed officers drill recruits, commanding them to turn precisely or stop as a group. Teams of soldiers manhandled large bales out of a building while other groups cleaned muskets or practiced aiming cannons. But the glint from their weapons set his teeth on edge. *They're so intent and purposeful—to what end? Oh well—at least I'm not here under suspicion, like last time.*

Many minutes later, the two soldiers who'd come to his cottage appeared, looking less sure of themselves this time. Sergeant Sommers nodded to the interpreter, who said in his halting French, "Colonel Markham sends ... his compliments. This way ... please."

André smiled inwardly. *Much more respectful. Today I look like a person of substance. We habitants might be poor but we have our dignity.*

Instead of being passed from soldier to soldier, with much saluting and stiff posturing, André was delivered immediately to Colonel Markham's office. This time he was allowed to wait inside. Others already sat on benches around the edges of the room. One after another, they were ushered in. Nearly an hour passed before the door opened and André's name was called. His escorts led him to the office and left.

André stood in front of Colonel Markham who glanced at a pile of documents on his desk, paged through them, picked out one and murmured as he read it, "Not that much farther, but ..."

Then he shook his head, set it aside and looked up.

"It has been a busy morning," the colonel said in French. "Sit, André Didier. What have you to report?"

André sat. "*Merci beaucoup, monsieur.* I have studied English. Please use that language if you prefer."

The colonel looked surprised. "No, we shall continue in French. May I know what you have learned?"

"The canoe will work well. It should be finished by tomorrow," André said. "But only five men have offered to paddle, so I would be the sixth, if we are to leave soon. To be frank, I have little confidence in them as a crew, sir. I need more men—or better ones."

"These men—tell me about them."

"Two know canoes and have useful skills. I've wintered twice with the man who has enough experience to be the *gouvernail*. The other is a tribesman from the area we travel to. Of the rest, one is young and untried but willing, a ... friend from my school days. The last two have wintered but are old, maybe forty—and I'm concerned for their stamina. However no others have applied. No one has been a *devant*, and I cannot claim those skills." André waited for the colonel to react. *So many ifs. Will he end the venture with such a weak crew?*

"Stamina is only one thing. Are they reliable enough to be trusted with a child?"

"*Oui*. I believe they're good, honest people and a child would be safe with them. The *gouvernail* I trust with my life. I know little of the others. All have committed to this journey and will not desert for their own whims." *Unlikely as they are, I feel good about them, including Michel, and even the old guys.*

"Essential qualities, as is your judgment. Will they follow you?" Colonel Markham asked.

André knew he had to speak about his greatest fear. "I'll have to work to ensure their loyalty. *voyageurs* aren't like soldiers, used to obeying orders—comradeship binds us, not authority. With great pride in our strength and ability, we only defer to the experience and wisdom of the *devant* and *gouvernail*, which I do not possess. Good *voyageurs* alert each other about dangerous situations. We work together because we share a goal. So, if my canoe has someone who does not work with the others, who is disagreeable or selfish, the whole mission suffers. Perhaps military men do not understand this." He held his breath, wondering if he'd doomed the venture.

Markham listened thoughtfully. "It is not so different from an officer's lot, bending the wills of ordinary men into life as soldiers. You are dealing with this sensibly. But I am placed in a difficult position—my regiment will leave this area soon and I must send the child. Are you prepared to lead, Mr. Didier?"

Mr. Didier, indeed!

André paused. Making the whirlwind arrangements had distracted him and he'd forgotten to mention Mama and Papa in his first interview. "I want to, but I ... My foster mother has been sick and my foster father injured his shoulder. All spring I've needed to tend them. She's slowly improving, but I'm uncertain about leaving them. And I've never led a group—especially one transporting a child. There are many things I don't know." *I said it. Now I'm sure I won't get to go.*

"I appreciate your honesty. From what I have heard, you are resourceful enough to make new decisions if your first plan doesn't work. That's of great value to me. I believe that you will rise to leadership, but if better men become available, or if you decide to stay here for your foster parents, it may be that you only organize this expedition. That remains to be seen."

The colonel was silent for a long time. When he spoke, it was of something far different. "I have fought the French many times. It seems the British and French are always on opposite sides. I know the French to be daring and dauntless and steadfast. There is something in their blood that makes them meet danger and hardship with their heads up. Sometime I should like to be on the same side and work with them, not against them. Perhaps this is a beginning."

André imagined the thrills and challenges of the journey. He felt his heart leap.

Colonel Markham continued: "I know there is risk. None of us can see ahead, as to how a thing may turn out. And who knows about tomorrow? You're very young, if you believe life is something you can be sure about. Soldiers know nothing is certain. A leader plans, and if that fails, he plans again. Whatever comes, whatever he faces, he can only do his best. And that is what I have heard about you."

André glowed with the compliment. *On this trip, I won't simply be an underling clerk—leading would show my ability, that I am respected. Perhaps this will be my career.*

"Sir, may I continue to seek other paddlers? I hope to make the journey as successful as is in my power."

"Do so—take another day. Now then, I will authorize the standard rates of pay for middlemen and steersmen, though you will have only the boy's baggage to carry."

André wanted to lead this express canoe, more than anything. He sat straighter.

"Please tell me about this boy we are to transport."

"His name is Danny Ashton. He is ... let me see, he is ..." Colonel Markham pulled out a sheet of paper. "Nearly seven years old."

"That's very young. V*oyageurs* are accustomed to a rugged active life. Can this Danny Ashton bear being away from everyone he knows, in the company of rough men?"

"As his father is a soldier, the boy has grown up in a military household and knows how to accept orders. Recently, his mother and infant sister succumbed to ... measles, I believe. It was his mother's dying plea that her son be sent to his father, stationed at Fort St. Joseph. I promised to help, especially as none here could take on his care. I have met the boy—a typical child, curious about the world and wanting to experience everything."

"Will he still be grieving for his family?" André persisted. "Or is he used to comfort? Can he eat the food of the trail, the only kind we bring? Can he endure being in a canoe for a dozen hours and more each day? Can he travel for day upon day, weeks and months without someone he knows?"

"Excellent questions. *Voyageurs* are known for ... how should I say it? ... robust behavior. Danny will need a companion, a person of his class to accompany him. I have taken the liberty of inviting a gentleman to speak to you. His presence would ensure that all behavior is appropriate for a child."

That irked André. *Why would a gentleman make us more "appropriate?" All the voyageurs I know are wonderful uncles who yearn for their own sons and daughters.*

"A gentleman? Does he know the boy?"

"Not yet. I am interested in your estimation of him." He rang a bell. A thin soldier anxiously answered the summons, saluting sharply.

"Clark, ask James Thatcher to join us. He's in the vestibule."

Chapter 11

A young man entered, not many years older than André. Though it was summer, he wore a heavy black woolen cloak lined with red silk, trimmed with colorful embroidery and dark silky fur around its neck and hem. He drew it off with a flourish to expose rich green knee breeches, a short tan jacket, a brown brocaded vest and a white shirt with lace-edged ruffles.

André's spirit sank. *A gentleman, yes, but those fancy clothes are wrong for a journey like ours.*

Colonel Markham spoke in English. "James Thatcher, thank you for coming. This is André Didier, who will guide the canoe."

The young man bowed to the colonel. He lifted an eyebrow at André's homespun clothing and then at André's calloused hands. Thatcher paused.

"Do sit, both of you. Didier has questions for you."

André had not been prepared to interview, but sat down and scrambled to think what he needed to know. And to speak in English as well.

"I believe I should have been accorded the honor to sit first," Thatcher said.

That started the meeting badly, but André defended himself. "Mr. Thatcher, in the canoe *voyageurs* must react first to the currents and winds. I am responsible for the canoe and its safety, so the men must first attend to the commands I give, to keep us from danger, not because of any rank or privilege."

Thatcher stiffened. "I was educated to lead."

"Tell me about your experience in canoes."

"None, if canoes are those strange bark boats being loaded some weeks ago. I noticed a great many of them upon my arrival from England earlier this month."

"Our canoe will be similar but smaller. In order to travel quickly, we carry little personal baggage, mostly provisions. My men will handle the canoe and its supplies and food. But each adult on this voyage must carry his own baggage—limit it to forty pounds so you can carry it in one load. We have many long portages."

"Then I must have a servant. I have never carried my own things." Thatcher was affronted.

"Each adult must also paddle."

What André was suggesting felt heretical and he feared the colonel's reaction. He glanced for confirmation, but Colonel Markham remained silent, following the conversation with interest.

"I don't know how to paddle. Could a servant do it for me?"

André's stomach hurt, imagining Thatcher and a befuddled servant, both unaware of the work he and his crew were doing, the problems they could cause, how they would complicate the voyage. Then again, perhaps a servant might develop useful canoe skills. He hedged. "Perhaps. Might I speak with your servant?"

"I don't have one yet but a person in my station always has a servant."

André struggled—nothing was going well. The colonel wanted to hire this man, so he strove to find common ground in the discussion. "What is your interest in this voyage? Do you know geography, or animal or plant life?"

"No. I studied military strategy. I hope for a commission, to lead our troops against the savages."

"The natives aren't savages, but skilled tribesmen," André answered angrily. "We'll stop at Indian encampments along the way, both for information about the route and to trade. Native people are of immense help to us. Without them, we wouldn't survive in the woods or on the waters. Our crew includes a tribesman who speaks several of their languages."

"Oh, my! Savages ... with us? I don't know ..." Thatcher looked shocked. "I expect to teach the boy his daily lessons—poetry, grammar, mathematics, Latin."

"Books are a problem on canoe voyages—water quickly ruins paper." André's recalled losing Father Goiffon's booklet when his own canoe swamped. His heart sank, imagining what could happen to this man's books. *But perhaps teaching is something Thatcher could do.* "We need someone who knows children. Do you have younger brothers?"

"I am an only child, sent to boarding school at age six."

Fair enough—I don't have younger siblings either. But the colonel is convinced that James Thatcher should be on this trip. I hate the thought of him relaxing and enjoying scenery while the rest of us stumble up rocky portages or being furious when our paddle splashes spoil his expensive book.

André was silent, searching to keep them from being at odds. The journey would be at risk if they couldn't respect each other.

But Thatcher had lost interest. "Sir, I have many misgivings about this venture. While the wages would be helpful, I cannot accept the position. You must seek another person."

André held his breath, and almost sighed audibly in relief as Thatcher was escorted out.

The colonel stood, indicating their discussion was done. "Interesting questions, Didier. I shall seek a more suitable companion for young Ashton while you search for other crew members. I shall draft your letter of commission and provide funds for the canoe, the supplies and provisions and the men's advance wages. Come back tomorrow to tell me of your progress."

Chapter 12

"Interesting questions." The words rang in his ears and André felt warmed by them. He'd expected Colonel Markham to side with Thatcher after André bluntly exposed problems, ruining his own chances for the voyage.

Instead the colonel had supported him. Compliments were rare.

I picture an entire compound of redcoats standing at attention while Colonel Markham commends my bravery, my masterful way of solving problems. The assembled soldiers cheer for me and fire an honorary salute—muskets and cannon. Denis, impressed, acknowledges my acumen with pride. The fur trade partners vie to sign me on as chief trader.

Just as he was to accept their pile of splendid gifts, he felt a tug on his sleeve.

"Slow down, André," Michel panted, rubbing his hip and grimacing. "I can't keep up. What news?"

André set aside his fanciful dream. "I've engaged a man I paddled with, Pretty Mouse, and a tribesman—they're exactly the kind of crew I'd hoped for. This morning two old guys inquired—they have experience but not much strength. However, no one else has approached, so the colonel gave me another day."

Then he realized he didn't know much about Michel. "How can you leave your apprenticeship?"

Michel's lip twitched. "Uncle ousted me. I was handy while my cousin was little, but now he's twelve and is being trained to take over the brick-making business."

"Why did he oust you?"

"When I told him Cousin wasn't strong enough to lift the heavy forms, Uncle said I was ungrateful to argue. He yelled at me to leave his house and never return."

"When did that happen? Where do you stay?"

Michel shook his head violently.

"What do you eat?"

Michel clamped his lips.

What doesn't he want to reveal? Maybe it's better I don't know.

"If this venture is able to go, tomorrow I'll get advance money. You can paddle *milieu*," André said, glad he'd committed to hiring Michel.

"*Merci*," Michel said humbly.

"Your limp—it could be a problem. Our loads won't be large like most brigades, but portaging our provisions and supplies uphill over rocks and roots will quickly make it worse. And you'll have to help tow the canoe over shallows, which means balancing on slippery boulders in cold water. Are you sure you can handle this?"

"My bad hip, it only happened … a few days ago. I fell … out of the tree where I was napping. It was how the redcoats caught me."

Clearly this was a different Michel than the one he'd known.

Chapter 13

"Coming through. Out of the way, you louts. Move."

The next morning, two British soldiers marched shoulder-to-shoulder, crowding a French-Canadian *habitant* in front of them, with a third redcoat pointing a bayonet at his back. They were headed for the British military headquarters half a league beyond. Where André would meet the colonel for the last time. Where he'd have to report his failure to attract one more paddler.

André's gut clenched, worried as much about his own woes as the fellow villager in trouble. Intent on what he planned to say to Colonel Markham, André tried to step out of their pathway, but the soldier closest to him thrust out his elbow as they bustled past. André lost his balance and fell in the mud.

"Poor man—God help him. Now, do you need a hand?" he heard a voice say.

Which caused André, surveying his best trousers, to look up at the sympathetic speaker.

A *voyageur*, with a red and blue sash wrapped around his narrow waist, offered his arm to André. A white plume arose jauntily in his red knitted *tuque*—which the man whisked off as he squared his strong shoulders and lifted his chin. His dark eyes sparkled with energy as he pulled André upright.

"You are perhaps André Didier? The one who leads a single canoe to the west?"

André nodded, standing taller.

"Oho—just the one I am looking for. Me, I am François," he said, his voice full of bluster and pride. "I grew up with a paddle in my hand. Big waves, rocky currents, storms—they hold no terror for me. I carry—up to three packs. Whatever you want, I can do. I am your man."

"What rivers do you know?" *This man sounds exactly like the voyageur I want.*

"All the waters from here to Grand Portage and the north side of Superior," he said, gesturing with both hands expansively. "The tricky rapids, the portages, the best places to camp—I know them, every one."

"Which brigades were you with? Who were your *devant* and *gouvernail*?"

"Me, I worked for a private group. Out of Nipigon."

Nipigon? Too bad I don't know anyone wintering there.

"Why didn't you sign on with the brigades this spring? You have good paddling years ahead."

"The man I planned to work for, he did not get the money to go again. The big brigades, they are not for me. A single canoe—that's the life I like."

"Do you steer? Or guide? Or interpret?"

"Not that I ever got paid for it, but I know how."

"Why do you want to paddle with me?"

"Here, in towns and farms, are too many rules, but on the rivers, that's where I belong. I like the *pays d'en haut*. And I need work."

"Were you at the *rendezvous* in Grand Portage?"

François answered sourly. "Only once. Me, I was stuck at the post while others went."

"Will you slip away to find your old mates? I won't pay the remainder of your wages until we fulfill our duty."

"*Non,* not me. I have honor. *Je suis un voyageur.*" He seemed insulted at the thought of not completing his obligation.

They shook hands. To André's eyes, François seemed an excellent choice—strong and experienced, a man of action and adventure. This one made the difference. Finally he saw his canoe filled with paddlers—not the strongest ones, but enough. Enough to do this task and prove himself.

Chapter 14

André described François to Colonel Markham. "On my way, I accepted a man who will be an asset to the venture. His experience, energy and strength make up for the weaknesses of others."

"Excellent. Then we shall set a leaving date and final preparations." He signaled a clerk who brought in several letters of credit and a bag with coins.

The colonel summarized each clause as André sounded out the English words.

"The amounts are generous," André said. *More than generous. I could do many things with this much money—get an education, become a merchant, buy land, invest, things I never dreamed of. Of course it's not all for me, but perhaps if I'm careful and don't need to spend it, I will have most of it left when we've completed our task.*

"Circumstances may require more money, so I have tried to think ahead." The colonel tapped at some notes on his desk. "Dispatches have been sent by ship to Fort St. Joseph to inform Captain Ashton of his wife's death and to expect the boy. I'll write the commander a letter of introduction so you will be well treated at the fort. If you wish, you and your crew might winter there, and leave with the spring brigades."

Colonel Markham leaned back in his chair. "Father Goiffon was correct in his estimation—thoughtful, adaptable, honest. Such a one as you, André Didier, would be an asset to any fort."

Welcome at a British fort—instead of being branded a collaborator! Such commendation. This man understands the risk and respects me.

The unexpected praise gave André real pleasure. He folded the signed papers and placed them in an oilskin pouch. Then he stood to take his leave.

"One final item. I have selected Henry Leonard as a companion for Danny." He fixed André with a straight man-to-man look.

"Henry is too young to paddle. But he will make it easier for Danny. I hope he can help in other ways as well. Some of your extra pay will cover the difficulties of Henry's passage. Both boys will be outfitted."

André sucked in his breath. He had forgotten the need for a companion. *Fortunately no person could be as problematic as the gentleman James Thatcher.*

"At Fort St. Joseph, Henry may decide to stay or he may take a ship passage back here. Or he may need to continue on to St. Louis. Captain Ashton will assist in that decision. Indeed, I shall prepare letters to assure it."

A young companion added problems—but he would certainly be better than Thatcher. Still, how could he refuse? It would not be ideal, but he could make it work. "I will look upon them as my own brothers."

"You have my deepest gratitude. We meet at the Lachine landing on the morning your canoe leaves." He clasped André's hand with real feeling.

André made his way homeward. *Being entrusted with so much money says this is a child of importance. I wonder how to be the best big brother. Would he be interested in steering, or knots, or whittling, or animals? Though I'm not the best at any of them, among the group of us, someone will know and can show him those things.*

◈ ◈ ◈

Michel held the *livres* in his open hand, fingering the coins, marveling at them. "I've never had my own money before. *Merci beaucoup.* Thank you very much."

"Most men get shirts and trousers and a sash. A *tuque* for your head. Plus a knife. The colonel is supplying your blanket, your paddle, your food—and the rest of your wages, when we finish."

"Advance money, before I've proved myself. How can I thank you? Oh, André, this gives me hope. No one's ever been interested in me. What woman would marry a person with no prospects for a future? But now I have work and my life opens up. Maybe I too will return with heroic stories of shooting the rapids. Anything I can do for you, I will."

"Michel, remember that you're the newest of the crew. You'll get the worst packs to carry, the jobs others don't want. They'll test you every day."

"Doesn't matter."

"Without experience, you don't know anything useful so when I make decisions I won't consult you ..."

André was about to say more but Michel inhaled sharply and he squared his shoulders. "I will prove worthy, even if I am untried." Then he turned and walked away.

He's grateful and I've spoiled it. Antoine wouldn't have said it so badly.

CHAPTER 15

On the morning they left Lachine, it was bright and sunny, but quiet. A month earlier, the many *voyageur* brigades heading to the *rendezvous* had sped off with great drama and excitement—church bells, shouting and singing, laughing and crying.

Today it was only their single canoe bobbing at the edge of the river. Father Goiffon blessed the crew, chatted briefly and then dashed off to visit his sick parishioners.

"*Bon voyage*," Emile said. "Me, I envy you, wishing I were along. Even when you must fight against the current, or wait in a downpour, I envy you. But I promised my Marguerite I would stay and I am a man of my word."

Papa, who'd also come to watch them depart, appraised André's crew who carried the canoe's food and supplies to the waterfront. "Not much strength yet, but they'll get better."

"On this voyage, you're lucky you don't have to hurry," Emile said. "Antoine, he always rushes to be first at the *rendezvous*. 'Rise early, paddle late,' he says."

"With the summer wasting away, I'll still push to go quickly. We'll need to find work afterwards, in case we can't return this autumn."

Under Pretty Mouse's direction, four of the crew—Gabriel and Baptiste, Reynard and Michel—placed the barrels of provisions and supplies in the canoe, stabilizing and balancing it after each addition. Within minutes, the men had finished their task. François forcefully objected, pointing out their canoe-loading errors.

"Is he telling Pretty Mouse what to do?" Emile asked, incredulous.

"I see they all purchased clothing with their advances—now they look almost like a regular crew. Some were so threadbare I worried the colonel wouldn't approve," André said.

"But after weeks of towing the canoe and carrying packs, those new shirts will be stained and torn," Papa said.

Pretty Mouse approached André anxiously. "We have no cargo so this canoe, she floats too high. Always before we sink to here," he said, pointing to a line mere inches below the gunwales.

True, their load was much smaller than usual—only two half-bales of trade goods, a few barrels of provisions, a pair of kettles, rope and a tarpaulin, rolls of birch bark and spruce root *wattap* to repair the canoe, plus the blankets and packs for the crew.

"You're used to hauling sixty bales. Don't fret," Emile said, putting an arm around Pretty Mouse's shoulder.

"And our paddles, they're too short." Pretty Mouse was alarmed.

"*Oui, c'est vrai.* 'Tis true your canoe will catch the wind differently," Papa reassured him. "But the canoe, it's so light that you can tow it up the small rapids instead of portaging. With so little gear, you might even cross portages in a single pass."

At that, Pretty Mouse lifted an eyebrow—perhaps paddling this canoe had advantages.

"It'll be fine. Remember our passengers will also bring baggage to weigh us down," André said.

Papa turned to André. "Everything you need to know, you already know. With a problem, take enough time to think it through and you ..."

"Can work out the answer," André finished his sentence with a smile. "The impossible, it takes longer, that's all. And trust your mates—I will remember. *Merci,* Papa."

"*Bon voyage.* God be with you."

CHAPTER 16

Much later, Colonel Markham made his way to the riverside, escorted by five soldiers laden with trunks and baggage. Two youngsters straggled behind, holding hands—the older, perhaps twelve or thirteen, looked resolutely ahead while the younger craned his neck at the canoe floating in the river and the half-dozen colorful *voyageurs* milling around. By the looks of the boys' pale skin, they'd spent much of their lives indoors.

At the sight of the British uniforms, André's crew stiffened.

"Redcoats!" Baptiste rasped. Gabriel froze.

Michel leaned over, speaking quietly. "Not to worry. They only tote for the little boy and his companion."

"You're sure?"

"André told me. That man in the fancy uniform, the one who's shaking his hand—he's paying us. The soldiers, they do his bidding. So we're safe."

Still, the *voyageurs* stayed alert as the soldiers set down a large pile for two small people—a tent, several bulky chests, a few softer packs and two small canoe paddles.

At Colonel Markham's signal, the soldiers pivoted smartly on their heels and marched away with precision. When their backs could no longer be seen, the brigade released silent sighs.

Pretty Mouse studied the shapes of the additional cargo and rearranged the new freight into the canoe. François, unsatisfied with how Pretty Mouse was adjusting the load, made alternate suggestions with each change.

Colonel Markham placed his hand on the younger boy's shoulder and spoke in English. "Danny, this is André, the leader of these men who will bring you to your father. Your journey will take many weeks so you must ask him whenever you need something. He'll tell you the men's names in due time. André, meet Danny Ashton."

André rose to full height, hoping to appear like the leader, and smiled as they shook hands formally.

Danny wore a miniature *tuque*, the red knitted *voyageur* cap ending with a tassel, and a boy-sized sash wrapped around a plain white shirt. Around his neck was a bag of possibles, which fascinated him. After inspecting its contents—among them, a cameo of his mother, a small ball and a brand-new knife—he tucked the bag inside his shirt. Minutes later he withdrew it to show the other boy before tucking it in again.

Danny looked around at his new companions, seeing their color and movement. When he spied Reynard, his jaw dropped.

Reynard had removed his shirt and wore only a breech cloth and high buckskin leggings. Around his neck was a leather strip threaded with sections of bone and a single bear claw. His oiled black braids were held by an elaborately beaded headband. And inside the garter that tightened one legging was a long knife with a carved handle.

Reynard nodded to Danny, with a brief smile.

The boy seems curious about us. He's not weepy, afraid to leave—I like that spirit. When the newness has worn off, he'll likely miss his mother or have bouts of homesickness. I don't know what to do then—I guess we'll figure it out.

Then the colonel indicated the older boy, standing aside. "Henry Leonard is Danny's companion. While he won't paddle, I hope he will prove useful to you. He might teach Danny, though I daresay the youngster's mind will be interested in other things."

Colonel Markham handed coins to Danny and Henry. "Not far out of the city, *voyageurs* traditionally stop at the little shrine of Ste. Anne, where they ask prayers for a safe journey. These coins are for you to offer at the shrine."

Danny examined the coins with amazed delight, like rare treasures.

Henry slid his coins into his bag of possibles with only a short "Of course." He kept his head down.

The colonel and Henry walked a short distance away. Colonel Markham put both hands upon Henry's shoulders and spoke in tones that were encouraging, although his words could not be heard. Henry's face showed stoic acceptance of a responsibility greater than his young age.

André looked more closely at Henry who was pale, with a slender frame. His clothing fit poorly—a too-large shirt hung loosely over his slight shoulders, covering a second shirt underneath, and equally baggy trousers. A faded *tuque* covered most of his dark hair. His jaw jutted out with determination.

He could be about thirteen years old, the same age as I was on my first brigade. Looks like he hasn't been outdoors much. Thankfully he's not arrogant like Thatcher.

Colonel Markham handed André letters for Captain Ashton and the fort commander, and a small bag of coins to cover the boys' additional needs. He glanced at the crew, Pretty Mouse standing ready at the bow. "He is to be the *devant*?"

"I can better attend to the boys if I'm closer," André replied. *Should I have told him that Pretty Mouse has more experience in canoes and was honored to take the lead position?*

"I wish you a safe—and uneventful—journey."

"Thank you, sir. I will do my best."

André pointed to the places where Danny and Henry would ride. Before Danny could jump in with both feet, Pretty Mouse slipped his hands around the boy's waist and lifted him high, settling him lightly on a bundle of blankets.

"Take care, little one. Big jumps make holes in the canoe —not good to start a voyage, especially when soldiers are watching us," Mouse said, in French.

Danny looked confused so Henry whispered in English, and the boy nodded. Then he craned around to wave to the colonel as Henry slid into his place.

Chapter 17

André waved to Papa and Emile. When he pushed off from the stern, the canoe swung out into the river.

"Pretty Mouse, give us a song!"

With his gleeful energy, Mouse started songs, loud and joyous, to weld them into a unit. Each lively tune further steadied the paddlers into the rhythm of a stroke to every beat of music. Soon the men at the landing were no longer visible.

When they sang "*Alouette*," Danny tried to join—perhaps somebody had taught him this French song. His high pitch and French pronunciation amused the men.

Finally under way, André relaxed. He glowed with satisfaction.

"Me, I will be the best bowman ever," Pretty Mouse had promised fervently. "You will see, André. Just think, I, Paul Doyon, I am a *devant*. The leader. I never thought I would become so important."

Mouse made good on his promise. Besides leading songs, his eyes scanned the currents for any unexpected riffle in the river. When he saw one, he called for the middlemen to hold their paddles, or to look alive and paddle faster.

From his stance in the rear as *gouvernail*, André considered the men before him, plying their paddles with vigor, though with little grace or smooth coordination. He felt satisfied with having paired them according to their strengths.

François knelt behind Pretty Mouse, paddling alone. *He's strong—the others will match their strokes to his. But he's bossy.*

He won't see to criticize the others if he's that far forward.

Behind him were Michel and Baptiste. *Baptiste will teach Michel. I should've talked it out with Michel but I'll wait a day or so, until he's accustomed to paddling.*

In the next row he'd placed Gabriel with Reynard. *They won't need words to work together.*

Henry and Danny occupied the row in front of André. Danny squirmed and twisted, leaning over the edge of the canoe, often rocking it as he pointed. But, an hour later, the morning's excitement tired him—he slumped against Henry and drifted off to sleep.

Naps? Do children that age need naps? He's been so active I'm glad he can sleep in the canoe—less for me to worry about. How do I teach him to sit quietly when he's awake? Mama would know about handling young children, if I had asked her. Oh well, I'll try to be a big brother, not a scold.

Even with Danny sprawled over him, Henry hardly moved. He didn't paddle, though he had been provided with one. He idly trailed his fingers in the water, and looked out at the rocky shores of the river. The scenery didn't seem to inspire him —he looked lost, resigned, focused on his own thoughts.

What's wrong? Colonel Markham said he wouldn't paddle, but I wish he'd try. That will help him feel a part of us. I'll try to find ways that Henry can enjoy this trip.

CHAPTER 18

Danny awakened in mid-afternoon, and whispered something to Henry.

"When do we stop? Danny needs to eat. And, uh, to do something else," Henry said loudly.

His English words meant nothing to the crew, who only spoke French.

André answered in English, "It's only a little past noon, so we won't stop until tonight, when we make camp. Brigades eat twice a day—about nine o'clock in the morning and seven or eight in the evening. Didn't you eat a hearty breakfast before we left?" But immediately he knew he'd given the wrong answer.

"Not until tonight? And only twice a day? Maybe you can go long hours without meals, but little boys can't," Henry snapped. "They need food several times a day."

The idea of stopping for frequent meals shocked André. He didn't have a response.

"Surely you have bread and jam. Or cheese. If he doesn't eat soon, he'll cry."

"We have neither. Those foods go bad quickly on a journey like ours."

"Not even bread? Well, you must find something for him. And for me also."

"Pretty Mouse, our boys are hungry," André said, returning to French. He felt desperate—no food could be found while they were paddling. "I only requested standard rations. What can we feed them—since you won't cook pea soup until tonight?"

"Pea soup? That is dinner?" Henry asked.

In English, André said, "And also our breakfasts, which are the remains of the evening's meal. Usually we eat during the second or third pipe break in the morning. Mostly we eat in the canoe." Each phrase made his answer worse.

"That won't suit us. Growing boys need more kinds of food than pea soup. You'll have to provide something."

Fortunately, Pretty Mouse had an idea. "Me, I have just the thing, deep in my pack. Let's stop on the shore so I can find it. We could let them run too. *Oui*?"

Not long after, Pretty Mouse spied a small inlet with a meadow surrounded by shrubs and trees, and André steered the canoe toward it.

"We'll take a pipe break, men."

While the men pulled out their long-stemmed white clay pipes, Pretty Mouse rummaged through his pack and dug out a hard roundish slab, brown and grainy and smaller than his fist. "Maple sugar. It's good," he said in French as he passed it to Danny, who studied it uncertainly.

When Danny glanced up, he saw Pretty Mouse wink and pretend to lick something in his hand. Danny copied him, tasted it and his eyes lit up.

Henry looked horrified.

"But Henry, it's good. You'll like it. Try some," Danny said, holding the maple sugar cake out.

Henry shuddered. "I'm not hungry."

Pretty Mouse escorted the boys into the nearby bushes, in case they were shy about relieving themselves.

"Eeek! What's that?"

André and Pretty Mouse ran full-tilt to where Danny stood, pointing, white-faced.

Just as they arrived, André saw the tall grasses move. He watched for a moment before reaching down to grab the small green snake which curled around his hand in an attempt to slither away.

"*Un serpent? C'est un petit serpent?*" André said.

Danny nodded, wide-eyed.

André looked confused as he released the snake some distance away. *This little snake caused them fear? I never imagined that, but I suppose town boys haven't often been around wild creatures, even little ones. With all the animals we see, this whole trip will be a trial until we ease them into the wild.*

Which Pretty Mouse had already begun, as he noisily walked them back to the canoe. Though Danny didn't understand the French explanation, he looked where Pretty Mouse pointed out several toads and a rabbit hiding from them.

In the canoe again, André returned to pondering how to provide midday meals. *They could eat when we stop for portages or tow the canoe at décharges. But what food could we offer? If we trade for fish or dried meat at every Indian settlement along the way, doing that will slow us.*

Some time later André realized that Henry had understood the French words he'd said to Pretty Mouse. *That will make it easier to communicate. But Danny only speaks English, so I'll teach him French.*

CHAPTER 19

After their brief stop, Danny napped again, lulled by the canoe's motion. When he awoke, his head twisted around at things that caught his attention. Instead of seeing people, houses, churches or shops, or parts of town life he was familiar with, he gazed at the deep green forest that surrounded them and the occasional dead tree floating past them in the wide river. The earthy woods smells and the bird songs were new to him.

It was awhile before they arrived at Ste. Anne's shrine. The men pulled the canoe ashore and hastily donned their shirts—while it was too warm to wear them while paddling, they intended to properly honor Ste. Anne. They dashed to the shrine to ask her protection for their journey.

Seeing the boys still at the canoe, Pretty Mouse turned back and led Danny to the alms box where he could place his coin. Murmuring his own prayers, Mouse showed Danny how to make the sign of the cross.

Henry had stayed behind, sitting on a stone bench to watch. In English he said, "He's Anglican, you know. Not Catholic. His father won't take kindly to your teaching him religion."

André was glad Pretty Mouse couldn't understand the words. *It's one more reason to ask Ste. Anne's graces.*

Chapter 20

Not far from the shrine, their canoe entered the Lake of Two Mountains where numerous islands crowded their view. André lost his bearings, bewildered at figuring out which were islands and what was mainland. He'd spent so much time on other preparations that he'd neglected the route's early challenges. He dug for his compass.

Nor was Pretty Mouse sure where to go. "Always before I've been a *milieu* and me, I can never see anything when I paddle in the middle. Today's the first time I'm the *devant*."

"I would've thought you'd at least ask how to get through if you didn't remember," François muttered. "We should have turned west immediately, before those little islands."

His tone made André testy. "My plan is to stay to the east until we pass all the islands. Then we'll bear west, to cross the lake at the narrowest part."

"*Non, non,*" François argued. "Your way, we'll catch all the big waves. But if you turn and skirt this next island to our left, and then go between the next two, we could avoid the worst of the breakers. Keep the western sun ahead of us—always."

André felt stung that his first decision had been challenged. "What breakers? There aren't any. Stay to the right, Mouse."

"If we charge straight ahead, we'll hit them. Can't you feel the wind?" François persisted.

They sped straight ahead, edging the eastern shore. When they cleared the islands, they met whitecaps on the bay, raised by winds, as François had predicted. When they finally turned westward, waves beat against their side, threatening to swamp them on the rocky shore.

A hard paddle and side winds were perils to avoid, especially their first day. Neither he nor his tiring crew were ready for the onslaught gusting across the expanse of the Lake of Two Mountains. François was right and he was wrong and now they'd all pay the price. André gritted his teeth and they paddled on, fighting the waves.

By late afternoon, André's back and arms felt stiff, though they'd not put in a full day. A glance at Michel, Gabriel and Baptiste showed them plying their paddles with little precision and strength.

They're exhausted and can't match the pace set by Pretty Mouse and François. Their arms can't take much more. But we're nowhere near the usual camping sites.

Emile advised me not to push as hard as Antoine because we aren't headed to the rendezvous. But we do have to hurry—we're alone on these waters, no other brigades behind us to help. Our food will last for six weeks. If we don't make haste, we'll run out, and being hungry makes us less efficient paddlers. There are so many things to consider—making decisions is harder than I expected. And today is only the first day.

"The brigades, they always camp early the first night," François said. "Isn't that right, Mouse?"

"*Oui.* My stomach, it tells me it wants supper. André, how much longer today?" Pretty Mouse called out.

That made it easier.

"Be on the lookout for a campsite. Tomorrow we'll have to paddle the length of this lake," André decided. It would make everyone happier. He was back in charge.

Chapter 21

"Me, I know a good place for one canoe," François said. "The land, it juts out to a nice point with a little bay beyond. Maybe one pipe away, or maybe two. I'll know it when I see it."

André felt insecure not knowing the route like François did, especially after he'd been wrong about avoiding the brunt of waves sweeping across the widest part of the lake. *The men had to work harder because I didn't know where to cross. At least we'll stop early tonight. That should ease their work. Leading isn't as easy as Antoine made it look.*

Finally when they'd passed the third point after their pipe break, André saw a bay with a tiny open area for overnight camping. He was relieved that François remembered it correctly. It was hard to calculate distance and remember exact places.

To protect the canoe's fragile bottom from the gravel, Pretty Mouse leapt into the water, followed by the men. After they stabilized the canoe, Pretty Mouse lifted Danny out and then pointed to where Henry could step.

"In the water? My shoes will get wet!" Henry was incredulous. But because he spoke in English, no one understood. Irritated, he removed his shoes, peeled off his socks, rolled up his trousers and stepped gingerly through a foot of water to dry land.

André chose where to place the canoe for overnight and called out assignments: unload and stack the food barrels and trade goods; flip the canoe over—shelter for the crew if it rained; erect the boys' tent; gather wood; light the fire; stow personal gear and blanket bundles.

Pretty Mouse waded into the river with an iron pot to scoop water for soup. Finally able to recover, Baptiste and Gabriel rubbed their arms, groaning, and Michel stretched his muscles.

André liked that his campsite was as orderly as Antoine's.

Then he heard Henry accosting a confused Gabriel, demanding that his baggage be carried to their tent.

"*Non*, Henry!" André said firmly in English. "On this trip each person carries his own baggage." Then he looked at the large pile of chests and sighed at their bulkiness—Henry was right and Gabriel or the others would have to carry them.

Among the trunks was a rectangular wooden box. Made of smoothly-finished dark wood and closed with shiny brass hinges and a brass lock, it looked like what high-ranking partners and *bourgeois* of the fur trade used to keep journals and records while in the canoe. "Is that a traveling desk?"

"Does it matter?"

"No. But it has no handle, so it'll be clumsy to haul. Gabriel, tie a rope around it to carry it. We'll manage all your heavy and bulky trunks," André said. "But your own blanket pack and small things—they're your responsibility."

"It's not that many more things for him to carry."

André's eyes blazed into Henry's gray fires blazing back at him. "There are no servants on this trip, Mr. Leonard. We're a small group. We've started late. We're alone, far behind any other canoes, with great distances to cover. We must work together. You must obey my orders, as everyone else does. And my order now is that everyone will do his share. That includes you. Or you will be put ashore at the next settlement. You decide."

"Insulting." Henry spun away. But he dragged two small packs from the pile and hoisted them. When Gabriel delivered the curious traveling desk, Henry disappeared inside the tent.

I handled that with authority, like a leader. Nobody ever challenged Antoine's decisions, even if we didn't like his plan. But I've made Henry angry. How do I get him on my side?

Chapter 22

At the fire pit, Pretty Mouse demonstrated to an enthralled Danny how to make pea porridge, step by step. As the water boiled, he guided Danny's hand, explaining—in French—how much to measure, how to toss dried peas into the pot. An hour or so later, Mouse ladled portions of the supper, first onto Danny's and Henry's wide pewter soup plates, with rolled rims that looked like ropes.

Danny gazed in wonder. "Ooh, look—it's new and shiny. I never had one like this before. When I dropped Mother's pretty china dishes, the maid would scold me. But this one won't break."

The men smiled at Danny's babble, unsure of what he said, but aware of his pleasure.

He shoveled a large spoonful of porridge into his mouth.

"Oww. Hot!" He spit it out and ran to the shore, overturning his steaming dish on Baptiste. Pretty Mouse leapt up to soothe him. Baptiste shrugged and wiped the mess off.

Minutes later, when Danny and Pretty Mouse returned to the campfire, they saw André had refilled Danny's dish of pea porridge and let it cool, and François was telling a funny story.

Henry stirred his porridge with distaste. "This is barely palatable. You were paid to provide better," he said in English.

"Henry, we cannot bring town food with us. The fresh things you are used to, they draw hungry animals or get rancid," André answered, in English. "If we hunt or fish each day, that slows our travel. Pea soup is what *voyageurs* eat, every day. It's the only food we brought."

"I do not know how we shall abide it."

"What do you suggest?" That *voyageur* food was beneath Henry and Danny irritated André.

"I am not the cook. That's your problem."

"My soup, he doesn't like it?" Mouse said. Though he didn't know Henry's English words, he understood the critical tone.

Henry stiffened but said nothing more.

"Me, I know a few tricks. Tomorrow, I make a better one. You will like it."

"When we come upon native encampments, we will try to trade," André said. Perhaps it would soften Henry's anger.

The men ate in uncomfortable silence.

Gabriel rose shortly after he'd finished eating and headed for an opening in the woods. Fifteen minutes later he returned, holding out his neckerchief to Danny and Henry. It held a dozen tiny red raspberries.

"*Les framboises!*" he said, pointing beyond their tent to a grassy meadow. Raspberries.

Danny peered "Are those raspberries? Yes! Henry, look!" He stuffed a few in his mouth. "They're good."

Henry gratefully accepted the remaining berries. "*Merci.*"

"*Beaucoup des framboises. Là.*" Many raspberries. There. Gabriel pointed to the meadow. He gestured for them to follow.

"What did he say—' lay from-bwaz'? What is that?" Danny looked confused.

"*Les framboises* is how the French say 'raspberries.' That man says there are more where he found them," Henry explained.

"Then let's get more, Henry. Come on." They followed Gabriel, taking off their neckerchiefs to collect berries.

Half an hour later, all three returned, the boys' hands stained red and their mouths sticky from having eaten their small harvest. André smiled in appreciation to Gabriel.

By then the sun was setting. André sat with the men who smoked their pipes, watching lavender and gray clouds streak the golden sky.

All in all, our first day has gone well. How kind of Mouse to take Danny under his wing. From here on the trip should get easier. I'll think of other ideas to help the child—and maybe even his grouchy companion.

"Mouse and Gabriel, you did well for our boys. Tomorrow should be clear and sunny," André said, adding loud enough for Henry, who'd retired to the tent, to hear, "We rise at dawn, so let's go to sleep."

On this balmy night, the men sought out comfortable sleeping places outside and used their blankets for pillows—Michel slumped near a tree, François curled under the canoe, Reynard farther away.

Later that night amid the forest sounds, André thought he heard whimpers and crying, and the quiet voice of Henry. *Of course Danny is struggling at leaving the safety of his home—it's good that Henry can help. I hope he'll feel better tomorrow. Because I don't know how to comfort him.*

Chapter 23

Only a narrow gleam of light of the morning sky showed when André awoke. He stretched his stiff shoulder muscles and examined his hands, relieved they weren't yet blistered.

On the first brigade, Pretty Mouse dressed my bloody palms more than once. He took good care of me. I should've checked with Michel, so tonight I'll see if he needs a treatment. That might mend the coolness between us.

He smelled the delicious aroma of roasting food—it surprised him. He twisted around to discover Reynard near the campfire, tending something speared on a long stick.

André joined him. "Fish?"

"Fish," Reynard said in a low voice. "They hide when the big brigades come through, but we are small, only one canoe. So this fish came back. Last night I saw it in the shallows. The boys can eat a little now, and we'll have plenty for us later."

"*Merci.*"

A moment later, Pretty Mouse's head popped up, sniffing. "I smell something good. Oho, the little one, he will like this. The other one, too, I hope. Good work, Reynard."

The noises of their movement and the scent of food woke the rest of the crew. They yawned, eased the muscles that had tightened overnight and rolled up their blankets, ready to leave.

"*Reveillez-vous. Allons-y,*" Michel said loudly. Get up. Let's go. Whistling and breaking twigs to make noise, he strode toward the tent to wake the boys up, continuing in French. "As soon as you're out, we can fold up your tent."

Hearing his voice, both boys groaned, followed by muffled commotion as they bumped against the tent's wall to prepare for leaving.

"It's too early—we're not ready," Henry called out in English.

Michel didn't know the words, but guessed at their meaning. "I'll look for *les framboises*. Maybe there are more berries around here," he said.

Danny heard the first French word that he'd learned. Immediately he stood, his head pressing on the tent roof until he stepped out. "'Lay from-bwaz'—is that raspberries? Wait for me —I'll help. Henry, would you roll up my blanket? Please?"

The sun had risen by the time Henry emerged, rubbing his neck. He trudged toward the canoe with his roughly-rolled blanket and personal pack and then returned for Danny's. "I didn't sleep well—animal noises scared Danny and there was a rock under my back. Do we always leave at dawn?" At the campfire, he sniffed the cooked fish with interest.

"We try to," André answered in English. "But this morning Reynard caught a fish for us. If you want to eat a little now, we can wait. The rest of us will eat in a few hours."

While the boys ate, the crew dismantled the tent, hauled their bulky gear to the canoe and helped load the barrels and supplies, chests and packs into the canoe.

Right before Henry climbed in the canoe, he looked sharply at how the items were stowed. "Yesterday my desk was out of reach. Today I want it close to me—I'll need it every day. See to it."

Startled, André felt the sting in the demand. He wanted to explain that it had been placed forward in the canoe because of its weight and size, but directed Pretty Mouse to move the desk and re-balance the rest. He needed to avoid a duel of wills, especially in front of the others.

He'd planned to describe the route ahead and to demonstrate the ways they would maneuver the canoe. But that teaching pleasure disappeared. "Today we follow the edge of the lake. Like yesterday, the waves and rollers will push us toward rocks so you must keep Danny still in the canoe. We'll stop only at safe landings."

"I am to contain his energy? That's very hard, for little boys are ..." Henry began.

André cut him off. "It's hard for us all, and it will soon be harder. In a day we'll hit the first rapids of the Long Sault—and then miles and miles of them. You two must stay in the canoe while we pole and tow it, if the water level is high enough for that. But when we have to carry the canoe and all our gear over portages, you'll have to walk—and carry your own blankets."

Henry's jaw set. "I see."

Chapter 24

To Henry's credit, he dug out a book of history from his desk and read to Danny while the men paddled. But Danny increasingly observed the wilderness with curiosity—birds with strange calls and colors, fish swimming below in the clear water, frogs basking, squirrels leaping from tree to tree, waves curling around sunken branches, the earthy scents of cedar and pine. He'd nudge Henry, pointing at something new and different, but whispering as if he feared to use his voice.

The men paddled for two hours—taking a break each hour to smoke their pipes—before stopping.

"Pretty Mouse, watch for a place to pull up. We'll take breakfast on shore so the boys can run."

At their landing, Reynard cut the fish into pieces, offering it first to the boys. Pretty Mouse ladled the remainder of last night's pea soup in the men's plates.

Henry carefully picked off the skin and separated the small bones. Still hungry after he finished his portion, he held out his plate for more. "*Merci,*" he said to Pretty Mouse and Reynard. "*C'est délicieux.*"

"What did you say, Henry?" Danny asked in English, confused.

"It's French, the language the men speak. *Merci* is 'thank you' and '*C'est délicieux*' means 'it's delicious.'"

"Say it again. I want say that too," Danny said. When he had practiced the new words, he held out his empty plate and pointed to it with a big smile. "Mercy. Say de-lee-cee-you."

That pleased Pretty Mouse, who had waded in the river to scrub the soup pot. He grabbed Danny's plate, scoured it with a handful of sand, rinsed it and handed it back.

Henry looked appalled. "That's how you wash dishes?"

"Sand cleans well. Besides, soap doesn't last long out here—it dissolves around all this water," André said in English.

Henry glanced at Danny's plate, and his own, horrified.

"If you scratch your initials on the bottom, you can find that same one each time. Will that help?"

Henry closed his eyes and sighed. "I suppose."

André had felt proud of the pewter plates, a refinement that most brigades didn't enjoy. His first brigade had used only wooden noggins, large spoons each man had carved to scoop out portions of soup from the common kettle. Now he wondered what else might be wrong with his planning.

"Boys, they have such small bellies that they need to eat often. Later, I've got dried venison to feed them," Pretty Mouse said to André. "What is that little one's name again?"

After eating, Danny again napped to the rocking motion of the canoe, so Henry unlocked his portable desk, removed a small leather-bound book, not the history he'd read to Danny, and re-locked the desk. Then he read, totally engrossed. While the men sang, while they paddled and shouted directions, he read. Though the waves became big rollers, threatening to crash them into boulders that lined the shore like teeth, Henry turned page after page. He only looked up when water drops sprinkled his pages.

I wonder what he's reading. I wish I could have brought a book, but where would I have gotten one? Montreal, maybe, but that's a whole day's walk. Would I have had enough money?

When they stopped for a pipe break, he broached the subject with Henry.

"A partner loaned me 'Robinson Crusoe' on our last voyage. I read it aloud many nights. Maybe you could read to us on this trip?"

"I didn't bring foolish novels. Moreover, I'll thank you not to spy over my shoulder. What I read—and write—is private."

"I didn't mean to ..."

"Do stop splashing on the pages. I don't want water drops to spoil it."

André gritted his teeth. *I've never met anyone like Henry —he's so haughty. Impossible. Papa said that when something is impossible, it just takes more time—but thawing him might take forever.*

❖ ❖ ❖

Danny woke in the canoe and twisted around, forgetting the need to sit still, uninterested in Henry's history book. He squirmed and wiggled, pointing at things he saw.

It's great he's curious about the woods—but I'm nervous every time he leans over the canoe. What if he were to fall into the river? It seems harsh to punish him for being active. How will we get him to sit more quietly?

At the next break, Baptiste didn't immediately take out his pipe to smoke, but instead unraveled a piece of yarn from the fringe of his sash. He broke it off, wound it around his fingers and turned around, offering it to Danny, explaining in French. Danny looked confused.

André translated. "Danny, Baptiste gave you this string— each time you see an animal, you tie a knot. We'll tell you the animal's name. Would you like that?"

"Oh, yes." Danny grabbed the yarn and twisted around to spot a creature so he could tie his first knot.

"Because we're big, we scare the small animals and birds, so the less you move your arms and legs and the less noise you make, the more animals you'll notice."

"Mercy," Danny said, smiling at Baptiste and André. Though difficult, he tried to move his eyes instead of his body.

"*Merci beaucoup*, Baptiste. That was a good idea to help him—and us," André said. *Papa said to trust my men—I'm grateful they see ways to help. But I wish I'd thought of it first.*

❖ ❖ ❖

When they neared a large turtle with a high-domed shell, sunning itself on a mossy root, Reynard gestured toward it. At Danny's gleeful yelp, the turtle slipped below the water's surface.

"Oh, now it's gone. Can I count it anyway?"

Gabriel nodded. "*Une tortue. C'est une tortue.*"

"Set toon tortuh," Danny mimicked, and tied his first knot.

When an eagle soared overhead, Danny watched it hover on updrafts.

"*C'est un aigle,*" Michel said.

Danny tried. "Set tan aygle." He tied his second knot.

When a pair of otters chased each other in a stream, Baptiste said, "*Les loutres,*" and Danny copied with "Lay lootray." As he touched each knot, he chanted "*Une tortue, un aigle, les loutres.*" The constant repetition annoyed Henry, but Danny remembered the new words and searched for other animals.

When he spied a fish, he learned to say *une poisson;* a loon, *un huard;* a fox, *un renard.*

All afternoon Danny pronounced the new French words and proudly tied knots. Soon he would need a longer string.

Chapter 25

When Danny wanted to say more than an animal's name, he whispered in English to Henry.

"Danny, you can tell me what you need. I speak English and the others might know a few words," André encouraged him. "We'll teach you to speak French."

Henry turned angrily. "His father would not approve."

"Perhaps, but in his new surroundings at the fort, Danny might rub shoulders with French speakers. It will help him to tell others what he needs," André said. "But since you understand French, maybe you could translate for him."

Henry snapped his mouth shut. "Teach him French then, but I will report any inappropriate language to his father."

"Our maid, she was French," Danny said. "She called me ... *cher enfant*. What is that?"

"It means you were a dear child," André said.

Danny was disgusted. "Huh. I'm not a child—I'm nearly seven. She should have said 'big boy.'"

At the bow, Pretty Mouse seemed distracted. He liked pointing out things to the boys, but then he'd miss a rock shelf or dead branch hidden beneath the surface, which their canoe barely escaped scraping.

While it made André anxious, he reasoned that he and Mouse were yet learning each other's method of steering—they'd both improve.

Because of stopping several times during the day, André realized they wouldn't achieve the daily number of miles he'd planned for. Besides, his six men didn't have the strength of ten prime *voyageurs* in a brigade.

We can't hurry like Antoine does. We have to go slower—Danny and Henry need to spend time out of the canoe and they need more sleep, Gabriel and Baptiste take longer to recover and Michel can't shoulder a full load. I hardly have time to think. But I ordered only six weeks of food supplies. I hope Reynard can supplement that by fishing. I hope we have enough trade goods—we'll need them more than I expected.

CHAPTER 26

After they found their evening's camping spot, unloaded and had settled in, André dug into his pack for a small pot of Mama's salve and strips of doeskin. He sought out Michel to bandage his hands.

"On my first brigade, Pretty Mouse nursed my blisters. In a few days, yours will be fine."

Once the stinging eased, Michel relaxed. "*Merci.* Paddling on the same side all day, it's hard, more than I realized. But I'm getting stronger, I promise you."

André was relieved. A simple kindness bridged the gap of hurt that he'd unwittingly opened between himself and Michel.

When he offered the ointment to others, Baptiste and Gabriel were as grateful as Michel, but Reynard had his own treatment and François didn't need it.

Danny's stomach growled. He looked longingly at the pea soup, barely bubbling in the pot.

"You want this?" Pretty Mouse asked holding out a bit of hard biscuit that he planned to use to thicken the stew.

Danny grabbed it, stuffing it into his mouth.

"This little one, Dannee, he is famished." Pretty Mouse's eyes misted.

"After supper we'll look for *les framboises*. That might fill him up," Gabriel said.

"I like that. And then, when we start portaging, he can pick berries while he waits for us," Mouse said.

"He needs something to do. That ball he plays with, it

bounces everywhere off these rocks. I've caught it a time or two—I'm afraid it'll float downstream," Michel said.

"In a week or two at the most, blueberries will ripen along the portages," Baptiste said. "He can pick *les bleuets*."

François said, "Better check for signs of bear. I thought I saw a fresh track today."

◆ ◆ ◆

"Supper's ready," Mouse announced an hour later. He banged his ladle on the kettle with loud clanks. "Time to eat."

The men needed no prodding, and Danny lined up with them. He shouted towards the tent, "Henry, I've got your dish."

Henry poked his head out of the tent and reluctantly came to supper.

Danny handed him a plate, which Henry immediately examined for the initials he'd scratched on the bottom.

Henry shook his head and reached for the one Danny held. "You're holding mine." He peered into the kettle with a grimace and at Pretty Mouse carefully ladling a portion into his dish. Then he found a fallen log to sit on, far from the others.

Today has mostly been better but Henry still seems uncomfortable. Maybe it's because there are so many new people—I'll join him.

But as André neared Henry's perch, Henry muttered, "How can I eat this day after day? It's poor people's food, or worse." He took a small spoonful and shuddered.

Pretty Mouse, watching for Henry's reaction to the improvements he'd made in cooking supper, realized it was not the success he'd hoped for. His shoulders dropped.

André felt his gorge rise at Henry's rudeness and Mouse's disappointment, and found another place to sit and eat. *What a disagreeable fault-finder—but he's not going to ruin my meal. This is only our second day—the fort feels very far away.*

Chapter 27

After supper, Michel whittled with his new knife, getting suggestions from François, Reynard scraped a long root making a thin rope and Baptiste and Gabriel mended their moccasins.

André stood to discuss his plan for the next days. "In the morning we'll paddle out of the Lake of Two Mountains."

"Finally no more big waves?" Michel said.

"But on the Ottawa River, the current squeezes between narrow banks, so we face whitewater, starting with the Carillon Rapids. After that, the Long Sault is twelve miles of rocks, rapids and chutes with boulders and dead trees to give us trouble. If the current is high enough, Pretty Mouse and I will decide if we can *décharge*. If so, François and Reynard will attach our long towing ropes to the bow and stern. While they do that, Michel, Baptiste and Gabriel may need to unload—partly or fully, depending on how deep the water is—before they help tow. Strongest men will stand in front. Mouse and I will steer from inside the canoe, to hold it steady. Questions? Michel?"

Michel shook his head, so André continued. "I hope we can *décharge* most of tomorrow. But when it's too shallow or too risky, we portage everything. We carry when there's no other way. Sorry, men, I despise it too—it's hard on our knees and backs and so much slower. When we must portage, Mouse and I carry the canoe, and you all split up the cargo."

When he ended, his men glanced up and nodded their agreement. Michel looked ruefully at his pants and shirt, the first new clothes he'd owned.

Danny and Henry he addressed in English. "For the first two or three *décharges*, you must stay in the canoe, until we are working efficiently together. After that, whenever we unload, you may choose to ride or walk."

❖ ❖ ❖

Henry returned to the tent to smooth the ground and remove stones from beneath his blanket, but Danny tucked himself between André and Pretty Mouse to watch the flickering embers in the campfire and the stars twinkling in the darkening bowl of sky.

André looked for familiar constellations and pointed them out to Danny.

As they sat, a long wail rose—and fell.

Danny's eyes widened. An animal? A big one?

A few seconds later, a longer, louder call answered, swooping up in pitch.

Danny buried his head under Mouse's elbow. "What's that?" he whimpered.

The next wail became a jittery tremolo, like a horrible laugh. Echoed by another warble, and another.

"Hide me!"

"Oho, it is the feared *wiindigoo*," François said in French, making his voice scary. "Coming for unwary *voyageurs*, to eat them, especially wicked little ones. Have you lied? That's who the *wiindigoo* looks for first."

Smoking companionably, the men chuckled.

"Town boys, they know nothing of the woods. Not like us," Baptiste scoffed, continuing the jest in French.

The animal wails escalated into screams, like the pained calls of furious beasts in battle.

With each one, Danny shivered, hiding further under the safety of Pretty Mouse's arm.

When I first slept in the wilds, I remember how strange the night sounds were at first. I was new, a town boy who feared everything. Others told me wild stories about the Ojibwe wiindigo and I believed them all. Teasing the newcomers is a rite of passage that won't hurt anything. He'll figure it out, like I did.

"The *wiindigoo*, it is early this year. Mostly it comes in winter. Maybe it smells a tasty bit, the right size to steal away," Gabriel said.

"Me, I say it is more than one *wiindigoo* and they haven't eaten since last winter. The big brigades, those guys are too tough to eat. But we carry two tender boys." François was warming up. Baptiste and Gabriel guffawed. Even Pretty Mouse grinned.

Danny heard the animal shrieks and sobbed, his breath ragged and panicky.

Sensing Danny's terror, Michel broke in gruffly. "*Non! C'est les huards. Là!*" They are loons. Look there.

He tapped Danny's arm and pointed across the river to the bird raising its wings, protecting its young. "Danny, it's not a *wiindigoo. C'est les huards. Là!*"

Hearing his name, Danny timidly poked his head out to search in the darkness. When the loon screeched again, he squeezed his eyes shut and turned away, to the men's laughter. All except Michel. When Danny could look again, Michel pointed to a pair of birds, swimming low in the water.

"What is it?" Danny said in English, his voice quivering.

"*Les huards,*" Michel said. Loons.

"Lays hwards? Like the one we saw this afternoon? I see them now," Danny said, sighing in relief.

He watched as one loon dived and rose close to them, and listened as they yodeled and wailed again and again, until it finally became a long wavering call.

"*Je suis désolé*, Dannee. *Très désolé.*" A bereft Pretty Mouse hung his head. "I'm sorry, very sorry. I forgot how it is to be scared."

Mouse put out his hand in apology and Danny accepted it.

"Danny, come to bed," Henry called out from the tent.

When Danny stood, Reynard handed him a small net that he'd woven from the long root he'd been scraping. "It will trap bad dreams so they cannot reach you."

Danny looked at it curiously while André translated, and then held it to his chest. He smiled and nodded. "*Merci.*"

He walked back to his tent, dream catcher amulet in one hand, Pretty Mouse holding the other. André heard him tell Henry in English, "Did you hear those terrible animal cries? Like one was in trouble? I was a little scared and the old men teased me, but I didn't understand what they were saying. Then, the youngest one, I think his name is Michel, anyway he said they were loons, *les huards*. He showed me a pair that swam far away—one dived and came up almost by the shore and now I'm not scared. You don't have to be either."

A moment later loons yodeled again.

"That's what I told you about," Danny said. "They sound scary, but it's not a *wiindigoo*, whatever that is. And then Reynard, he's the Indian with braids, he made this to keep us from having bad dreams."

André felt ashamed. *I should have done stopped the teasing and showed him the loons. Danny's much younger than I was on my first voyage. Why did I think it was funny when I hated being teased? It took Michel to stop it. Once Michel was a bully, but he was kind tonight.*

That night Danny didn't cry himself to sleep.

When they heard animal cries—the long baying or yipping of wolves, the screech of a lynx or the pained howl of its prey—Danny's eyes widened, measuring how close it was. But he no longer feared night noises.

CHAPTER 28

At the Carillon Rapids, André found lower water levels than he'd hoped, but deep enough to *décharge*. So began the hard process of struggling against the fast current. The men towed the canoe over shallows, one after another, sometimes unloading first. Being constantly wet, they became tired and cranky, the opposite of the joyous crew André had hoped for.

The cold water pained Gabriel's knees and hips, shoulders and hands, decreasing his usefulness. His feet couldn't find solid ground and he fell often, becoming a liability. Though the afternoons were hot, he barely warmed up.

Baptiste assisted his friend, keeping him upright in the current, but that meant neither man focused much on towing the canoe.

To support Gabriel and Baptiste, Reynard had to abandon his station near the front.

As *devant*, Pretty Mouse nervously called out every ripple and stick that broke the surface, relevant or not.

In confusion, Michel reacted to each direction anyone shouted. "Is this right? François said for me to stand here."

Confined to the canoe, Danny and Henry heard the men's cross words and felt the tension.

At one *décharge*, André' dropped his setting pole which disappeared in the whitewater. He stumbled while trying to grab another pole from the bottom of the canoe.

That jerked the ropes away from Michel, Gabriel and Baptiste who accidentally lost their hold and stood helpless as the canoe slipped toward the current. Instantly it floated back downstream toward the rocky chute they'd just navigated it through.

Near the bow, François and Reynard clutched their ropes even harder, though the effort burned their shoulders.

"What should we do?" Michel stood frozen as disaster loomed. "I can't swim."

Danny and Henry twisted around, looking alarmed.

"Mouse, drive your pole deep and hold it. We need you to steady the canoe while I get a pole," André called.

"I'll try, but I can't hold it long, only a few more seconds," Mouse yelled.

Finally André seized a new pole, and could swivel them back in position. "Grab on, men, and drag us to shore. Tie the canoe to anything. We need a rest."

When the canoe swung around, Michel and Baptiste grasped for the ropes they'd dropped and followed his command.

In the pause after the near-accident, François snarled that the other crew members didn't haul together. Gabriel and Baptiste slumped in shame. Michel was shocked at how quickly the canoe got out of control.

Reynard protested that his strength would be better used at the stern where he could react and make last-minute adjustments.

André felt discouraged as they caught their breath.

Reynard is probably right about the order of where they should stand to tow. Maybe Michel should be between Baptiste and Gabriel. We'll need more time to regain our strength and confidence before we face the brunt of the Long Sault.

I'm glad Antoine wasn't here to watch us—he'd have laughed himself silly. I'd be the joke of the rendezvous. And the Carillon Rapids is only the first of our tests. Those miles of fast-flowing current through rocks and islands will test my skills and our teamwork. I have to be at my best—but will my best be good enough?

Chapter 29

The first few days they'd enjoyed clear, hot, dry weather, but clouds gathered. One morning they woke to heavy gray clouds that threatened rain. By their second break to smoke their pipes, the occasional mist became light showers. Already damp from the *décharges*, they charged ahead.

However, Henry, outraged that the voyage continued, angrily stuffed papers in his desk. "If you expected rain, you should have told me. My books will be spoilt. I doubt I can dry them properly."

Wearing damp clothing irritated him. "We'll all catch our death. Can't you rig up a cover to protect us?"

André shook his head. "Not while we're moving. It's better to take off your shirt, like we do. Then it'll be dry after the rain."

Henry refused.

The canoe barreled ahead as showers became a steady drizzle and then pelting rain. They stopped only when they saw flashes of lightning, waiting on the river bank until the dark clouds lifted and they could paddle on.

But they'd barely restarted when mosquitoes swarmed in force to feast on them.

Les moustiques! Danny learned the word very quickly.

Because the men's hands were always busy with paddles, ropes and packs, they couldn't swat them, so they swore.

Henry shushed them. "Your language is highly improper for young boys to hear," he said, in English.

While the men didn't understand his words, they recognized his intent and attempted to curb their profanity in Danny's earshot.

Bitten constantly, the men were resigned to mosquitoes biting them while they paddled and portaged and towed. It had always been so. Their camaraderie returned over the never-ending battle with their common enemy, the mosquitoes.

"Makes me glad I have a beard. Too bad Michel and André are so young," François teased.

"Me, I've tried everything," Pretty Mouse said, clapping at a mosquito buzzing his ear. "Once I slept in the water, but they found my nose."

"I traded for skunk urine at the *rendezvous*. Whew!" Baptiste said.

"Me too. But it didn't work for me," Pretty Mouse laughed. "Was it Mad Pierre that sold it to you?"

If being sticky and wet made Henry irritable, the mosquitoes infuriated him. He slapped and swatted, but strove not to scratch himself. "Don't scratch, Danny. Put on your shirt with long sleeves," he admonished.

"That makes me too hot." Danny slapped and scratched. Red welts formed on his face and arms and sweat made it sting. He cried.

André wished he'd asked Mama for one of her remedies. Unfortunately he had none.

❖ ❖ ❖

Michel held up a piece of thin cloth, his old shirt sleeve. "Would this work for Danny, if we tie it over his face?"

"It looks like a veil. Boys don't wear it." Danny was adamant.

Pretty Mouse took the cloth. "Come, Dannee. Let me … ."

"*Non!* I'll look silly. No one else does."

"I will," Henry offered. That surprised everyone—he'd been unwilling and uncooperative before. "We'll take turns. I'll go first." He tied the thin cotton to protect his face and neck so only his eyes were visible.

On the portage, Danny reluctantly agreed to take his turn.

"If I can't see animals, how can I tie knots on my string? Besides mosquitoes bite my feet and my neck and everywhere else, not just my face."

But, at the end of the portage, the sleeve had mysteriously disappeared.

❖ ❖ ❖

"Here. To keep *les moustiques* away," Baptiste said, holding an oily, smelly cake of something to Henry.

Henry sniffed and grimaced. "What is it? What do you do with it?"

"Bear grease. Rub on your arms, your neck." He demonstrated.

Henry shuddered, but applied a layer of the grease to both Danny and himself. And after the new treatment, *les moustiques* bothered them less.

When they camped that evening, Reynard added damp grasses to the fire, and a sharp-smelling smoke filled the air. He positioned Henry and Danny to sit downwind. "Let smoke get into your clothes and hair. Mosquitoes don't like smoke."

"*Les moustiques*, they're not so bad as black flies," François said. "Nothing works when we run into black flies. *Las mouches noires*, they bite through leather! We're lucky a hatch hasn't found us yet."

❖ ❖ ❖

He was right. They discovered black fly bites left bigger welts that itched even more when sweat dripped down their necks. Danny, unable to resist, scratched with abandon.

Pretty Mouse showed the boys how to dip their shirts in the cold water to ease the sting, but Henry only sloshed water on his face and arms.

Chapter 30

André's two previous experiences as a *milieu* paddling the Long Sault had been uneventful. But his group was not smooth, like Antoine's highly-experienced brigades.

They now faced portages, unloading everything and hauling it by foot over rough trails, which required much more effort than *décharges*. The increased grumbling from his men spiked over the next miles of white water which challenged their abilities.

Inspired by Papa's suggestion to cross a portage in a single pass, André urged his crew to try, but they required two trips and sometimes a third—usually someone had to return for a forgotten item.

On their first long portage, André and Mouse surged ahead with the canoe while François organized the bales, barrels and chests. He foisted the heaviest bale plus a full barrel of provisions onto Michel, who trudged across with an immense load, not realizing that Gabriel and Baptiste ambled over carrying light packs and supplies.

Finally, near the end, Michel dropped to his knees.

"I dropped the barrel, couldn't hang on," he gasped, sweating and unsteady and embarrassed at making others wait.

André confronted François. "Did you …?"

François shrugged. "But of course. This is his first real portage—all new guys carry extra heavy loads their first time. It's how they prove themselves. Didn't you too? We'll even out the loads on the rest of the portages."

André nodded, recalling that rite of passage when he was twelve, and Pretty Mouse had protected him from the worst. After this first carry, he would help Michel fend for himself.

Later that day at a *décharge*, Michel, trying to be helpful, tied a sloppy knot connecting the bow and stern. His knot loosened and the canoe bow entangled itself into a fallen tree caught along the shore. Extricating the canoe from the snarl of branches cost them more than an hour. André gritted his teeth with frustration at the mistake and the delay.

"God help me, I thought everybody knew knots that hold," François grumbled. So that evening, he taught Michel three different knots and their uses, including one that wouldn't loosen.

At another portage, Reynard offered to carry Henry's bulky desk, but stubbed his toe on a root and dropped the desk on rocks. The lock sprang open, strewing papers, packets, bags, quills and a bottle of ink which smashed—to Henry's fury.

"I'm sorry. I'll pick up your things," Reynard said.

"No, you've done quite enough damage," Henry retorted, gathering the ink-splotched papers.

During *décharges*, Henry preferred to ride. He paid no attention to the men's effort and drama, speaking only when splashes of water threatened his reading.

Danny, however, asked to walk so he could look for rabbits and squirrels. He yearned to touch one, but it was hard for him to be still enough.

When the boys stayed in the canoe, Danny's eyes would light on a bird or raccoon and he'd lurch and point, altering the canoe's balance and direction. That caused them to scrape against submerged stones. The men growled when they felt it and André tensed until he could check that they hadn't cracked open a seam in his new canoe.

Danny skipped across portages and played with his ball—until it bounced too near the water's edge. When others rescued it enough times, he tucked it into his bag. Needing something to do, he poked around in the forest. Colorful rocks attracted his attention, and the prettiest were in the shallows of the river.

Which made André nervous, because he and Pretty Mouse were carrying the 300-pound canoe and neither could give him the attention he wanted.

Mouse, more concerned about Danny's whereabouts, often stopped abruptly, forgetting to alert André, whose head was under the bow.

Portaging after a rainy morning, André lost his balance in slippery mud, skidded and fell. Mouse couldn't hold the canoe aloft by himself.

"Ohh," yelled Pretty Mouse and they fell head first into a brush-filled thicket.

Danny giggled at their mishap. He held his belly and laughed until he cried. "Oh, your faces were so funny I couldn't help laughing," he half-sputtered.

When the two leaders crawled from underneath the canoe, the crew barely contained themselves to see their leaders' hair full of twigs and grasses. They whooped with abandon. It had been too long since anything tickled them so and it was hard to hold it back. They guffawed watching Mouse and André attempt to retrieve the canoe.

Michel, who was drinking water, snorted it out his nose. "I didn't mean to laugh at you," he said. "But I can't remember ever laughing so."

André and Pretty Mouse looked at their scratched arms and then at each other's bloody faces—no real damage aside from their pride. They shrugged and grinned.

"You're bleeding," Danny cried.

"Dannee, my boy, 'tis nothing. Each of us will fall, and today it was our turn. Help me get the leaves out of my hair," Pretty Mouse said.

"No need to apologize. It's good to laugh again," André said.

When they finally righted the canoe and brought it to the river, they discovered thorns had scraped deep furrows in the birch bark and loosened a few stitches. Mending it was not one of André's skills—yet.

Fortunately repairs were minor, but their canoe began to show wear.

Laughing at our mishap strengthened our camaraderie but I hope we don't fall down more just so it brings us together. Antoine's brigades always laughed and joked—how did he encourage it?

At first I hoped we'd catch up to another brigade—it'd be easier and safer to travel together. My pride can handle being embarrassed but I'd rather others didn't see us straggle.

The next days in the Long Sault, André's ill-assorted group began to function more smoothly. Mouse shouted alarms less often, and André grew strong enough to pole away from danger.

CHAPTER 31

Danny basked in Pretty Mouse's attention, calling him "*Monsieur Souris.*" Mr. Mouse.

Deeply honored, Mouse doted on the boy like an uncle, showing him things and tending to his needs. Though he spoke only French and Danny English, they communicated.

"*Monsieur Souris*, I want to paddle by you." He didn't wait for an answer, but clambered over others to reach Pretty Mouse in the bow.

Henry grabbed Danny's shirt, halting his forward progress, and shook his head sharply, In English, he said, "Don't you see *Monsieur Souris* is working and cannot answer you? He's the canoe's main steersman, the *devant*. You can only speak to him when the canoe isn't moving."

"Oh." Danny slumped back to the place next to Henry, his lower lip starting to quiver.

André thanked Henry when they next stopped.

At the beginning of a portage, Danny tugged on Pretty Mouse's sash and raised his arms. "Carry me?"

"Oho, my Dannee, that I cannot do, *non*, I cannot," Pretty Mouse answered sorrowfully, shaking his head vigorously to compensate for his lack of English. "Me, I must carry this canoe over my head, you see. Both of my arms, they are working."

Which Henry translated.

"But ... but ... but in the canoe, can I sit by you?"

Pretty Mouse shook his head. "*Non*, my boy. When we paddle, I stand in the canoe, so I can see deep into the water. The rocks, they hide and try to break holes in our canoe. Me, I must spot them and move us away, oh, so fast. When we stop at night, first we cook our soup. But after supper, when I sit with my pipe —that is when you can sit with me."

Danny sighed and took out his ball. "Tonight after supper, then I will sit on your lap."

How did those two become so attached to each other? I'm a little jealous because I thought I'd be like a brother, but he goes first to Mouse, especially when I'm taking care of canoe problems. Is there anything I do well enough to teach him, because the others, they know more than I do?

Chapter 32

Pretty Mouse had begun the voyage by leading songs with enthusiasm, but now watching for undercurrents and submerged shoals occupied more and more of his attention. Often André reminded Mouse to sing, to keep their paddling in rhythm.

Pretty Mouse apologized. "Me, I can't sing when I search for rocks or rapids. I can't do both."

"I don't mean to overload you, friend. Your first task is to be our *devant*. Singing is an extra for us because you bring such enthusiasm."

"In Antoine's brigades, some middle paddler, any *milieu*, could call out the verses—if they knew the songs," Mouse said. "Me, I'd rather join on the choruses, but not lead."

"Gabriel, he could be our singer," Baptiste volunteered after a break to smoke their pipes. "He likes it."

"Does he know enough songs?"

"But of course. I can help him. There's extra pay?"

André nodded. That was fair, but he felt a momentary pang at the loss of the coins that Colonel Markham had so generously provided.

Gabriel eagerly began with "*A la Claire Fontaine,*" the *voyageurs*' anthem to lost love. He moved on to "If My Old Top was a Dancing Man" and "Behold, the Fair Françoise," but skipped a verse or two. After "A-rolling My Ball" and "The Return of the Soldier Husband" and a dozen others, he'd exhausted his repertoire until Baptiste—or François—suggested others.

All day they sang to Gabriel's lead. As his energy flagged, he sang slower—so they all paddled slower and slower. Their momentum stalled.

Henry accosted André. "*Voyageur* songs are not for a small boy's ears, even if they aren't in English. Danny is picking up enough French to understand the meaning. At his age, he shouldn't be hearing 'The Return of the Soldier Husband.'"

"He likes 'A-rolling My Ball' and his family's maid must have taught him '*Alouette*,'" André countered.

"Fine, but the one 'When a Christian Decides to Voyage' describes such fearful dangers—you wouldn't want him to believe that about this journey."

"Tonight I'll ask the men all the songs they know. If you give me paper and ink, I'll list them," he said stiffly, trying to compromise. "Tomorrow you can read from it, if you would, and we will sing what you choose."

Henry turned away.

He intended to be sharp, but maybe he won't be so unhappy if he has a useful task. I hope this works, because I don't know how to make this trip better for him.

That evening, André wrote down every song anyone could remember and handed the sheet to Henry.

"I can hardly make out the handwriting," Henry muttered.

"*Oui*, because the rock underneath was lumpy."

The next day, Henry called out the songs, but he didn't realize how various tempos and rhythms energized the crew.

"Henry, give us a fast song for pulling hard against the current."

"How should I know which are fast?"

"Look on top. I put them first on the list."

Henry read the top entries, but none quite suited their need. Eventually, choosing the song became a group effort, with Gabriel, François and Baptiste taking turns to lead the verses, while the rest joined in on the chorus. Henry returned to reading his book.

Danny was eager to become a full *voyageur*. When he could repeat a chorus, he did, whether he garbled the words or not. He paddled and searched for ways to help the men, especially Pretty Mouse. He soaked up every moment as an adventure, hardly needing Henry as a companion.

Henry had no such aspirations. He kept all interactions short, responding sharply to requests. Each evening he slipped into the tent early to write or read, coming out for supper and returning soon after. He ate with little appetite. On days when Reynard had caught a fish or they traded for game, Henry appreciated the change in diet and accepted larger portions.

It was actually easier when Henry didn't participate. The crew avoided him, fearing his sharp tongue. He might accuse them of some wrongdoing. His glares eroded their interest in forming a relationship.

Which André accepted—Henry wouldn't be the kind of brother he'd envisioned.

But it infuriated him when Henry occasionally angled his paddle blade in the river while the men labored. Henry would study the water as it purled around and eddied away. His oblivious experiments got in the way when the crew was struggling against a tricky current and their paddles crashed.

One evening André took advantage of the crew's search for dry wood to speak quietly to Henry, who stared moodily away.

"If you're going to paddle, you need to keep time with the others. That's why we sing," André said in his best English.

Henry flared, lifted his nose haughtily and hissed. "Don't give me orders, canoeman! I don't have to listen to you—I'm a paying passenger and not required to paddle. Furthermore, I tell you what to do."

The men stopped collecting fuel, and stood, now listening.

But André didn't care. His anger surged so strongly even his ears felt hot. He bit back hard on the words that wanted to come out. He had tried not let Henry's stinging contempt upset him, but this was too much.

André struggled to keep his voice even. "Colonel

Markham said you would help with Danny, but also do what I ask, because to be successful this brigade needs each of us to work together. If your paddle is in the water, it must not collide with ours. So far I haven't asked you to gather wood for the cooking fire or do small tasks to make it easier for the others now that we're portaging each day, but I may need to. Remember—on this brigade, I am in charge."

Henry glared, speechless.

The next day, Henry played with his paddle only after they stopped for pipe breaks. But he was clearly insulted.

I had to say that, but now he's even more unfriendly. I try to be a good leader—he's the one not fitting in.

But though the crew follows my directions, there's not much joy to hold us together. They don't mesh yet. It's folly to compare our single canoe with Antoine's seasoned brigades—but that's all I know to measure us against.

CHAPTER 33

On the afternoon after they'd maneuvered through most of the Long Sault, Pretty Mouse noticed smoke and followed a tributary a short distance off the Ottawa River. At a rocky point a pair of Indian men pulled fish from a net, looking up as the canoe neared. Part of their hidden campsite came into view.

André noticed that their scalps were shaved, with a narrow band of hair front to back. Both had tattooed foreheads. "These people are new to me. Reynard, what can you tell us about them?"

Reynard gazed for some seconds. "They could be Hurons at their summer camp. I see corn and beans in the field. And yonder are the beginnings of a longhouse but with no palisade surrounding it, so it's not their main village."

"Are Hurons friends?"

"We always come as friends."

"Let's break for a pipe," André called, and dug in the trade goods for tobacco to offer. "I want to ask about river conditions, learn the news. Reynard, can you translate?"

Reynard shrugged but went with André. "If not, I will listen and watch."

"Me, I want to trade for food. With Dannee?" Pretty Mouse asked hopefully.

"I don't know the language so I'll stay with the canoe," Michel said. He picked up a stone and began polishing the whistle he'd whittled.

"So will I," Henry said. "Do ask about more bear grease for mosquitoes. Danny and I used most of what Baptiste gave us."

Henry unlocked his desk and sat under a tree with paper, an ink pot and a quill.

André and Reynard consulted with the elders, who wore the symbols showing their importance. One had a wide silver band circling his upper arm and a necklace of shiny silver coins, another a curious belt of small white and purple shells.

Is that wampum? If they tell us its story, this stop could take more time than I expected.

They sat smoking a ceremonial pipe and listening before André had Renyard ask his questions in sign language.

Pretty Mouse traded for a half-dozen dried fish, a duck, a handful of mushrooms and some wild onions, planning a stew. Afterwards, Danny chirped happily, curious about this Indian encampment, so they wandered slowly back to the canoe.

Until Danny noticed a child about his own age. Their eyes locked.

Mouse dug into his bag of possibles for a nubbin of vermilion, like a crayon, and handed it to Danny to offer it in return as a gift.

Nearby a grandmother pushed a cake of maple sugar toward them.

"Oh, I know this. It's good," Danny said gleefully, tasting the treat. Then he remembered his manners. "Mercy bow coo."

"*Miigwetch*," the grandmother replied, prodding the Indian boy to speak.

"Meeg-witch," Danny repeated, memorizing the sounds.

François had placed his own trade goods—fishhooks and chisels—on the ground. A young warrior examined the wares, nodded and pulled a skin from his pack. Baptiste and Gabriel traded needles and beads for new moccasins.

Michel tested his whistle, making adjustments until finally sound came out. He sat back, pleased with his success. A girl who'd been watching slipped over to him and reached out her hand to try it. When she understood how to make sounds herself, she took off her beaded wristlet and handed it to Michel. He smiled, surprised at making the swap without saying a word.

When, André returned to the canoe, he was pleased. "That worked out well. We know more about the upcoming rapids and the rest of you have made good trades."

Reynard was quiet but adamant. "We should leave. Now."

They paddled away, but André was mystified. When they had returned to the Ottawa River, no longer in hearing distance, he asked "What's wrong? I thought we'd made friends."

"I don't trust them—their moccasins look like those of the traditional enemies of my people. If they wish us ill, they may follow us. Tonight we should stand watch," he answered.

That evening, using a stick, Reynard drew a boot, wrapped with ankle ties and a smooth pointed toe. "Did you see? Their moccasins are like that," he said. "Now look at mine."

André glanced at Reynard's feet—the leather puckered where the toe section met the sole. He'd never paid attention to those details. "Perhaps they traded for them," he suggested.

"Maybe, but then I don't trust their trading partners. Or their friends. In the back of their encampment, did you see that large hill, one without trees and grass? It looked like a burial mound from their wars."

André had forgotten about battles between tribes who had long fought over fishing and hunting lands and trading rights. More recently, white settlers had pushed from the east, usurping Indian lands. He recalled seeing Pretty Mouse's scarred back, disfigured from years ago when his brigade was ambushed. But Mouse, focused on Danny, wasn't nervous in this village.

"André, I saw a British uniform hanging outside the wigwam. Does that mean they side with the British? Like collaborators or spies?" Michel asked.

"Uniforms are nothing to worry about. When I was the head clerk at a trading post, we called them 'chief's coats' and awarded them to the best hunters and trappers."

"So if Indians wear enemy uniforms, they're friends?"

"It's not that simple," Reynard said. "About those coats you bestow—we like them because they're warm and dry faster than wet leather. But the men you give them to aren't our real chiefs. We don't like having someone else name them chiefs—there's more to leading a band than being a good hunter or trapper."

Andre felt chagrined, remembering how he'd curried favor using chief coats.

Reynard continued. "Not long ago, the Shawnees changed their minds about white settlers because there are more and more each day. Some say that associating with whites contaminates us all, that we should destroy the blankets, guns, tools and all white goods which dilute our culture—it's why my people sent me to listen. I'm still thinking how to advise them."

It was the first time Reynard had spoken so long and passionately. His comments stunned André.

"I'm glad you told us—about the moccasins and the chief coats. I'll take the first watch tonight."

Our fur trade canoes always use their rivers, but we could face attacks like Mouse did long ago. Are we traveling through their land without permission? What would happen if they aren't our friends any more? I can't protect us—we don't have weapons except for our knives. Did I do wrong by giving gifts that changed the natural order in their tribes?

Those Huron elders today told us that British soldiers promised them a land free of settlers if they would ally with them when war broke out with the Americans. Not if a war started, but when. So they see another war coming. They said they refused to fight another country's war. But they too might follow the Shawnees in opposing white settlers. What message will Reynard give his people?

Why does this interior country matter? How much will it affect the tribes, or traders, or us? Will anything happen before we get Danny to his father?

Sleep came very late to André as he roused Baptiste for the second watch.

Chapter 34

"Can't we go any faster?" André urged the men. "If we sing livelier songs we can pick up our speed."

Due to their inexperience, it had taken four full days to traverse the twelve miles of near-constant islets, boulders and rapids of the Long Sault. Antoine's best crews could do it in a single day. Now that the river had widened out, André hoped to make up the time they'd lost.

Just then Danny tugged at Pretty Mouse's leg and pointed to a small frog basking on a log. As they watched, the frog's long tongue shot out and curved around a fly.

Mouse glared at André. "I need a break. Everyone needs rest. Except maybe you. Steering in the back, you could be enjoying the scenery for all I know. Now Dannee, he wants to show me something."

The criticism jolted André. True, he liked steering from the stern and no one could see what he did. He could think about what needed attention—the river, the crew, Danny, the provisions, the trade goods. He knew how to be a *gouvernail*. And he felt guilty not taking the position at the bow, the position Colonel Markham expected he would take as leader.

I thought Pretty Mouse felt honored being our devant. He's never held such an important job. Maybe he couldn't say no, since I paid off the contract he defaulted on. But I don't want to be the guide—I don't know enough.

He knew being a *devant* required constant focus to sense the patterns of water indicating small rapids or fast current, large boulders or submerged dead trees, in enough time to order "Lift paddles right," "Hold left side," "Double-time, all," "Back-paddle."

André saw that the tasks overwhelmed Pretty Mouse and made him nervous. Mouse had confused the crew, calling attention to each boulder or dead tree, even those that wouldn't cause problems. Worse, Pretty Mouse was making more and more mistakes.

❖ ❖ ❖

It came to a head one morning when Pretty Mouse froze in mid-stream, staring at high cliffs surrounding them. Immediately their canoe floundered.

Alarmed, everyone stopped paddling in unison—pointing out rocks and deadheads, shouting directions and questions, cursing, poling off rocks. Each one acted on his own and the canoe swirled out of control.

Still Pretty Mouse didn't move.

Without coordination, they drifted backwards toward the rocky shore.

Finally André jammed his setting pole between boulders and held on until the bow swung fully around. Then he yelled, "Right side, back-paddle. Left side, double-time."

The canoe pivoted, heading back into the main channel. Pale-faced, Mouse took over again.

As soon as they could stop, they did. André was furious. "What happened?"

Abashed, Pretty Mouse hung his head and wrung his hands. "That place we just were, it was where warriors attacked my canoe years ago. I told you, remember? Today I saw them again, waiting for me."

"I didn't see any warriors."

Pretty Mouse shrugged, looking at his feet.

That shocked André!

The rest of the day, Pretty Mouse seemed to put the incident behind him.

Guides can only think about the river, never anything else. But how can I chastise him for his lapse when his back has scars?

He won't ask to be demoted—he'll slog on, but what if he makes more mistakes? One of them will cost us. I've encouraged him because I was relieved not to be responsible. Maybe we should take turns at being guide.

❖ ❖ ❖

In the evening, while Pretty Mouse was washing up after supper, André suggested a change. "Mouse, should I be our *devant* tomorrow? You could take a break for a day—I should have thought about this earlier. We could take turns until ..."

"Oh, André! So happy you have made me," Pretty Mouse yelped. "When I steer from the stern, I can sing again, and make better soups. And watch little Dannee up close—he needs me. Oh, André, it is what I want the most. Guiding as *devant*, I hate it—I didn't know how to tell you. I don't even like steering as *gouvernail*, but it's not as hard as in front, responsible for everything. Wheee! I can be me again." He leapt up and grabbed André's arm and swung him around, dancing for joy.

I expected Mouse to refuse and try harder to please me, or at least consider it for a few days before deciding. Pretty Mouse is free, but I'm stuck with that weight, that yoke. I hope I don't make any mistakes.

❖ ❖ ❖

The next day, André stood in the bow as guide, watching constantly, aware that his crew were studying him closely. His mind was full of the increased responsibilities.

Why does the water move like that? Is that the main current or an undercurrent? Should we pull up or portage? Where is the portage trail?

Now that the river had widened, they faced less-complicated challenges. For that he was grateful, but the effort sapped his energy. Mouse shook his head when André asked to swap back for the following day. Exhausted and grouchy, André fell asleep shortly after supper.

Switching positions encouraged others to air their preferences. "Me and Gabriel, we work better in the same row, so I can help him." "My left shoulder, it's sore. Better if I paddle on the right."

Michel and Reynard exchanged their portage loads. When André noticed, Michel said, "It makes our work easier. We didn't think you'd mind. Did we need to ask permission?"

François especially had suggestions for André's steering: "Main current's on that side—deeper too. We should paddle over there." "Canoe's not balanced. Move the chests aft now that our food barrels are getting lighter."

Danny's chatter and activity interrupted Reynard's need for quiet.

Everyone cringed at Henry's sharpness.

To their numerous suggestions, André responded with "Perhaps. I'll think on it."

Now that it's all on my shoulders, I hardly have time to decide. They bristle at my directions, when they're angry, when I push them to hurry or make a portage when a décharge would have sufficed, when they think I'm wrong. Do their comments mean they don't trust me as a leader? How did Antoine manage?

Chapter 35

"I like being a *voyageur*," Danny said. "Our maid, she got mad when I didn't keep my clothes clean—or my hands. Oh, look! A squirrel—I wonder how I could catch it."

In the canoe, Danny struggled to sit quietly. On land, tossing his ball bored him after it bounced awry. Then he'd would poke at worms in puddles, peer into holes and trees, search for the few raspberries birds hadn't eaten and wander. He'd find rocks, selecting ones to save—which the men added to their loads.

Of the crew, only Pretty Mouse, freed from the weight of guiding, enjoyed the journey. He kept a rolling patter, in French, with Danny who answered in English, or a few words of French. Whether either understood each other's exact words mattered not, because they connected deeply.

However, as the daily routine settled, the faults of others worked on the crew. But no one spoke directly to André.

Instead the men provoked each other. François pointed out Michel's deficiencies. "Hurry over the portage—*voyageurs* dog-trot, not shuffle." "I thought everyone could hoist a barrel."

Michel felt Baptiste and Gabriel shirked their share of the loads. He heard their snickers and smelled high wines. Baptiste and Gabriel couldn't match their strokes with anyone. Reynard spent his evenings away from the campsite.

Henry said little, but when he spoke, everyone stiffened. To keep him from finding fault, they erected the tent first, delivered his food—and ignored him. André felt a personal sting in each of Henry's criticisms.

CHAPTER 36

The afternoon heat became stifling. To take advantage of the cool mornings, they tried to set off before sunrise, though it was hard for Danny and Henry to rise that early.

Often a mist hung over the river, not yet evaporated, and the men paddled silently, hating to break the quiet so Danny and Henry might doze. Until the sun's warmth dispersed the fog, the men could only glimpse treetops and an occasional bird.

Once, after they had rounded a point where a stream fed into the Ottawa, André spied a dark shadow shifting among reeds. Then it was hidden by the gray cloudy mist.

His heart thumped.

What is that? Real or shadow? The Iroquois that Pretty Mouse feared? Enemies of Reynard's people? A beast?

He quietly signaled to hold all paddles and they slowed, gliding through the vapor, seeing almost nothing. He held his breath trying to decide what to do.

A second later André discerned a long black head. Black eyes followed their progress. He saw huge ears, eyes and nostrils, its body still hidden by the raveling mist.

"What is it? A bear?"

"A *wiindigoo*?"

"*Un orignal!*" breathed Gabriel. A moose. "Not since my year in the woods have I seen such a moose."

Antoine had once regaled them with a story of barely escaping a moose, which had been surprisingly fast and notoriously cranky.

As they silently drifted closer to its ominous presence, André's heart raced. Alert to danger, each man's arms were poised to move.

The mist parted and they saw the moose plunge his head into the water. When he raised it, bands of green grasses crisscrossed his wide nose and dripped from his velvety stubs of antlers. He chewed the succulent plants for several moments and contemplated the nearing canoe.

"Dannee, look!" Pretty Mouse whispered, prodding him lightly.

Rubbing his eyes, Danny twisted around and yelped.

André shushed them.

At the sudden noise, the black shadow shifted. The moose stopped chewing. Without warning he lunged toward them. His powerful shoulders propelled him with astonishing speed. In a trice the moose was only a few yards away.

"Double-time!" André ordered. *Did I wait too long?*

Instantly their paddles dug into the river and they shot into the main current.

All paddles except Reynard's, who gazed directly at the moose and intoned quiet syllables.

The moose paused in its swim, eyeing them until the canoe disappeared. Then it returned to the marshy shore to forage.

"Moose, they can be ornery. That one we saw years ago, Gabriel, it didn't like us then and this one didn't like us now. Me, I think they are brothers, these moose," Baptiste said.

When they were a safe distance, André confronted Reynard, "Why didn't you help paddle? A few yards closer and that moose would have smashed our canoe to bits."

Reynard hesitated. "This *naabe-mooz*, when I saw its head lifting above the mist, I knew it had something to tell me."

"It meant to attack us," André retorted.

"This one gave me a message—that my people are calling to me. I asked him not to harm our little canoe as we pass through."

André didn't press—Reynard had interceded for them.

Maybe he was like André's friend Thunder who had developed unusual skills following his vision quest.

"You spoke to the moose, almost like a prayer," Michel said.

"Animals don't like us disturbing them—they disappear while the big brigades paddle through. But the *naabe-mooz* is special to my family—we see them when others don't," Reynard said, fingering a piece of antler strung around his neck.

"Dannee," Pretty Mouse said. "Tie a big knot for that *l' orignal*."

"I learned Reynard's people call it a *naabe-mooz*," Michel said. "Time for me to start my own string."

Chapter 37

Having challenged himself to carry all his assigned pieces in one load, Michel arrived first across a portage. While he waited for the others, he picked up a round stone—flat, smooth, just the right size. He spun it over the river and watched it skip.

Grinning, he selected another and flung it farther across the waters. It skipped twice before its final plunk!

Danny arrived to see its last bounce. He watched, amazed.

"*Comment?*" Danny said shyly, unsure of his French. He wanted to ask how Michel had done that.

"Like this," Michel said, unsure of his English. He demonstrated. "*Comme ça.*"

Danny reached down for the closest rock, a lumpy one.

"*Non, non. Comme ça.*" Like this. Michel handed him a smooth flat rock, which Danny pitched high. It didn't skip like Michel's had.

"Oh, well." He turned away.

"Danny, *comme ça.*" Michel showed again the sideways wrist motion needed to spin one and gave him a handful of flat smooth stones, the right kind for skipping.

Danny heaved a dozen or two, unable to master the skill even when Michel guided his hand. Dejected, he wanted to quit.

Until one pebble skipped—a single bounce.

Amazed, he looked at his hand.

"Did you see? My stone, it bounced," Danny was in awe.

Michel dropped to his hands and knees, joined by Danny, and they each selected small piles.

"Are these good?" Danny asked, showing the rocks he'd chosen, mostly because for their pretty colors.

Michel pawed through to choose good ones. "*Oui.*"

It took Danny many tosses before another one skipped—and he was hooked.

Michel added more pebbles to his pile and Danny managed to skip a few more. It was enough—he was elated.

A few minutes later, Henry arrived.

"Henry, look what we can do. You try it." Danny held out a rock. When Henry's first stone didn't skip, Danny said, "Like so. Ah … ah … *Comme ça*," demonstrating.

Henry's second stone didn't skip either and he turned away to look for his book.

"Henry, *comme ça*." Michel showed him more slowly.

When one of Henry's stones skipped, he looked surprised.

Michel handed him a pile of smooth pebbles.

It took Henry at least twenty tries before another one skipped. He too was captivated. When he'd depleted his pile of stones, he searched for more of the right kind.

As the others trudged in carrying their packs and blankets, chests and barrels, they saw the three skipping stones.

"Oho. Me, I haven't done that for years." Baptiste said. He quickly deposited his loads and grabbed a handful of stones, followed by Gabriel, François and even Reynard. Some of their tosses skipped many times before dropping.

Finally Pretty Mouse and André arrived with the canoe.

"*Monsieur Souris*, look," Danny called. "Michel showed us. Watch me."

The stone Danny threw skipped twice—to the cheers of Pretty Mouse.

André was astonished to see his men playing. "We can take time to toss a few more—if we paddle longer tonight."

Henry, of all people, is having fun. Too bad I'll have to break it up.

CHAPTER 38

While the men labored over portages or *décharges*, Danny and Henry now scurried to the end, searching first for berries on the trail and pebbles once they'd crossed. After Henry had skipped a few stones, he propped open his book.

On the other hand, Danny strove to skip his stones even farther over the river. He selected better pebbles, strengthened his arm, refined his technique, perfected his aim and occasionally saw his stones skip more than one bounce.

He reasoned that standing on shore limited his throws—and climbed rocks or low trees to lengthen his reach.

Then, he spotted a perfect branch leaning over the river. He glanced back to locate the men laden with their packs and concluded he had enough time.

Filling his pockets with stones, he clambered up, crawled along the branch, seated himself and began pitching them across the water. He enjoyed the final *plunk!* as much as the skip, kicking his legs back and forth in glee.

His pockets emptied, Danny needed more stones. So he jumped down, forgetting how high he'd climbed and how far over the river the branch extended.

At the moment of landing, he toppled into moving water.

Henry looked up at the splash. "Danny? What did you do? Help! Hurry—Danny fell in!" he screamed.

Reynard, toting both boys' trunks, dropped them and ran.

"Over there! Save him!" Henry pointed to where Danny's arms and head were swirling in an eddy nearing the waterfall the men had portaged around. Henry fell to his knees, his voice unsteady. "It happened so fast ... it's my fault ..."

Immediately Reynard bounded into the river, keeping Danny in his sight. He stretched but his arms didn't reach.

Michel arrived to see the tassel of Danny's red *tuque* slipping underwater. The current drew Danny farther away, close to the rapids. "I don't know how to help—I can't swim."

"Me neither," Baptiste said. "I'm scared to."

François cracked off a long dead branch and pushed it toward them. "Help me get this to Reynard."

They shoved it toward Reynard who grasped the end.

Its thin end broke in his hands.

Reynard grabbed again and wedged the far end between rocks while Baptiste sat on the near end to stabilize it on shore. When it was secure, Reynard used it to spring toward Danny.

The others held their breath.

Closer, but not quite enough—the eddy was swirling Danny farther out toward the fast-flowing current.

Gabriel rubbed the cross hanging inside his shirt.

Reynard returned to the branch. Taking a moment to see where Danny was, he surged toward him again.

This time his fingers grasped Danny's shirt. Clenching the fabric, he pulled the boy nearer until, with a great grunt, his other hand seized Danny's shoulder.

Turning Danny's head upwards and wrapping an elbow across his chest, Reynard made his way back to the branch.

But their extra weight loosened it. No longer secure, it swung into the eddy, drifting again near the rapids.

Reynard kicked but couldn't aim himself and Danny along the branch toward shore. It was all he could do to keep them away from the waterfall.

By the time André and Pretty Mouse arrived, François had organized a human chain—anchoring himself onshore with Gabriel and Baptiste. Michel found a place among the boulders.

Pretty Mouse waded in up to his hips, anxious about Danny and his uncertain ability to hold his own in the current.

"I can swim—I'll take the far end," André said, sloshing up to his chest and then kicking hard until he could reach the branch that Reynard clutched. Though awkward, he swung it around, pulling it closer to shore.

Once the branch was within reach, Pretty Mouse muscled it in and braced it. André drew near enough to stand and add his strength.

"Pull them in, men. Reynard can't hold on much longer against this current," François shouted.

Hand over hand, the men on shore pulled. When its small limbs snagged on boulders, they yanked hard.

Many minutes later, they dragged the waterlogged pair onto the clearing.

After an exhausted Reynard released Danny, Pretty Mouse searched for life in the boy's pale face. He lifted him, hugged him, moaning and rocking the boy like a baby. "Oh, my Dannee."

André didn't know what to do. No one had suggestions.

Baptiste paced, working his hands.

Gabriel clutched his wooden cross, looking skyward and murmuring pleas to Ste. Anne. Henry knelt in prayer.

Then, as if Pretty Mouse's hug were too tight, Danny convulsed, spewing out water, coughing and spluttering. He wheezed—and sucked in air.

Gabriel cheered and embraced Baptiste. "Mother of God, he lives!" They held each other in relief.

Danny gazed vaguely around. He fell back limply.

The men found it hard to approach the boy—they'd seen too many friends drown.

"*Miigwetch*," André said, extending his hand to Reynard and François in appreciation. Henry and the others followed.

"It's early but we'll camp here tonight," André said.

Pretty Mouse kept the boy close by, wrapped in his own blankets near the fire, talking to him constantly as he prepared the soup. "You need something lighter than porridge tonight. Maybe I should make wintergreen tea for you. With maple sugar?"

Michel brought him the tail of a gray squirrel.

"Here—I found it a few days ago."

A grateful Danny rubbed the fur against his hand and cheek, entranced at its softness.

Once the disaster had been averted, the men sat musing as they ate supper. André stayed by himself.

Like Papa said, depend on your mates, they know what you don't. Today Reynard knew what to do, and François. Their quick thinking saved Danny, lucky for us. I've worried about him falling out of the canoe since we set out—but I never thought he'd fall in from shore and us only yards away. Danny moves fast—he's hard to keep track of. Watching out for him takes valuable time. How can we manage that?

I know he wants to hold an animal, a live being of his own. I remember how important my sled dogs were after they brought me through the woods and the blizzard. Maybe we can find something.

I'm glad Henry felt guilty—he should see we can't pay close attention while we're working. I wish he'd take over. But I'm ultimately responsible—I promised to get him to his father. I thought this would be an easy voyage. Was I wrong!

There were no quick answers. He had to deliver this boy to Captain Ashton as soon as possible. Back to hurrying.

Before they left, André announced new rules. "First, while we portage, Henry must be responsible for Danny. Pretty Mouse has his hands full and can't attend to him. He can hardly answer questions while we're carrying the canoe. Second, Danny—no tree-climbing unless one of us is next to you. And both your feet must be on dry land when you skip stones. Every time. You can only get your feet wet if I am nearby."

From the silence, André guessed he had stepped on toes. Would Mouse and the others still follow him?

The next morning, Danny was quieter than his normal self. When they stopped for a pipe break on shore, he waited in front of Reynard. "*Monsieur* Reynard?"

Reynard looked up.

"I wish to say..." he searched for Henry, who had disappeared in the woods. He stretched out his hand to Reynard. "You put your life in peril to save me and I thank you. *Merci beaucoup.*"

André translated that as well as Reynard's response, "All of us took part."

"*Merci, Monsieur* Andre, I will be very careful. How do I say 'thank you' in Reynard's language?"

"*Miigwetch.*"

"Meeg-wetch?" Danny attempted and Reynard smiled one of his rare smiles.

CHAPTER 39

Baptiste showed Danny how he could tell trees apart by their different leaves—rounded or pointed, smooth or toothy, with veins radiating or parallel.

Danny listened politely until the lesson was over. It was interesting but he needed to run.

François taught whittling and knife skills to Michel and Danny, and occasionally to Henry.

Andre helped Danny to identify and make bird calls until he could mimic robins, hawks and jays with some accuracy. But the birds mostly flew away before he could find them in the trees.

They saw tracks along the river's edge, though the animals kept themselves hidden. When Reynard pointed out tracks of deer, fox, raccoon, muskrats, rabbits and squirrels, Danny became enthralled. He liked knowing what animal it was, where it was headed and how fast. He began to notice leaves that had been chewed or twigs broken.

He learned to walk slowly. He looked longingly at a brown rabbit that pretended to be invisible.

"Could I keep it?" Danny asked in rough French.

Reynard shook his head. "The animals must stay with their families."

"But couldn't I be its family? It could sleep with me and I could feed it pea soup."

Reynard shook his head again.

"What if the mother and father are gone? Then could I?"

Reynard simply gazed at him.

When they paddled around a bend in the river, Danny spotted a family of otters swimming near them. "*Les loutres!* Otters—swimming underwater! One went down there. But where will it come up? Oho, there, by that stream. They're playing. Animals are playing!" He was spellbound as they slid into the river, and eyed them jealously.

"They're playing in the water," he said plaintively to Henry. "I wish we could but *Monsieur* André won't let me get my feet wet. It's hot. We never have any fun."

"You're being childish," Henry admonished him. "You know we can't be in the river. Remember all those broken paddles lashed together? André said each one marks the watery grave of a friend. We almost put one up for you a few days ago."

Henry shivered. Danny looked sadly at the otters.

Oops, I only wanted them to understand what the paddles meant. We can't risk a repeat of his near-drowning but Danny needs fun. Fun? When did we last have fun? Maybe I could show them how to swim like Black Duck and her friends at the last rendezvous. Is that irresponsible, after Danny nearly drowned? Will Henry agree?

André tossed the idea back and forth. *Yes. No.* And finally, *if I see the right place, we'll stop so they can play in the water. And learn to swim.*

❖ ❖ ❖

"Oho, *les bleuets,*" Gabriel said. Blueberries. Holding a small kettle one evening at their campsite, he gestured for Danny to follow him. "Come. Get your cup."

"*Les bleuets?*" Danny asked, confused as if he should know something.

"*Oui, les bleuets.*" Gabriel held out his neckerkerchief with a few blueberries to show him.

Gabriel led Danny through a piney woods toward an open glade, and knelt by a low bush loaded with white blossoms, tiny green berries and a dozen large blue ones.

"Oho, *beaucoup des bleuets!*" Many blueberries. Danny was enchanted.

Gabriel smiled and cupped his fingers beneath a cluster of

the ripest berries, raking them into his hand. "*Comme ça.* Like so, do you see?"

Danny tried, spilling most. He tried to pick them off the ground.

"*Non.* Let them be on the ground—they'll grow new berries next year." They found another bush for Danny to harvest. Gabriel demonstrated how to hold his fingers like a claw and pull to capture berries in his cup. "Eat one, keep one for the cup. Eat one, keep one, eh?"

Danny nodded happily, snacking on some berries and dropping others with a satisfying *plink!* into his cup.

Gabriel filled his kettle with berries. He grinned, watching Danny scramble over rocks searching for more.

They presented their results to Pretty Mouse. "Oho, I'll make blueberry soup like my *grand-mère.*"

He rummaged among the trade goods for a nutmeg and added his maple sugar to the teakettle of river water, which he placed on the edge of the fire to bubble until after supper.

"Dannee, taste this."

"I like it. Our maid, she made this once. *Monsieur Souris, Monsieur* Gabriel, *merci beaucoup,*" Danny said.

Their addition to supper brought compliments from the men, especially Henry.

"Danny, tomorrow when we portage, you can look for *les bleuets* and pick many, many in your cup, *oui*? Now you have another thing to do if you cannot skip the stones," Baptiste said.

"*Oui, Monsieur* Baptiste. If *Monsieur* André says I may."

André nodded. *Both feet on dry land. No climbing. No wading. How could Danny get in trouble with that?*

CHAPTER 40

Two days later, well in the afternoon, André spied a brook with a wide sandy delta. He directed the canoe to pull up. As usual, his men took out their pipes.

"Peel off your shirts, boys. We're going to swim."

Danny looked first at Henry, who rolled his eyes. "No. It's not suitable."

"Please, Henry. It's so hot. We could ..."

"All my people swim," Reynard said.

"Fortunately for us—you never know when you might need it. It's fun. I learned a few years ago. Anyone else want to try?" André looked at his crew, who mostly shook their heads, glad for the break.

"I know how," François said.

"Okay if I join you?" Michel asked.

Henry relented. "Well, Danny, you may but I certainly will not. I will watch you. Because someone must, if André insists on allowing you in the river, after ... ."

"Oh thank you. Do come, *Monsieur Souris*. Please, please, please," Danny begged.

Pretty Mouse and Michel tore off their shirts and moccasins and splashed in the river.

"Seeing as Pretty Mouse is already wet, Gabriel and me, we'll start the porridge," Baptiste said.

André taught Black Duck's lessons—sit down in the water and let it come up to your chin. Hold your breath, then put your face in. Open your eyes to see the things under the water. Let yourself float, then fishtail or kick your legs if you want to propel yourself.

Reynard showed them water games, until Baptiste called them to supper.

"*Merci beaucoup*, André. *Miigwetch*, Reynard. *Monsieur Souris*, wasn't that the best thing?" Danny said, his eyes glowing.

"Your Papa, he'll be surprised to see you swim," Pretty Mouse said.

"*Oui*. My Papa, he will be proud. I don't think he knows how to swim."

"New rule, Danny. You can never swim alone. Never. If you even get your feet wet, one of us who can swim must be with you. You promise?"

Danny beamed. "But I can skip stones when I have both feet on dry land? And I can pick *les bleuets?*"

André nodded. He'd done something right.

CHAPTER 41

Too soon they hit the daunting *Chaudière* rapids.

André's stomach churned at navigating his first major challenge as *devant*. Wracking his memory for how Antoine had piloted them through the *Chaudières* brought no information. When he questioned Mouse, François interjected opinions.

Both remembered steep-sided gorges and exhausting nearly-vertical portages. But where should they approach it?

"We take the portage on the north side of the river. We always do," Pretty Mouse said.

"That's because of the heavy runoff of early spring," François argued. "Now, it's the middle of July and the water is low. Let's try the south bank. Big brigades, for them it's impossible, but ha! we are little, and we are *voyageurs*."

"*Non*, that side, it's never safe," Pretty Mouse insisted. "The worst obstacles for canoes, they hide under that placid water. Besides, because of our little boy, we cannot tip. His father is British, and he will have our heads if anything happens."

The reminder of Danny's near-drowning shut up François.

The closer they came, the louder the roar, the more crosses of lashed broken paddles were staked into both banks—and the higher André's anxieties mounted. An almost-dry boulder field on the south proved there wasn't enough current to float them.

André said, "The north—at the narrow waterway at the foot of the falls—that's where we portage. It'll be a wet carry."

"You'll need every one of us to haul the canoe over," François growled, grumpy at being overruled.

"Right you are. So on the second pass, Mouse and I will tote provisions and goods with the rest of you," André said.

Before coming to shore, they paused to glimpse the picturesque *Chaudières*—a lovely high white curtain of water tumbling over a wide thundering falls.

"It's a torrent, as turbulent as a cauldron—I must draw it," Henry said, mesmerized by the veil of water hurtling onto great limestone boulders, the shoreline edged by makeshift crosses.

Like the boiling kettles it's named for. I hope I can get us through the eddies and back-currents. Ste. Anne, watch over us all. Clenching his setting pole, but barely breathing, André guided them so close to the falls that they were drenched by its spray.

The portage was as difficult at François had predicted. Soaking wet from exertion as much as the spray, they returned for the packs and trunks to find Henry still sketching, unaware of their extreme efforts.

"Henry, you'll have to stop. This is our last pass over the portage. Can you finish later?"

Henry sighed and locked his things into his desk.

They paddled again against a relentless current that tumbled through narrow chutes and churned around slippery boulders. André poled as the men paddled hard against it. He studied every small purl for clues to dangers beneath the surface. Only when they stopped at the next carrying place did he relax.

How strange—I'm relieved to portage instead of paddle. Every man I know would rather paddle a dozen extra miles to avoid even a short portage because it takes so much effort to haul everything on our backs.

On the next portage, Pretty Mouse led Danny up crude stone steps. "Look, Dannee! Carved by tribes long ago."

The steps intrigued Danny, who climbed them and hurried down, several times, before continuing on the path. Then he ran ahead to search for blueberries with the hope of skipping stones.

"I'm going to sketch these steps," Henry decided, choosing his angle with care.

Chapter 42

The men slogged over another difficult carry, so narrow that they needed three passes to cross with boys' chests and provisions.

As they reloaded the canoe, neither boy was around.

"Where did they get to now? Someone, go back and check the steps." André felt frustrated.

"I'll go," Michel said and trotted to the beginning where Henry sat, drawing the scene. "We're waiting for you two. But where's Danny?"

Henry hastily collected his papers, looking guilty. "Finally I could enjoy doing something I like. Danny was right here—he played on the steps for a long time."

They didn't find Danny on the hike back.

"Danny promised he'd stay on the shore."

Pretty Mouse wept. "Ste. Anne, we need you again. Be with the little one until we find him."

"We didn't hear a splash—I'm sure he's not in the river." Baptiste gazed downstream over the roiling waters.

"But the falls are so loud we might have missed it," François said. "Skipping stones, drawing, playing? Don't they see how hard we work?"

André lashed out at François. "You knew what the task was before we left. But you signed on."

"Who knew what lads are like? They move constantly on land and in the canoe."

Their bickering bothered Michel. "We were that age once,

all of us. But too soon we forget what it was like."

Embarrassed, André bit back his response.

He's right—they're children. Danny disappeared so fast—what could've happened to him? A bear? A wolf? Wouldn't we have heard something? Or was he stolen by enemies of Reynard's tribe?

"How do we find him?" Michel asked, his face pale as he contemplated the dense black forest. "I've never gone deep into the woods before. The trees lock their arms against us."

Reynard organized the search. "We look where he might have gone. Gabriel, stay with Henry and watch the animals on the shoreline. See if they tell us something useful."

Henry frowned. "How can animals tell you where he is? That's no way to find someone."

"You see," Gabriel said, "if the boy wanders near a bird's nest, that bird will get upset. Then it flies up and caws and flaps. Animals, they won't come to drink if people are near."

"The rest of us, start back up the trail. Keep calling his name." André tried to bring order to the group.

That might ease Michel's fear of the shadowy forest with its dense twisted branches.

"*Non*, André, not yet. First we are quiet." Reynard sniffed the air and closed his eyes to identify smells.

Slowly he led them along the portage path, looking for trail signs, holding his hand up frequently to halt their progress, listening or smelling. He pointed out shrubs that showed where Danny had passed.

"He picked berries here," Reynard said, noting the crushed blueberries on the rocky ground.

"Then he turned off onto this game trail. You see the broken twigs? And his footprint over there? We enter here."

"What if we lose contact with each other? Can we call out now, Reynard?" asked Michel.

When Reynard nodded, they shouted Danny's name, stepping noisily, slowly, carefully in the thick brush, peering around for movement. There was no response.

"Halloo? Dannee?" Mouse's voice was plaintive.

André's anxiety spiraled, his stomach in a hard knot. *How could he get so far away in such a short time? Where would he go? Why can't he sit still? How long do we search? What if we can't find him?*

❖ ❖ ❖

Minutes stretched as they made their way through the thorny foliage.

"Are you hiding? Come out," called François.

"Speak to us, little boy," Baptiste echoed. "So we know where you are."

When there was no answer, they inched ahead, calling, waiting for some sound to locate him.

Sweat poured out of André. *First nearly drowning, now lost—and I'm panicking. Papa would say ... he would say "The impossible, it just takes longer. Think more." We'll find him. We must—but the sun will set in a few hours.*

Finally Reynard pointed to the ground—a few more dropped blueberries and a heel mark. "Here. He walked here—he followed a rabbit."

In all this forest, how did Reynard notice that?

They crept a step further—calling, waiting. Another step, calling, waiting. Again.

❖ ❖ ❖

Reynard stopped, put his finger up to his mouth for quiet.

He sniffed and listened. Then he pointed to a grove of tall red pine trees ahead.

At that moment, they heard a *hunff!*

Then silence.

"What was that?" Michel asked, nervous.

Reynard knelt to search for tracks. He sniffed and scanned the area. "Hush. Wait," he said. He stepped off the game trail and slipped around a massive red pine.

He motioned them to come quietly.

There they saw Danny, some yards away, curled between another tree's roots, sleeping deeply. His cup lay nearby, a few blueberries spilled out. A big berry patch surrounded him.

Found! Safe! The men breathed deeply and grinned. Their shoulders relaxed.

Pretty Mouse was about to speak when Reynard pointed to a large she-bear and two cubs contentedly feeding in the same patch.

Their eyes widened. The men froze, a second too late.

The mother bear abruptly raised her head, aware of the new scent of many beings that might threaten her family. She straightened and huffed a warning to the cubs.

One looked around and returned to eating. The other noticed the boy-scent and ambled closer.

The mother sniffed and grunted louder to draw her cubs back from the large beings. In a flash, she lumbered toward them both, her claws ready to cuff them for ignoring her.

But the curious cub edged near Danny and put out its nose to sniff the little being.

The she-bear raised up full height and growled, showing long teeth.

The men stood stock-still, Michel in a cold sweat.

We're between her and the cubs. How do we get Danny?

Reynard began a low chant, a haunting melody.

The mother bear cocked her head.

He continued the song until she dropped down on all fours and grunted loudly.

This time both cubs obeyed her summons at a gallop, disappearing with her into the woods.

Pretty Mouse dived toward Danny, scooping him up.

At that, the boy woke and shook his head with confusion. "Papa? Where did you go? Did you see the butterfly that landed on my finger? It was yellow and sat there. But now it's gone. And so are you."

Pretty Mouse carried Danny on his shoulders back to the canoe. "We have you again, my Dannee. Ste. Anne, she held you in her arms."

"Such a big mama bear!" Baptiste said to Gabriel. "With two cubs. And Danny between them, all enjoying the same berry patch. That'll make a good story for us all to tell."

"There was a mama bear? And cubs? Why didn't you tell me?" Danny demanded. "I could have tied more knots on the string. It was big?"

As they returned to the canoe, Michel asked, "Reynard, now I feel safer in the woods. But how did you quiet the bear?"

"It's the moose song," Reynard said. "I don't know a bear song so I asked for help from the Great Spirit."

He turned to André. "When I taught him to read animal tracks and signs in the forest, I wanted him to be at ease in the woods but aware."

"Who knew he'd feel so comfortable in the woods so quickly? Danny scared us all by disappearing, but we want him to find his own way, even if it means getting lost sometimes. Does he know enough to find his way back, if he'd waked up first?"

Reynard shook his head. "I'll need to show him how to leave trail markers."

CHAPTER 43

Once past the roaring *Chaudière* falls, André guided them through the *Deschênes* rapids. Here the river rushed between small islands and massive boulders at a hair-raising pace. There was no deep channel. At *décharge* after *décharge*, the men sought footholds on slippery chutes with water rocketing toward them. They couldn't take time to sing. The boys stayed in the canoe, to prevent another disappearance of Danny until they could teach him.

Constantly wet, sore and exhausted, everyone was vexed when they made camp. Baptiste and Gabriel set up the tent without ceremony, Michel and François roughly ripped up branches to heave into a pile of firewood. Pretty Mouse had little energy even for Danny. Supper was silent.

Though Danny begged to swim, the water was too fast.

They slept in their damp clothes, knowing they'd start the following day with too little rest.

Daily, André fingered the canoe's bottom, where it had grazed more than one rock shelf. There were no torn stitches, but each night he and Pretty Mouse daubed melted pitch on the stitch holes, using twigs with frayed ends. It was a messy chore.

Getting lost didn't inhibit Danny's curiosity. "*Monsieur Souris*, why do you put that black stuff on the canoe?"

"It keeps the water out, most of it anyway." When Mouse lifted his head, a thread of the pitch flew across his face, attaching to his beard. He batted at it, smearing his face and hands—and stifled an oath.

"I want to do what you're doing. Let me help."

"*Non*, my Dannee. Don't touch—it's sticky."

But Danny had already dragged his own twig into the warm goo and swabbed it on a section of the bark. A glob stuck to his hands, which he wiped on his shirt. He rubbed the dark stain, making it bigger. His eyes teared and his lip trembled.

"Ohh, now I've spoilt my shirt. The maid will be angry—Mama too. But ... but... Mama's ... gone. Maybe ... my shirt doesn't matter."

How can we admonish him for interfering when he's still coming to grips with his mother's death? Danny has hardly mentioned her since the first days—maybe Henry is helping. Maybe it's because Pretty Mouse is like an uncle and we're all watching over him.

Kindness is what he needs, not rules. Even me. I got cross when Pretty Mouse steered badly, but I'm not better. I hardly keep the canoe from smashing sideways into rocks—and the men have been kind while I learn.

CHAPTER 44

Once past the dramatic falls and the rocky rapids, the river widened again into a lake. It gave them a day or so of paddling with neither *décharges* nor portages. The men were glad to recover before tackling *Lac des Chats*.

Unfortunately Baptiste and Gabriel need more than one day to get their strength back. Do we push on or take the extra time? The slower we travel, the longer it takes to deliver Danny. We're not trading often to get more food, and Reynard hasn't had fishing time or luck lately. We'd best continue onward.

After supper's embers had died down, Danny and Henry retired to to their tent.

Michel whittled while the others smoked or mended, each one lost in his own thoughts. Their reverie was jolted by strange voices.

"Do I see a campfire? Halloo! We bring news."

The greeting came from four men paddling a small canoe.

André's crew alerted to an exciting prospect—hearing news was a rare event.

"You hungry?" André called back. The hospitality of the wilderness obliged those who had food to share it.

"Our pea soup is still warm." Pretty Mouse walked over to the pot.

Two middlemen hopped out and sauntered over, leaving the canoe to their steersmen.

"Upon my word, what a kindness! If you have enough, yes, we will gladly partake," the leader said, in rough French. He and the others untied cups from their sashes and Mouse portioned out servings of porridge. They hastily dug in.

They're eating our breakfast for tomorrow. Mouse will have to improvise.

"My name's George and this here's Franklin. We're nearly out of food but we've got high wine to return the favor," the leader said. He beckoned to a steersman. "Pierre, bring the keg."

At the offer of high wines, a few of André's crew whipped out their cups as Pierre poured liberally. Then he plopped down by Michel, watching him whittle. "You're new with the knife, I see. Me, I show you how to shape that?"

Liquor made André nervous—he'd purposely not brought any on this journey and he wasn't going to partake.

"You said you have news?"

"A few weeks ago, a storm came up quick and capsized a Montreal canoe not far from Sault Ste. Marie," George said. "Being close to the fur post, most of the cargo was saved. But the guns sank quick and deep, taking the canoe down. They had to order a new canoe. Held them up for five, six days."

François perked up. "Were any men lost?"

"Don't rightly know. Nobody said."

"Which company?"

"I reckon it was North West. McTavish, he's the head, right? He'll be mad to lose those guns and the canoe."

But André's crew were silent, wondering if any of their previous mates might have drowned, wondering why a canoe had swamped, wondering about the brigade. It unsettled them that the strangers were more concerned about losing guns than *voyageurs*.

François silently swirled his cupful.

André asked, "How deep is the river upstream? What should we watch out for?"

Pierre and the other steersman described the challenges in detail.

Then Franklin asked, "Tell us about the rapids up ahead, and the portages. We've not been there, but heard it's a back-breaker." He gestured Pierre to serve more high wines.

Pretty Mouse and François argued about the two approaches to the *Deschênes* and *Chaudieres*, pointing out André's decisions and the canoe's mishaps.

André cringed at their criticism. *They might be correct but I don't like hearing it, or others hearing it.*

"Big brigades went through a month ago. You've got no cargo to speak of, and too late to be carrying a bigwig to the *rendezvous*. And to be honest, you're not what I'd call an elite crew. So what's your errand?" George asked.

"Delivering a boy to his father," André said, proud of the assignment.

He was about to continue when Pretty Mouse sneezed, dumping the remains of his cupful on André. "Me, I haven't tasted such good high wine since we left. It tastes mighty fine after those last hard days, but I must be drinking too fast. Sorry, André, I've made a mess of your shirt. "

"You got my pants wet as well." Disgruntled at the interruption, André stood to air what had been doused.

"Me, I am so clumsy tonight. Want me to hang your shirt up on a branch?"

"It can dry on me," André grunted in acceptance. He wanted to resume his story.

"Must be important, to get a private ride. His father must be at a fort, then?" the leader probed.

Pierre lifted the keg but Pretty Mouse shook his head back and forth, as if to clear his brain. Mouse stood, giving André a long look.

André realized the message—he shouldn't have blabbed.

"What do you bet we know him? Who has a son in Montreal?" Franklin said. Their conversation switched to English while they mused on the topic, tossing out names.

"Anyone want to try this new twist of tobacco from Brazil?" François offered it to them. "So what brings you on the river? You don't have much to trade either, aside from rum."

"Sharp you are, for a Frenchy," Franklin said, glancing at him sideways.

"We're keeping the peace," George answered. "Rumors of a few dust-ups around here. Needed to see for ourselves."

"That's a surprise. Fur posts are quiet this time of year—everyone's at the *rendezvous*. Nor have any tribe encampments where we've traded mentioned trouble," François said.

"You heard of Tecumseh? A Shawnee down in Ohio country? Won't sign treaties and now his brother is stirring up his people against us," Franklin said. "We're here to listen in this part of the country—to see who's with us and who's not. A good thing to know, don't you think?"

Reynard turned slightly and edged closer.

"*Non*, never heard of Tecumseh," François said, his voice like ice. "Every single one of the folks along this way, every single one has been friendly to our little canoe."

André cleared his throat, but Pretty Mouse glared at him. François would take over the conversation.

No one else spoke. It was silent a long time.

"Well, that's good news, and a big help, it is," George said. "At the Fort—St. Joseph, that is—would you be so kind as to make a report? The man in charge should hear it from our lips, but we're headed the opposite way. Mention our names—I'm George Hobbs and he's Franklin Wheeler."

The others quietly nursed the remains of their high wines, not responding to the visitors' hints.

"Yes, sirree, at the Fort, they'll be glad to hear it from you," George said. "They'll offer you a meal or maybe a job, you folks being late and needing work for winter, I suspect."

When no one responded, Franklin excused their group. "Dark's coming soon, so we'll be on our way. Time to find a campsite—this one doesn't have room for another canoe."

Chapter 45

François waited until long after the strangers had paddled on. Then he confronted André. "What were you thinking, telling them our business?"

"You made me look stupid, telling them my mistakes, like I'm incompetent."

"You sometimes are," François said. "You don't listen when I tell you things."

"André, that's not the only problem," Pretty Mouse added. "You betrayed our mission—to strangers. Didn't you catch my look? I tried to shut you up."

"They were too free with liquor, and people were drinking lots. I was worried for you, Mouse," André said. "I didn't pack rum because of you. And Danny, of course."

"You think I can't handle myself, that you're my mother, doling out what I can or can't have?" Mouse was furious. "But you're the one whose tongue was loosened—without tasting a drop. And why was that?"

"So they'd see how important you are?" François said.

"But were you worried for Dannee?" Pretty Mouse shouted. "We're lucky he didn't wander out. Maybe they'd sweet-talk him. What if they insisted on taking him? Then what?"

"Don't you know a spy when you see one? They ask soft questions and wait for people to talk They use high wines to encourage them and they notice a lot in a short time."

"Even if they're not spies, they're strangers. They came fishing for information, and you gave it to them."

"Never tell more than you absolutely need to."

"And with a little boy, never ever."

"You've made your point." Embarrassed, André unrolled his blanket far from the others.

Late into the night, André wrestled with their remarks. *Ouch. I was so glad for guests and their news that I never thought about what they might be up to. François is right—I wanted to be important. He and Mouse saw through them—Mouse spilling high wine to stall me, François sharing his best tobacco, changing the subject. They were like a wall to keep me from telling more. Papa warned about others endangering a child's safety but I was the one who walked into this trap. They showed better sense than I did.*

What did those strangers really want, besides drumming up allies against us—or the Americans—in some war? They came from the fort so why weren't they in uniform? What else have I missed?

Chapter 46

The next morning, André apologized.

But afterwards, no one spoke about their evening visitors. Pretty Mouse wasn't light-hearted and François was brusque—they were pondering the consequences they might yet face. André would have to be watchful in new ways to undo the damage he'd unwittingly created.

The challenges of the river ahead didn't help their tension—*Les Chats* rapids began with a series of falls spilling over granite outcroppings and around small islands.

Henry refused André's suggestion that as the companion, he should be constantly responsible for Danny as they traversed *les Chats*. "Would you have accepted such a leash at his age?"

So André set Danny to counting its many waterfalls. "*Une, deux, trois ... quatre, cinq ... six, sept, huit ... Non*, I forgot where I was."

He started over and got to "*neuf, dix ... onze, douze ... treize*," but after thirteen, he'd lost track again.

"Why are they called *les Chats*?" Danny asked in French. "Aren't '*chats*' cats? I don't see any."

Baptiste pointed at raccoons napping in the crotch of a tree. "*Les ratons laveurs.* You know, they wear masks on their eyes and have stripes on their tails? See there?"

Because of their noise, the raccoons had slipped away. Danny didn't see them, but he now kept a sharp lookout. He was on his third knot string.

All that day the men dragged the canoe upriver over *décharges* and portages that wore them down. Gabriel and Baptiste complained they were near their limit and François griped about how it might have been accomplished better. Michel took all opinions as truth, uncertain of which to heed. Reynard ignored them.

And André chafed, knowing he was being watched—and judged—by his men. He'd made enough mistakes and couldn't afford more.

They trudged over a winding portage so narrow that, with the canoe on their shoulders, Pretty Mouse and André saw little as they zigzagged up. Michel, scouted for them, pointing out puddles and roots to avoid. Danny ran ahead, doubled back to watch a dragonfly and then ask Pretty Mouse about a flower he'd seen.

"Careful, men," Michel shouted. "There's nothing much on either side of the path—we're on top of a high ledge."

They'd crested a steep ridge when Pretty Mouse, carrying the bow, stopped to answer Danny's question. It would give him a moment's break before heading downward.

Unaware that Danny had already raced off, Mouse turned and stepped, without looking.

Nothing was there. The rocky cliff dropped straight down dozen feet or more. He plummeted.

He tried to regain his balance or find something to grab. Instead he tumbled forward, sliding on loose rocks, the weight of the canoe propelling him.

"Eeyaaahh!" Pretty Mouse yelled.

To slow his slide, he let go of the canoe, trying to hook his leg around a sapling. His head banged into the outcropping.

As the lone support of the 300-pound canoe, André's knees buckled, not strong enough to keep it aloft himself.

"*Au secours! Aide-moi!*" he gasped. Help me!

The bow—where Pretty Mouse no longer was—dropped hard, crushing André into thick roots across the trail.

Michel ran back to help them, unsure of where to grab. Moments later François arrived.

They lifted the stern and André squeezed out, groaning.

Everything hurt. His hands and face bled. "The canoe? Is it all right?"

"We saved it from that big branch. And lucky we were close," François said.

"Can you move this off the path so Baptiste and Gabriel can carry through?" André said.

When they lifted the whole canoe and brought it back up to the portage path, they saw Pretty Mouse still sprawled on rocks many feet below, his head tilted against them.

"Rest time is over," François called to Pretty Mouse.

Mouse didn't answer.

"I'll leave my packs here and help you carry the canoe," Michel said.

The two carried the canoe to the portage end. When they returned, Pretty Mouse hadn't moved. He was silent, pale, lifeless.

"Hey, Mouse? You having a nice nap?"

"Get up, lazybones. We did your work for you—you could at least say *Merci*."

"Is he alive?"

They heard a few irregular breaths—a good sign.

François' idea was to splash water on him, sit him up. "We walk him across the portage, where we've piled our packs. That should bring him back to life."

"*Non*, let him be. He needs more rest," Gabriel said.

"All of us need more rest," Baptiste said grumpily.

But Pretty Mouse lay unaware.

They each grabbed a leg or arm and hoisted him along the path, depositing him in a shady spot at the portage end.

Occupied by skipping stones, Danny spun around to see his favorite *voyageur* being placed on the ground.

"*Monsieur Souris*, what's wrong?" Danny repeated his plea at higher and higher pitches. He wept, his arm around Pretty Mouse. "Help him. *Monsieur* André, do something."

André shook his head. "I don't know how."

"We wait, Little One," Reynard said. "The Great Spirit is speaking with him now. We do not hurry this."

Henry tried to pull Danny away but Reynard held up his hand. "He will like Danny holding him. The boy should stay."

"Henry, can you bring my blanket and the … bunny you made me?" When Henry returned with them, Danny rolled his blanket into a pillow for his friend and tucked a gray knitted lump near Mouse's chin. Then he snuggled in Mouse's arms.

"We camp here?" Michel asked.

André nodded. He and François examined the canoe for ruptures from its dive into the brush. Baptiste and Gabriel provided supper, a dismal meal, as they listened to Pretty Mouse's ragged breathing. After eating, Danny reluctantly went to his tent.

"André, you do carry medicine?" Henry asked

"Only purges and vomits, and they won't help him. My foster mother sent herbal remedies for pain or rash."

"Smelling salts?"

"*Non*. But high wines might be pungent enough."

"If he doesn't wake up, what will you do?"

"Look for the next fur post or cabin, I suppose."

"And leave him in someone else's care?"

"*Non*, we can't—we need all of us to paddle."

I depend on Pretty Mouse for everything—his strength, his joy, his willingness to try anything. He cooks and sings and helps with Danny. We can't go anywhere without him.

The evening's brilliant sunset was fading when Pretty Mouse groaned, put his hand on his head and curled up on his side.

"Mouse, speak to us," André begged.

"That was quite the fall," François chimed in.

But Pretty Mouse was silent.

Twinkling stars filled the sky when Pretty Mouse grunted again, uncurled his legs and tried to sit. With effort, he opened his eyes. He shook his head slowly, breathing hard. All he could say was, "Ooh, my head." After a long sigh, he sagged. An egg-sized lump swelled under his *tuque*, near his temple.

André was next to him in an instant. "Are you thirsty? I'll get water."

"You want supper?" Baptiste grabbed a dish but Gabriel stopped him. "Not yet. Give him time to settle."

The ruckus woke Danny who rushed out of the tent in his night shirt and nestled into Pretty Mouse's limp embrace. "Are you better now?" He peppered Pretty Mouse with questions.

"Need water. Then sleep," Mouse rasped.

"Weren't you sleeping already?" Danny asked.

While Henry escorted the protesting Danny back to the tent, François and André raised Mouse to sitting to give him sips of water from a cup.

After a bit, he stood. When he tried walking, he reeled, his balance off.

They eased him to the ground.

Pretty Mouse sat, holding his forehead, squinting. "My head, it hurts. Can't see right."

He lay his head on his arms. "Sleep. Have to sleep."

They covered him with Danny's blanket.

Chapter 47

They rose to a beaming sun—André had delayed their departure.

Pretty Mouse stretched. "My head hurts—that high wine of Baptiste's never had such a bad kick before."

"*Monsieur Souris*, you're finally awake," Danny squealed, wrapping his arms around his waist.

Mouse shook his head, blinking, confused. "My eyes, they don't see right. What happened?"

When they told him, he only recalled slipping.

"Are you up to paddling today, Mouse?" André asked.

Pretty Mouse looked at his feet. He looked across the river, at the canoe, at his feet again. "Me, I hate steering. Everything comes at me too fast. I never want to steer again."

André felt panicky. *He isn't healed yet. Might not be again. And now I learn he doesn't like steering. Michel isn't ready to steer, and Baptiste and Gabriel can't. Reynard hasn't paddled these rivers. Though I don't work well with François, it'll have to be him. Maybe only for one day, though.*

He looked around at the crew, packed and ready to leave. "Steering is too much for Pretty Mouse today. We can go on—if someone else is *gouvernail*?"

François volunteered.

"How many times have you been over these rivers?"

"Eight. This is the ninth."

That's four more times than me. "What luck for us. I accept. *Merci*, François. You're our man."

"For more pay?"

André nodded. He'd forgotten that steersmen earned higher wages. Colonel Markham's hefty surplus for unforeseen circumstances was slipping away.

"Pretty Mouse, you and François switch places. You'll paddle behind me."

"*Non*, André. I can't help Danny and Henry if I'm in front of them."

"It's better if Gabriel and me, we paddle together, in the same row." Baptiste interjected.

Michel grinned at Reynard. "Works for me."

François took the stern and the others moved to new locations in the canoe.

André and François did not make a smooth steering transition. Both were certain they were right.

"We should edge the south bank," André called.

However, François aimed for the center of the river. "*Non*, didn't you see water curling around a submerged reef?"

A mile farther: "Current is speeding up over there."

"*Non*, André. Too many boulders that way. This way there's fewer. River is deeper too."

They scraped the bottom of the canoe more often. Each night when they examined the seams, they silently blamed each other for the new chafe marks.

When they reached the end of *Lac des Chats*, Mouse declined to steer again—headaches and double vision plagued him. André grudgingly accepted his new *gouvernail*.

I'll have to get along with François. Is this what it was like for Antoine, testing different steersmen before finally choosing me? His men didn't berate me, though my errors cost us time. I had no finesse. I don't have that much even now. It's my turn to show grace.

Chapter 48

"With so little water flowing this late in the season, it's harder and harder to find a deep enough channel. We're lucky to have such a light load or it'd be impossible to get through," François said.

"Which way do you suggest?" André shrank from admitting his lack of knowledge but the route ahead blurred together. *When my two previous brigades reached this part of the river, I was paddling as milieu and could hardly see ahead in the river. Now I have to learn what François remembers.*

"The usual—we paddle a few miles through rocky rapids. Eh?"

François was making him beg and André needed specifics. "What else?"

"Won't know until we get there, with at least six channels to consider."

"Six? Tell me." André's bravado crumbled. He was in over his head.

"When we reach a big island, let's test a few channels. We'll choose then. The one on the north side—it's usually the widest and deepest. Probably the far end of the island will be too shallow to *décharge*, so expect a couple of portages."

"And after that?" André was grateful. *Maybe François should be paddling as guide. Would Colonel Markham even care, far away and with his own worries? But I care—I want to prove I'm capable.*

"We're nearing the *Grand Calumet*. Oho, I have an idea.

Instead of killing ourselves over that portage, we could take a shortcut when we come to the white cliffs. Big Montreal canoes never take that passage, but we're light. We should try it."

André was skeptical. *I remember each awful step of the mile-and-a-half Grand Calumet portage. Antoine's brigade was in top shape, and it exhausted us. François has lots of enthusiasm and not enough hard information. But sometimes he's right. Not having to portage over Grand Calumet sounds wise. Who could we ask? Do I take a chance?*

"I never heard of another route. What's this shortcut like?" André asked.

"Little lakes, swamps, a river—steep portages but not as bad as the *Calumet*. We might even cut off two or three days."

"A few days shorter—I like that. When did you take it?"

"Me, never. The brigades I was in, we always carried big cargoes of trade goods, but a couple of the old guys, they showed me where it was."

"How do you know they told you true if you've never been on it?"

François frowned, aware that André distrusted him. "Ask Mouse. Or at the next trading post, if we see one."

Mouse, who loathed the *Grand Calumet*, hadn't heard of that route. Nor could Baptiste or Gabriel verify this new route.

André dreaded the decision. *Is that different from me being the guide on this route and not remembering each rapids in the river? Papa said to trust your mates.*

"Michel, should I believe François?"

"You're asking me? What would I know about routes, new paddler that I am? If François' route gets you to the right place in less time, you could write about it and become famous." Michel's voice had a hard edge.

He's hurt because I haven't treated him like a friend—me and my grandiose dreams of being a leader.

André felt sheepish. "Fair enough. I owe you an apology. Every day you're willing and steady. Thanks for sticking with me. I'm slow to learn how to lead so others feel included. I am sorry,

Michel, and I'll try to do better. I'm asking you now. I need your help to get to the fort without any more incidents."

"*Merci.* If you try this shortcut, what's the worst that could happen? We'd have to backtrack to the Ottawa, and then portage the terrible Grand Whatever-it-is. We might lose a few days."

"*Grand Calumet*, because the river bends like a pipe." André felt grateful for Michel's sensible comment. His wisdom would help him decide when they came to that place in the river —an uncharted route. It gave him slightly more confidence.

Before the new route, however, André and François had to choose the best channel among six possibilities—which had the fewest problems?

The next mile was rugged. By luck, they found the current deep enough to float them, but there were more rapids to be poled or portaged than François had counted on.

"Are we almost at the fort where my father will be, *Monsieur Souris*?"

"*Non*, Dannee, it's far and far away. Count each finger two times. That's how many days it will take—maybe more."

"*Monsieur Souris*, it's sunny but I'm cold."

He was right—they had turned north, bringing coolness and shadow to the bright July days. Moreover, the land was rising and the river narrowing.

"Dannee, you see that rock rising almost straight up from the water?" Mouse said, pointing out a high granite hill, capped by dark pines. "Here the great north begins. This is where we really start to paddle up the mountain."

"Paddle up mountains?" Henry sounded scornful. "Don't fill Danny's head with such foolishness."

"But don't you see, that's exactly we've been doing these weeks? The river, it tumbles to the sea, back where we started, but we paddle against the current, climbing with each waterfall and portage."

CHAPTER 49

The following afternoon they gazed at the white cliffs which signaled the route to the dreaded *Grand Calumet* portage. They slowed to search for the small trail leading away from the Ottawa River, and found it as François had described.

André's stomach churned as he debated. *A new uncharted route or the known rushing river and unforgiving Grand Calumet portage? Agreeing with François? I used to believe I liked change, that I trusted my men, that I liked adventure. It's time to prove it to myself.*

He took a deep breath and announced, "We're leaving the Ottawa River, men. We're taking the new route."

On every step of their first portage, scaling rocks as high as the white cliffs that loomed in the distance, André rued his decision. *This section is worse than the Grand Calumet—but I'm not ready to admit that yet. I'm not ready to quit either.*

The men grumbled as they climbed more escarpments, glaring at François and André. But from their towering vantage point, they could see part of the route ahead—another falls to portage around before they could start down the river. They trudged, uncertain, wondering where they'd sleep that night.

What if François is wrong?

But soon the land flattened. Instead of slogging around the *Grand Calumet's* thundering cascades, the portages became shorter and gentler. Instead of fearing a current that could smash them into boulders, they paddled over minor rapids and quieter waters, lake after swamp after lake after swamp.

The next days they paddled through a dozen small lakes bordered by leafy maples. Herons poised at the reedy edges. Fish jumped, breaking the surface. Ducks abounded.

François was right!

At the portages, Danny skipped stones across the river. He'd lost his ball when it hit a boulder at an off-angle, ricocheted into the water and floated downstream. Aware of the trouble retrieving it would have caused, Danny watched it go.

He was more entranced by tracks in the wet ground, identifying wildlife with confidence. He knew which animal came to drink—porcupine or raccoon, fox or skunk. At the water's edge, he gazed at leggy water bugs almost skating across the surface. He examined waves and ripples and the fish underneath, identifying each by its unique shape and coloring. On shallow sandbars, he studied turtles or frogs sunning themselves. But eventually he tired of watching.

While he kept his promise about not wading on his own, he begged to swim—or at least get wet. On days when André could find places, they stopped early. But it was never enough to satisfy him.

He needed more activity—and dreamed of an animal to keep.

One day he managed to capture a chipmunk. He held all day, fearing its escape.

"Oho, *mon suisse*. My little chipmunk, you will like the people in our canoe—especially *Monsieur Souris*. Watch the men who steer, André and François."

Henry refused to give up his traveling desk as its new home, so Danny swirled his blanket around it while he tossed out his least favorite rocks to make room in his trunk.

The chipmunk soon chewed its way to freedom, leaving a hole in Danny's blanket.

Danny bit his lip when he realized that his almost-pet had escaped. Undeterred, he began trying to construct a small cage for the next one he could catch.

Now that ripe blueberries abounded, Danny collected what he could, mindful to stay on the path or keep the camp in sight. While his harvest pleased Pretty Mouse, it didn't excite Danny.

While waiting for supper one evening, he ambled in the clearing not far from the tent, watching butterflies flit about pink and yellow flowers.

A dragonfly buzzed his head, alighting on grasses next to him. Reynard had taught him to be still in hopes that the dragonfly would land on his outstretched hand.

Danny tried not to move, but when he exhaled, the dragonfly lifted off, circling. Then it lit on a stump nearby, fluttering its wings as if to call: "Come. I know a game."

First Danny checked that he could see the tent—and then followed the dragonfly. The moment he got to the stump, the dragonfly swooped and flew high. When it reappeared on a branch, another dragonfly joined it. He followed them in a great circle, from branch to rock to twig to root, staying within earshot. The pursuit thrilled him. Maybe one of them would be his pet.

He shadowed the dragonflies until they disappeared into the deep woods—where he had promised not to go. He sighed, disappointed but staying true to his word.

Because he could still hear camp activity, he sat still and watched a pair of blue jays feed each other from a berry bush. When they too flew away, the game ended. He glanced towards the campsite waiting for Pretty Mouse to clang the kettle.

Danny knelt by the bushes, pleased the birds hadn't eaten all the ripe blueberries. He ate a few, dropping some in his cup. He picked the bush clean, nearly filling his cup, when he noticed another plant with a few dark berries.

Blackish ones, not exactly the same as the blueberries he knew, but larger and easier to pick. The one he tasted wasn't sweet, so he spit it out, and tried a second berry, hoping it was riper. It wasn't. He spit it out and dropped the rest in his cup.

Then Pretty Mouse banged on the kettle. Danny hurried back to the campsite, careful not drop his berries. He proudly held out the cup to Gabriel.

Gabriel looked into his cup, then looked closer He lifted one of the dark berries. "Little boy, did you eat?"

Danny hesitated before shaking his head. "*Non.*"

However, Gabriel frowned at the telltale blue stains on his lips. He took the cup and threw its contents as far as he could. "*Ce ne sont pas des bleuets, non!*" They're not blueberries. He puffed his cheeks and pantomimed spitting them out, vomiting.

Danny's eyes filled with tears, his whole cupful gone. "I thought you'd be happy."

Then he hoisted Danny over his shoulder and ran to the shore. "André, get a purge. Danny picked nightshade berries."

"But ... but I spit it out. It tasted bad."

No one heard him.

Gabriel held him over the water, thumping his back.

André pawed through their medicine box for a dose of purgative. He read the words on the paper packet to prepare it: "Mix with water in teacup. Drink entire contents of cup. Expect violent vomiting." *I wish we didn't have to do this. Will a little boy need as much as an adult?*

"But I didn't swallow any."

No one believed him.

Pretty Mouse insisted on holding Danny, while André gave him the cup. "Drink all of it."

Danny shuddered at its bitterness. "All of it? It's awful."

They waited, uncertain. Suddenly his body took over and expelled the contents of his stomach.

Gabriel poked at it with a stick. "There's berries. Could be nightshade, I can't tell."

Pretty Mouse didn't mind that the vomit hit him. "The shirt, I can wash it. But my little Dannee—will he be fine?"

Gabriel shrugged. "Don't know. I wish we could tell how much he ate. But we should keep him awake tonight, in case it's not all out of him."

Danny was confused—the different berries, the attention, the frustration of not being believed, the exertion of emptying his stomach—all extracted a toll. He drooped.

When the others could pry him from Pretty Mouse's arms, they took turns singing to him.

"Give him more water," François suggested.

"Keep him warm," Baptiste said.

"But he's sweating," Michel said. "Maybe we should cool him in the river."

For once Henry did not admonish them for negligence.

"Reynard, what do your people do?"

Reynard shrugged. "I wasn't often around the healers."

"My foster mother would know. I wish I'd asked more." André fretted that Captain Ashton would punish them, remembering the British prison once again.

"She never talked about nightshade to me," Gabriel said.

By twilight, Danny hadn't shown any signs of poisoning. Whatever he'd ingested had been expelled.

"Can he sleep by me?" Pretty Mouse asked Henry. "Under the canoe, where I can watch him?"

Henry nodded and delivered Danny's blanket and the small gray sock, twisted into a lumpy rabbit.

The men woke at dawn. Today they delayed leaving until Danny roused.

"I'm thirsty."

Michel dashed to the river to scoop out a cupful of water. The men stood in a ring watching him drink, taking a collective deep breath of relief.

"Would you walk with me when we cross the portages today?" Henry asked.

Danny frowned. "I'm fine. But if you want, I will."

He's survived drowning, getting lost, a threatening bear, poison berries—how many more ways can a little boy get in trouble? Henry's earned his keep today.

But André knew he was the person responsible to Captain Ashton—and Colonel Markham.

Chapter 50

The detour around the *Grand Calumet* portage saved them two days. Even better, it helped to restore their energy. When they once again reached the Ottawa River, they were gleeful at having explored the shortcut. It was a good enough story for them to earn a pint of ale, whenever there was any to be had.

"Now about the route ahead, André," François said, "do you recall that in only one day, we reach Baptism Point?"

"Oho, *la Pointe au Baptême*," Pretty Mouse interrupted. "I remember that's where I became a true *voyageur*. André, we must baptize our new recruits, now that they have lived in the wilds."

André was surprised. He'd forgotten. *On my first brigade, I was the only new paddler. In fact, because Antoine only hired experienced paddlers for his brigades, when they passed Pointe au Baptême, others scorned the rite. What ceremony they would have had with such a silly cub as me—scared of loons and owls, who thought my light hair attracted mosquitoes, who feared a wiindigoo, the Indian cannibal ogre, would capture me?*

"All I remember from *Pointe au Baptême* is that Antoine dispensed extra rum—nothing more. Is it that important?"

"*Oui*, so it is. Our brigade, we carry three newcomers—Michel and Danny and Henry."

"We won't do anything that requires high wines. Since I don't know what it involves, can you take over?"

"I'll help you," François said, surprising Mouse.

After supper the next night, Henry was returning to the tent when François stopped him. "Henry, stay. We have come to this place, *la Pointe au Baptême*. Tonight, it is a special night."

Henry looked questioningly at André, who nodded. The others sat, nonchalantly smoking or mending or whittling around the campfire.

"We are far from home. Danny noticed the big hills, did you also?" Mouse said in his most dramatic voice. "Because now we, we have arrived at the very place where all new paddlers are honored for having proved themselves as real *voyageurs*. You have lived almost a month in the wilds. Tonight you three will become true men of the north."

François stood. "But first, go into the woods to find some small thing. It may a stone or bone, a broken egg, a bird nest. You will know it when you see it. Return with it. Quickly now."

"Oh good," Danny chirped, excited at the permission. "If you're afraid, Henry, you come with me. I know how to track in the woods."

Henry took his hand. Michel followed at a short distance, keeping an discrete eye on them.

As soon as they were out of sight, Pretty Mouse said, "That will keep them busy for a bit. What's next?"

"Baptiste, cut some cedar boughs, and Gabriel, find a stick to beat the rhythm and think of a song or two," François said, directing his grinning co-conspirators. "Reynard, you've got those tiny feathers, eh? André, today dig out the good tea."

André and the others set to their tasks.

Before long the three returned to the campfire.

"Show us what you found," François said. "Danny, you speak first."

"It's an old broken blade. I wanted to find a bear claw or wolf tooth—that would be exciting. But I only saw this rusty knife caught between boulders," Danny said, disappointed with his find. "Mother once told me about a boy who pulled a sword out of a stone and became the king."

"Even broken, your knife is important. We need knives to cut our fish or shape things like Michel does." Reynard tied a blue feather to it, whispered a blessing and handed it back.

151

Danny examined the blade with new interest.

"Henry, what did you choose?"

"I looked for an unusual rock, but instead I saw this strange thing." Henry held out a dried transparent rope-like tube. "What is it?"

When Reynard identified it as a snake's skin that had been shed, Danny's eyes got large. His fingers ached to touch it. His rusty blade became less appealing.

"Henry, you have grown taller and wiser on this trip. Like this snake, you no longer fit into your old skin." He tied another blue feather to the snakeskin and returned it to Henry with a murmured blessing.

"And Michel?"

"I've also grown bigger—my new shirt is almost too small," Michel laughed. Then he produced his item, a brown arrowhead smaller than his thumb.

Reynard fingered it. "No arrow shaft?"

Michel shook his head. "On each side of it were three white stones, in a line."

"This arrowhead was well-enough made that the hunter hoped his friend would bring it back to him. It carried a message, telling what direction to travel. Like him, you must choose which direction you will go."

Danny gazed with longing at Henry's snakeskin. "Could I hold it?"

"Since you also have grown, perhaps it should be yours." After a glance of approval at Reynard, Henry accepted Danny's rusted knife in trade.

Michel said, "Henry, I could make this useful—clean the blade and fix a handle. Or would you rather have my arrowhead?"

Henry's eyes lit up. "Yes, the arrowhead—because I also must choose a life path. *Merci*, Michel."

They held their new objects with an appreciation.

Satisfied, Pretty Mouse asked them to solemnly recite the *voyageurs'* oath, phrase after phrase, promising to fulfill the responsibilities.

"Now I, Baptiste, will baptize you. Isn't that apt?" Baptiste was pleased with this role as he dipped fragrant cedar branches into the river and snapped his wrist, sprinkling them with cool drops of water.

François announced, "You are now true *voyageurs*, men of the north."

"*Non, non.* First they must dance," Pretty Mouse said. "Gabriel, a song?"

While the crew sang "They Have Me Scared, Those Wolves" and two more songs, Gabriel beat time on the soup pot, and the three danced around the fire. Then they all joined in.

When Gabriel said, "I'm thirsty," Mouse pronounced the final element. "We're all thirsty, André has a small libation to commemorate the occasion." André poured their best tea into each cup. To Michel's cup, Mouse added a dram from his small flask.

Danny teared up. "Oh, *Monsieur Souris*, I'm a *voyageur* like you. This is the best day of my life."

"*Merci beaucoup*," Henry said. "I'm very grateful you included me. I never thought it possible to become a *voyageur.*"

Michel was the most pleased. He was accepted as a full member of the crew.

Chapter 51

They sat, sipping their tea, as the moon rose.

"Why do they call you *Monsieur Souris*? You're not a mouse." Danny's French was improving.

"Once, Dannee, once long ago, I was good to look at, but my story, it is not so pretty," Mouse said. "I was at a *rendezvous*, the summer gathering for fur traders, *voyageurs* and the fancy partners. This friend and I, we played a knife game: how close can you throw a knife past someone without cutting him."

"Weren't you scared?" Danny's eyes got huge.

"So I was, you are right, but I trusted him. That day we had sampled high wines and his aim was off. When I flinched, his knife nicked my nose. Blood got on everything—my shirt, my best sash, everything. And my nose, it hurt. Then he laughed—you know how it is when you don't mean to laugh but your body does it anyway. That made me mad and I hit him. He pushed me back and I fell, so hard my poor nose, it broke."

Danny sobered at the awful thoughts. Even Henry, who usually shushed the men before improper things could be uttered, stood rooted to the ground, his mouth open.

"Back then I was handsome," Pretty Mouse said, oblivious to their shock. "But now, well, it doesn't matter. I paddle, I cook, I sing, I dance—even if my face is not pretty any more. I have many friends—and you are one of the best."

"Our nicknames, they tease," François added. "Pretty Mouse, he is not so pretty any more. And such shoulders as he has —not a mouse either. You see?"

"You are François, but that's not a teasing name."

"In the big brigades, many men have the same name, like François, or Pierre, or Jean-Baptiste, so the teasing names help keep us straight. We called one Baldy ..."

"Because he had so much hair?" Danny guessed, gleeful to solve the puzzle. "What did they call you?"

"Silent Pierre," he said, feeling sheepish.

"Always there were two or three Jean-Baptistes, so my friend here, he became Twig though he was big and strong. Me, they called Fish because I don't like the water," Gabriel said.

"I was *Bon à rien* the first trip," André said. "I was weak and very foolish, so maybe naming me Good-for-Nothing wasn't teasing. Last time the men called me Scarface."

That made sense to Danny—André's face was young and unlined.

"I am Reynard, which means fox. When I was little, my mother called me Turtle, because I was slow and quiet."

Danny nodded. "Michel, what's your *voyageur* name?"

Michel looked surprised—there hadn't been a need.

"But we were baptized so we must have *voyageur* names," Danny insisted. "Michel, he could be Grandpa."

Michel smiled.

Pretty Mouse said. "Dannee, we'll call you Giant. You must have grown a half a foot since we left."

"Giant. I'm Giant!" Danny was thrilled—not only was he a full *voyageur*, but he had a name to prove it. He repeated it, and laughed each time.

The playful rites united the brigade again and infused them with spirit.

The next morning they rose ready to paddle and sang with more energy, Baptiste and Gabriel carried their share, Michel understood which comments to disregard, Henry didn't make a face at supper and André felt no threats or competition from his crew.

CHAPTER 52

Later the next day, André remembered that Henry had not been given a *voyageur* name. He mused on a few possibilities. *Honey? That doesn't feel right. More like Wasp.*

The same thought occurred to Baptiste on a portage trail. "Gabriel, we forgot to name Henry," he said. "Wouldn't you say he's like a Thistle—full of prickles?"

Gabriel snickered. "So he is, so he is. But you can see a thistle and move away. How about Nettle? You hardly notice it at first, but even a little touch burns for hours."

They mentioned it to Michel who was ahead by a dozen steps. "Black fly. Always with us. Those welts last for days."

Bear, red ant and hawk were considered, to much laughter.

"Wolverine. It's small but it never lets go" was Reynard's choice.

François' favorite was Porcupine. "Because they're unpredictable and those quills keep working their way in."

André laughed. "Sometimes porcupines are helpful." The malicious revenge, a chance to strike back, felt oddly satisfying. He was about to suggest Rosebush but they had arrived at the portage end to start loading the canoe.

The men were suddenly quiet.

Danny was crawling in the dirt, inspecting animal tracks.

But Henry stood off the trail, his arms tightly wrapped around his belly, his head down.

André's heart dropped. *Oops. We were talking loud. Did he hear us?*

Henry raised his gaze briefly at André, his lips pressed in a thin line. He said nothing.

André felt ashamed. *He's hurt from what we said, or me anyway. For a moment, it felt good to be mean. We thought it was funny. But I encouraged bad blood and conflict. What kind of leader does that make me?*

"Let's use our given names. That makes it easier to work together as friends," he said. But he couldn't look again at Henry's pain.

CHAPTER 53

Each day the land rose more dramatically and the river narrowed.

Whenever André measured his canoemen against Antoine's brigades—how efficiently their camp was organized (acceptable), how smoothly they paddled together (sometimes), how quickly they portaged and made *décharges* (never), how far had they gone (not enough)—their best was poor. He tried not to let it bother him.

He watched the days getting shorter—summer wouldn't last forever—and fretted again about their falling behind. Their food wouldn't last for the entire trip.

André steeled himself at what would be an unpopular choice—they would have to rise earlier and paddle longer into the evening. Papa had warned him, and it was up to him to make it work for the whole crew.

At their mid-day stop to feed Danny and Henry, André planted his feet and faced his crew. "I've been calculating the amount in our food packs and I've made a tough decision. I don't expect you to like this but we must put in more hours on the water each day. Either that, or we run out of provisions before we get to the fort."

He paused, took a deep breath and went on. "Early on we stopped often, because of the boys and, honestly, none of us were in shape. Mornings we usually leave late and evenings we stop though the sun is still high. Now that we're stronger, starting this afternoon, we'll take only two breaks to let the boys run. Danny and Henry, you'll have to manage during *décharges* or portages. Tonight we'll paddle as long as we have daylight. Tomorrow, plan to leave at daybreak. Are you with me?"

André hoped he sounded as sure and reasonable and decisive as Antoine.

No one answered, though Reynard nodded.

"Back to it, then."

That evening, André calculated they'd worked two extra hours. The following day, they'd added three more hours—almost a half-day. André smiled to himself. He'd acted like a proper leader with a sensible decision. His men were behind him.

But one morning, they rose to a pelting rain.

"As long as there's no lightning, we leave when it lets up," he ordered. Three hours later they took off. It sprinkled much of the day and by nightfall, they were thoroughly wet.

At dawn, Michel called, "Tent's soaking wet, André. If we roll it up, it'll start to smell bad."

"My blanket's wet," François echoed.

"*Oui*, but that smells for a different reason," Gabriel said, which made Baptiste laugh.

André sighed. "We wait."

For another two hours they sat while the sun dried their things. Afterwards, they paddled longer and limited their breaks.

As each portage brought them higher, the river now was hemmed in by towering pines, rough and rocky shores. It triggered flashbacks that darkened André's mood. Soon they would see the thundering rapids of *Roche Capitaine*—where his friend Gerard had drowned.

That day, two years ago, because Antoine's brigade had arrived ahead of schedule, the men had been given an evening to revel with high wines.

The next day, the steersman Gerard had been catapulted out of the canoe and sucked into deep churning waters. His crew mates, slow to react, were unable to save him. Though they searched a whole day, they never found his body.

Weighed by memories, André became silent. Birdsong sounded lonely and distant, not cheery. The place held sadness.

When they came to the rugged *Roche Capitaine*, Henry took out paper to sketch the turbulent falls and massive outcrop that dominated the middle of the river.

The men struggled under the labor of hauling the canoe and their supplies upward.

André glanced up for the cross of lashed paddles where the brigade said their goodbyes to Gerard. No new crosses stood nearby. Sadness and loss washed over him. He wanted private time to reflect.

Gerard taught me to steer by listening to the river's sounds and looking beneath the surface. And by imagining the pole as fingers that feel between rocks, pry loose ones, slide us past immovable others and steer through whirling channels. He never laughed at me. What a good man he was.

I was scared when Antoine asked me to say something at Gerard's memorial—but I did it. Then Antoine tapped different men to steer—it took him a week to ask me. Without Gerard's death, I wouldn't be steering today. Tonight I want to tell the others about him.

"Men, let's make this portage in two carries. I'm sorry, Henry, it won't give you much time to draw."

While they ate their supper at twilight, André shared memories of those days with Gerard. Pretty Mouse squeezed André's shoulder and André nodded an acknowledgment, biting his lip to keep a sudden tear from escaping.

CHAPTER 54

The longer work days didn't ease André's anxiety about the distance they yet had to travel. He checked—and rechecked—their decreasing food supplies, counted the number of known portages left on the Ottawa River, guessed at the number of days before arriving at the fort. They didn't balance.

When André's canoe had capsized at *Roche Capitaine*, they lost part of their food so Antoine had insisted that other canoes share provisions. Everyone had eaten less and tightened their sashes. André remembered how hard it was to paddle when they were hungry.

André wondered how his men would accept limiting food. He hoped Pretty Mouse would support him.

"I'm changing how much we serve at supper," he announced after they finished one breakfast. "Our provisions were meant to last for six weeks, but we'll be lucky to get to the fort in seven. Fishing takes too much time. With tribes at their summer camps, we've seen few people to trade with. And they haven't harvested wild rice yet. We must save more of our rations or we'll run out. Starting tonight, Pretty Mouse will cut four cups out of the pea porridge each day—a half-cup for each paddler."

"Are you mad? We need every spoonful," Mouse said.

"*Non*, André. You're making a big mistake. With less food, we'll get more tired. We'll slow down," François added.

"True, that may happen. Nonetheless, it's better for each of us to eat a little less every day than to run out completely. I remember what starving feels like. And so does Mouse."

Michel hunched. He'd never eaten so many regular meals.

The others gazed glumly at the pot, never to be as full.

That evening, Danny noticed. "But *Monsieur Souris*, you aren't using enough peas! You said one quart for each person."

"Sharp eyes, my boy. Right you are, but André, he fears we will run out. So now we will eat less to save some for later. He is our leader, with the right to decide."

Danny frowned. "You can eat part of mine then."

"I will also share my portion," Henry said.

Pretty Mouse's eyes misted. "You're kind, both of you. But all of us will eat. Just a little less. We'll hardly notice."

André was grateful for Mouse's support.

Supper didn't seem smaller, but the mood was watchful.

When Danny and Pretty Mouse served breakfast, however, the men eyed the kettle, measuring their helping.

All day they paddled and portaged and made *décharges*. Supper was again smaller, but no one complained.

Late that night, André woke, hearing a rustling in the grass, then whispers and snickers. He sat up, alert. "Who's there?"

The sounds stopped.

When it's this quiet, someone's up to no good. Could someone be stealing food?

As the men rose the next morning, André sneaked a peek at their faces. None of them looked guilty, no one looked full—or hungry. The kettle was the same as always.

Except for the initial outburst by Pretty Mouse and François, the subject did not arise again.

But André felt nervous. François was right—less food didn't encourage them to move faster. But he had no other choices. They had to work longer days and eat smaller meals until they got to the fort.

Chapter 55

André studied his crew. Reynard had healed from the disease that had ravaged him. Michel was heavier, having developed muscle in the weeks of regular meals. With Pretty Mouse and François, those four were in top form.

Gabriel and Baptiste had improved, but they were his weakest paddlers—the canoe could only go only as fast as they could push themselves.

From the first, Baptiste had sheltered Gabriel, helping him portage the lightest bales, do the fewest tasks. After days when they'd waded in the cold current, Baptiste applied a salve and wrapped his friend's legs. Lately Gabriel's knees were worsening. He needed rest after most portages. At supper, he claimed a seat nearest the campfire. But now at least, he spoke without halting, so different from the day André had met him.

With each portage, Baptiste puffed and coughed and wheezed as if he wouldn't make it. They both sighed at the ends of pipe breaks and spoke about finding Baptiste's nephew so they wouldn't have to return to Montreal.

Now that I've made hard choices, no one is talking to me. Pretty Mouse is entirely taken with Danny, and I hardly know what Michel thinks. François probably thinks I'm a fraud, not knowing things I should.

Relaxing was a luxury denied André. Each decision weighed on his shoulders, and many had to be made in split seconds. When he needed his crew's attention, he spoke abruptly, curtly, to prop up his uncertainty. He didn't like being the leader.

"Watch out where you set that gear, Baptiste. The ground is wet."

Baptiste looked around for another place, muttering "It's just canoe supplies, not blankets."

"Pretty Mouse, when we carry the canoe, don't slow down to look around for Danny Ask if you must, but don't stop."

Mouse called out to Danny, but when he didn't get an answer, he slowed—to André's irritation.

"Gabriel, don't set up their tent under a tree. Move it."

"I thought they'd like shade. It's hot," Gabriel said as he dutifully moved the tent.

"That tree limb will smoke when we burn it. It's too green. Get a drier one, Michel."

"I've gathered wood before," Michel answered. But he picked out better fuel for the fire.

"Reynard, we need more fire wood, now."

Reynard did what was asked without question, without drama. He shut them all out, attending to some inner voice. But then he'd disappear into the forest, out of sight.

Each time I open my mouth, I criticize. It feels ugly but they aren't earning compliments.

Alliances shifted among the crew. Michel spent time with Reynard and François, whittling, learning woods lore. André felt lonely, without a friend.

Simple decisions—when to end the day or where to camp—weren't simple. André felt the blame for each negative outcome.

Last night's site on an island seemed ideal, though, of course, François had another idea. André maintained his choice, but mosquitoes swarmed incessantly after dark. Danny and Henry batted and slapped at insects that found their way inside the tent. In the morning they rose, covered with welts. When François muttered that André didn't pick decent camping sites, Reynard agreed.

As if I made the mosquitoes come.

Henry picked at his pea soup. François groused that his

contacts at the supply warehouse would have included tastier foods. Pretty Mouse nodded.

François griped that André's guiding made them paddle harder than necessary. Michel agreed, but kept to himself, looking exhausted.

They're right—sometimes. Do I dare to say that?

It eroded André's confidence.

Whenever the canoe stopped at the infrequent trading posts, his men traded, some for high wines. Only a few nights ago, André was beneath the canoe examining the canoe's inner lining when he saw Gabriel's feet sidling over to Pretty Mouse with a guilty giggle. André heard the chink of coins and they disappeared soon afterwards. André looked in the other direction, not wanting to know.

I'm the youngest. How could I insist that they not imbibe?

CHAPTER 56

"Tomorrow we arrive at the confluence of the Mattawa River," François announced.

"The Mattawa!" Pretty Mouse grimaced, moving the pot of soup off the hottest part of the fire before crumbling hard biscuits into it. "That rock-filled ..." He started to swear, but remembered Danny absorbed his every word. "The Mattawa, Dannee, it is not my favorite river. Everywhere boulders hide, waiting to slice our canoe. All the time we portage, all the time. In a week or so, this stream, it will become so narrow that you—even you—can reach across and almost touch on both sides."

In disbelief, Danny stretched out his arms—earlier the Ottawa River had been hundreds of yards wide in places.

Nor could Michel imagine the river narrowed so much.

Baptiste said, "Me, I hate the Mattawa. It's a bog dammed up by beavers with a bare trickle meandering through, usually so shallow a man can hardly paddle it. We go back and forth, back and forth—it takes twice as long."

Gabriel nodded. "Rocks everywhere."

"Like it or not, it's the only route to Lake Huron." François glanced at Michel. "Now the French River—it's one wild ride downstream after all the hills we've climbed."

Michel was not reassured.

"You'll be fine—the French, it's not bad," Pretty Mouse said. "It'll take us a week to get to Lake Nipissing, the start of the French. I hope André gives us a day of rest first. We all need to recover, to be ready for the fast water."

As François predicted, the next day the narrower Mattawa flowed over menacing boulders into the once-grand Ottawa.

Before leaving the Ottawa, Reynard tossed a handful of tobacco into the oncoming current.

Danny noticed. "Why did you do that?"

"I offer tobacco to the spirits of these waters and ask them for safe passage over their waters."

"Can I do that too? But I don't have tobacco."

Michel reached into his bag of possibles and gave a pinch to Danny, who tossed it high into the air.

Henry rolled his eyes but said nothing.

Each day they faced bigger rocks, faster rapids and portages one after another. Uphill they pushed and hauled, dragged and carried, from morning until night. No one sang.

While the men trudged over muddy portages, Henry took out paper to sketch.

"Current's not bad this year. I can see where boulders hide," François said. "In high water, we paddle so fast, we hardly see what's below. This slow, it's easier to dodge boulders."

Slow? It's dangerous—I'm tired of watching constantly, deciding where to go. But I'm remembering a few places, and steering with François is more predictable. It's different, though —the water levels, the current, our light little canoe.

Every rugged portage climbed higher and the river tapered, proof that they neared the height-of-land.

Studying the steep crags and dark pines that edged the river, Henry said, "We're so closed in by these cliffs—I don't like feeling."

Count on him to find the negative. He must know we can't change the land. But I'm just as tired of the challenges of rising land and constant rapids. Maybe we're not so different.

Instead, André said, "It'll open up when we get to Lake Huron. Then you might wish for the safety of trees and a river."

CHAPTER 57

Only Danny appreciated the granite cliffs. "What's that?" he asked, pointing to reddish marks high up on the face of a cliff.

Reynard studied the ocher and vermilion symbols, memorizing them. "Picture rocks. They tell a story."

"Who put them there?" Danny persisted.

"Long, long ago, the grandfathers of my grandfathers painted them. My people lived here since the beginning of time."

"Are they here now?"

"When white people came to live here, we needed more space and claimed another place for ourselves farther west. Now we live not far from your father."

"One part looks like a canoe. Does it have a story?"

"Sometimes picture rocks mark a dream. Or a lesson to be learned. You'll have to wait until winter, Danny. That's when our elders tell us stories."

"Only in winter do they tell stories?"

"Maybe that kept us from complaining about the cold."

I never noticed those picture rocks before—Danny's sharp eyes found them. And I didn't realize stories were only told in winter. When I visited Thunder or went trading for furs, tribes always told stories. But I wasn't there other seasons.

At the next portage, Danny spied a cave opening into a great rock. "*Monsieur* André, can I explore it? I promise to..."

"Not today," André said. "We have another long portage."

"We cross the height-of-land soon," François said. "André, will we be ... um ... doing anything special?"

"The usual—tossing out our steersmen's setting poles before heading downstream. But no high wines, if that's what you were hoping for," André answered.

I know I have to switch to the long paddle when we ride with the current, but, oddly, I'll miss my setting pole—it's propelled us ahead, pried us away from boulders and held us steady in rapids. Change is hard.

When they arrived at the continental divide, Pretty Mouse said, "Dannee, something amazing happens here. Watch."

He tossed grasses on the stream and they watched as the pieces slowly slipped into the Mattawa River behind them.

"That's not a very big surprise."

"Wait. There's more." Then Pretty Mouse moved yards upstream where he tossed more grasses which slowly moved in the opposite direction, drawn by a current ahead of them.

Impressed, Danny ran back and threw his own grass, watching again. "Henry, come. You'll like this."

Pretty Mouse continued his lesson. "Do you remember, Dannee, on one of the early days, when you asked how far we were going? I said we would paddle to the top of faraway mountains, and then we would paddle down."

Danny nodded. "*Oui,* but me, I was confused. You can't paddle up mountains!"

"That day it made no sense," Henry added. "But you were right—we've been doing it this whole month."

"Today we reached the highest point. Now we start traveling back down."

"That sounds fun. Will we go fast?" Danny asked.

"Today not so much. But each day we pick up speed. And very soon we will go so fast it will make your head spin."

Henry looked alarmed.

To honor tradition at the height-of-land, André and François removed and saved the "shoes," the iron ferrules that strengthened the ten-foot setting poles, and pitched the wooden poles as far into the river as they could. The men cheered, especially Danny. Even Henry participated.

Pretty Mouse sidled up to Baptiste with a grin.

But Andre felt down. *They feel joy, but I'm tired, I'll be glad to turn Danny over to his father, and Henry too. Maybe only a week left on the Mattawa, a day on the French River, and a week or so on the big waters of Lake Huron to Fort St. Joseph. If weather and luck hold, this trip could be over in three weeks.*

Then, after I pay the men, then what? Reynard returns to his tribe, Baptiste and Gabriel take a ship back to Montreal, maybe Michel too. François might find his old mates. And Pretty Mouse and I might head toward the New Fort on Lake Superior. Maybe we'll carry dispatches or mail to inland posts—and we could visit Antoine. Or we could go to Michilimackinac—Papa talked about it. Colonel Markham even wrote a letter of introduction to get hired by the British.

We ought to discuss our future, before we deliver Danny and Henry. I should've made a better plan, but I was so flattered to be a leader, so glad to be paddling again.

The next morning, André and François reached for the extra-long paddles to steer downstream. At first the river changed little, with shallow marshes and small rapids, until they came to the Talon portage, surrounded by swirling currents around the double cascade nearly forty feet high. The portage was grueling, even with minimal cargo.

Even so, André felt buoyed remembering his first days of steering. Besides the Talon, he recalled the picturesque names of the portages he had navigated—the Turtle portage, *les Musiques* and three Muddy ones. He could do it again. A day at a time.

For more than a league they paddled through a cedar swamp on a stream barely wider than a ditch. Danny delighted in trying to touch brush or reeds on both sides at once.

Chapter 58

It was early in the afternoon when they entered Lake Nipissing and edged a wide bay to look for a campsite.

"Paddling a lake might look easy to you but you'll miss the security of the river," François said to Michel. "In a blow, waves whip up fast. Look yonder at those crosses—they are new, from this year."

Michel saw a dozen paddles lashed into crosses crowning a low island. In the clear water below, too deep to retrieve, lay pieces of broken birch bark, metal kettles, ax heads, beads and a long box of muskets. He shivered at the thought of his fellow canoemen swallowed up by the lake.

"We'll take all day tomorrow to regroup and plan, and then head downriver the next day," André said.

Gabriel and Baptiste whooped. "Oho, a day to recover!"

"We all need it—me too. Last trip we whooshed the whole seventy-five miles in a single day. I was terrified. I get shaky remembering it."

Michel pondered how such a long day would test him.

André continued. "Once we start, there's no time to think, but if we all know what is ahead, we can navigate better. François has the most experience on the French. Tonight we recall everything we know about the river so we know how to run it."

"People in that canoe might be helpful." Henry pointed to an Indian grandmother and two youngsters paddling toward them.

After Pretty Mouse bartered for their fish and wild onions, André asked Reynard to find out about river conditions. The grandmother shook her head—it wasn't a route she would take with children.

André opened the discussion after supper. "To keep ahead of the current, expect to paddle double-time much of the day. Or else the water takes us where it wants."

"Right into a rock," Gabriel said, grimacing. "That happened to us, didn't it, Baptiste?"

Michel paled. "Double-time. What else?"

"Even triple-time," François added. "We only have split-seconds to react."

Reynard said, "Our canoe is light, with no trade goods. That makes us tippy. We should lash the boys' chests inside the canoe with everything locked."

"Maybe I could have one book?" Henry asked hopefully.

"Not if you care about it," André answered.

"We go, oh so fast. Henry, you won't miss reading—it will be too exciting," Pretty Mouse said. "Dannee, this day keep your little paddle inside. We take no chances or we end up in the bottom of the river."

François named several rapids that required great skill and then he described the four main portages.

"Oho, I remember the Little Gut. And … was one called *Recollet* Falls?" Gabriel asked.

Baptiste agreed. "*Oui*. But they come later. First are *la Chaudière des Français* and *le Parisiens*."

Pretty Mouse said, "Some brigades shoot the whole river in a day, without stopping. I have run a rapids or two instead of portaging. Do you think we'll do that?"

François didn't bluster. "Running rapids, that's only for top crews—and only when the water is high. Me, I say we rest at each portage. We need that more than bragging rights."

Michel agreed loudly, seconded by Gabriel and Baptiste.

André squared his shoulders and asked directly, "I've never been the *devant* on the river. Mouse, do you want to paddle *milieu* or steer? I'd be glad if you did."

"*Milieu*. François is better at steering than I ever was."

Taking a breath to steel his resolve, André turned to François. "How about you? Would you rather guide or paddle *gouvernail*?"

François looked surprised. It took several seconds for him to respond. "*Gouvernail* suits me. *Merci*. You're doing fine."

The affirmation humbled André.

"We will stop at four portages. What else?" Michel asked.

André said, "At the end, just when we need to relax, we have to find the correct channel into Lake Huron. There are several. Watch for the one past the old fort."

"By that time, big winds from the lake will blast us," François added. "We'll get pushed from front, back and sideways."

"I've wanted to ride the current instead of paddle against it. I wanted to see Lake Huron. Now I'm not looking forward to either," Michel said ruefully.

"Same here. I'm not ready," André said. "But I'm glad we're all in this together. You want to help us check all the canoe's seams?"

Chapter 59

After taking the whole next day to recover—and reinforce the canoe's seams—they ate an early breakfast and emptied the soup kettle. Henry locked his desk and sealed it with wax. Blankets, tent and chests were lashed together and tied inside the canoe.

Before they left, Reynard tossed a tobacco offering to the river, singing his plea to the Great Spirit. Danny copied him, using grasses he'd picked.

Baptiste and Gabriel pulled out wooden crosses from inside their shirts and murmured prayers, ending with "Watch over us, Ste. Anne. In this little canoe, we need you."

"I've said more prayers on this voyage than I ever did at home," Michel said, pacing.

André and François clarified their final plans, and the whole crew shook hands.

Danny grabbed Henry's arm—the canoemen's reaction to this river was alarming, though they'd navigated mile-wide cataracts, thundering over boulders and crashing around islets.

But for the first hour, they paddled leisurely across the still waters of Lake Nipissing, listening for the noisy rapids that signaled the beginning of the day's downstream adventure.

When they saw a great flat boulder marking the French River, they paused and stopped singing.

"Are we ready?"

"Let's go."

"*Allons-y.*"

"Dig in, men!"

In unison, the crew drove their paddles deep and pulled hard. André and François steered into the river where the strong current grabbed them.

They approached their first rapids.

"Double-time right side," André called. He levered his paddle against boulders to propel them into deeper waters.

They steadied the canoe at the top of a small falls, and shot over—almost flying for terrifying moments. When they dropped, the splash drenched them.

André's stomach knotted—no sudden leaks, the canoe seams held. He hoped not to fly over again.

"Go left—current's deeper there," François shouted.

"Left it is. Double-time—both sides. Now, triple-time," André answered, swerving.

The men paddled furiously.

André finessed them over submerged granite ledge after ledge. They zoomed down narrow flumes and plunged through sprays higher than their heads.

I'm not seeing the boulders fast enough.

The canoe rocketed through tight curves one after another and plummeted over more dizzying falls.

"Lift right side—big deadhead coming."

Danny spied a turtle resting on moss and put out his hand to catch it, narrowly missing smashing his fingers as they swung past. His eyes grew huge. "I won't do it again," he breathed.

The river widened briefly before a turn, but once they'd rounded it, André saw they were headed straight toward rocks. He swerved around, back into the deepest water.

Again and again.

He glanced up to spot a small opening in the forest. *A portage trail? Their trail?*

"That's it—our first portage!" François shouted above the din of the rapids.

André steered the canoe toward it. "I've never been so glad to see a portage."

"Me too," Michel said when they pulled up, slapping each other on the back. "You did it, André and François."

François swaggered. "But of course. *Nous sommes des voyageurs.*"

"Me too. *Je suis un voyageur!*" added Danny with his own swagger. I'm a voyageur.

"Ste. Anne, she was with us," Baptiste grinned.

The men untied the gear, unloaded it, portaged it and the canoe and lashed it all inside once again.

As he smoked, Gabriel judged the sun's position. "Took a couple of hours so far."

"*Monsieur Souris*, do you have any maple sugar?"

"*Oui*. And I have one more, if Henry wants it?"

"*Merci beaucoup*. For later." Henry gratefully took the lump of brown candy, tucking it in his bag of possibles.

While they rested, André and François discussed the complications of next section. All too soon, it was time to continue.

CHAPTER 60

"One portage done, three to go. Are you ready?"

Michel took a deep breath before shouting "*Oui*" with the others. Danny squeezed his eyes shut when the canoe slipped back onto the current.

André's heart thudded as he angled them toward the rushing river.

He pried against shoals to keep the current from forcing them into dangerous eddies. *I get only a second to keep us from going broadside, or else we smash.*

They sluiced between close boulders. Today they scraped more often, caroming off, but no water gushed into the canoe.

Tonight we reseal every seam.

They raced through winding spillways, ending in clouds of frothing waters. At each tight bend, André and François responded intuitively.

When they'd hurtle over a cascade, each person prayed for a soft landing.

"Ledge on the right—André, watch it!"

André bit his lip, relieved François saw perils that he'd missed. "Back-paddle left side."

The canoe rocketed over rapids, careened through narrow passages, edged around a spectacular falls, plummeted into the air again.

"Hold, hold, hold—now paddle again. Double-time."

At one bend, the current sucked them toward a large dead tree caught on rocks, roiling waters hidden by white foam.

"Go right, André. Veer right." François voice boomed over the deafening roar of the river. "It's the next portage—I see it just beyond that dead tree."

Intent on studying the immediate problem, André hadn't spotted the portage. He steered around the deadhead into a side channel where the river became a glassy black—deceptively quiet surface waters. They pulled to shore, grabbing onto low-hanging branches to steady themselves as they floated toward the carry.

Gabriel and Baptiste dipped their cups in the river and drank deeply. After his drink, Baptiste tossed a cup of water on his shoulders to cool himself.

When Pretty Mouse splashed water on his face and shirt, Danny mimicked him.

Instead of unloading, the men lifted the entire canoe like a basket and toted it over the short portage. At its end, they quickly pulled out their pipes.

"Whew! I'm beat. Two portages left. How far to the next one?" Michel asked. He stripped off his shirt, dipped it in the water, draped it over his face and chest and lay sprawled on rocks.

François said, "To *Recollet* Falls, a couple hours."

"We can reach Huron by the day's end. Is everyone rested?" André asked.

"Nous sommes des voyageurs!"

"Nous sommes des voyageurs!" yelled Danny.

"Let's go, men."

The current sped like a mill race—rapids, mist, rocks, tight turns in dizzying succession.

They sped around tapering curves, descended over rapids through billowing white spray.

Once the channel was so narrow that they all poled against the rock walls.

Exhausted, André called directions to hold, paddle double- or triple-time, keeping ahead of the current. One after another after another, the men responded to each challenge that the river threw at them.

"I see the portage," André yelled.

"*Oui*, it's the *Grand Recollet*." François said as André slipped the canoe out of the current and pointed them towards the shore.

"Thank God," Gabriel gasped.

"I never want to do this again," Baptiste said.

"Nor I," Michel said. "I haven't breathed since we stopped at the last portage."

"Well, I liked it. Someday I'll paddle this river again," Reynard said.

But André was blinded by a reflection in the water and miscalculated. He hadn't seen the wall of barely submerged boulders directly ahead.

He didn't slow and the canoe plowed into them at too high a speed.

Water sloshed in the bow—right where he stood—and began soaking their blankets.

In a trice the men leapt out, hauling the damaged canoe to shore, hoisting it on land, emptying it.

My error, no one else to blame. And here I was, congratulating myself that we'd made it this far without a canoe mishap.

Chapter 61

François did not poke at André's lack of knowledge. "I'll hang out the blankets that got wet."

Gabriel and Baptiste offered to catch fish for the meal. Michel and Reynard erected the tent to dry it out, and carried trunks for Danny and Henry.

"You and me, we'll keep out of their way. Dannee, I will show you how to tie knots," Pretty Mouse said.

André glanced forlornly at his crew, all busy with small—but important—tasks. *I'm over my head and need help. But leaders have to figure it out themselves, especially because nobody is volunteering.*

He fingered the broken canoe shell now turned upside down. He felt defeated as he examined the tear in the outer birch bark. When he crawled beneath to look at the inside, he bit his cheek to prevent tears from seeping out.

The rip is worse than I've ever seen—I don't know what to do. I've strengthened canoe seams but never made this major a repair. Now what? How long until someone comes down the river that can help us? Or do we end the brigade now?

He stayed hidden, head in hands, feeling miserable, angry, afraid, abandoned.

Then he noticed Michel's moccasins and his voice. "Can I help?"

André caught himself before blurting out an insult. "Don't know yet. But you could bring over the roll of birch bark, an awl and the basket with pine pitch. And *wattap*."

"Remind me, what is *wattap*?"

"This. *Wattap* is what we use to sew the canoe." Reynard lifted long loops of spruce root to show him and placed the other supplies next to André.

Gratified, relieved, surprised, André's anger softened.

"*Merci. Miigwetch.* I thought I was alone in sorting this out."

Reynard ran his fingers along the torn seams and the split section. He studied the canoe for several minutes. "Turn it right side up again."

When the three had flipped it over, he removed a dozen cedar slats lining the bottom. Without those inside layers, he peered closely at a long gash. Besides the broken hull, two lines of stitching had torn loose.

"Do you know what to do?"

"Not exactly. In my tribe, others did this work. But I watched. We can figure it out."

André looked westward. "How long will the repair take?" *The work of cutting, marking new holes, sewing it with the long spruce roots and sealing could require days.*

"Doesn't matter. We do it right, however slow we are. If it leaks, we do it again until we get it right. If we take enough time now, we won't have to stop as often on the rest of the journey."

André sighed.

"First we layer a new piece of bark over the gash," Reynard directed.

Michel was about to carve off a piece with his knife but Reynard shook his head. "Bigger. Don't cut yet—bigger is better, in case we make a mistake. We can pare it down later."

Michel increased the size. When Reynard nodded, he cut.

Step by step, the three placed the patch, pierced holes with the awl and stitched it to the canoe with *wattap.*

They sealed it inside and out with the pine pitch and let the goo set.

Hours later they replaced the cedar slats that strengthened the bottom.

"I'm afraid to try it," Michel said.

Reynard shrugged. "The river will tell us what else we have to do."

Water seeped in during their short test in the river.

André felt discouraged. "All this work for naught."

"But only from a few holes. More gum—and hardening it overnight. Then it will hold."

"At first I thought this was impossible."

"Nothing is impossible if you take enough time to think it through—and trust your mates," Michel said. "Isn't that what your foster father said before we left?"

André smiled. "Right. You two have been a godsend, helping to think it through. *Merci. Miigwetch.*"

CHAPTER 62

The next morning the men carefully placed the canoe back in the water. No water oozed in the new stitches.

They reloaded just as carefully. Still no leaks.

Danny and Henry took their places. One by one the men got in the canoe. The repair held.

"*Merci.* I'll watch where I stand today," André said. "Now, about the last section of the river, what do we need to remember?"

François said, "It's like a gut. Skinny, twisty, fast."

"It widens and slows down when we get to Huron. But it's been years since I did it," Baptiste offered.

"Where we see fallen logs of the fort, bear right," Mouse said. "Feels like it's not the best channel but that's what we do."

Can I can get us to the old fort without wrecking the canoe again—or losing one of us?

"*Allons-y*! Let's go! Time's wasting," François called.

The newly-repaired canoe made them nervous.

Without confidence in himself, André felt particularly anxious. *Ste. Anne, keep the water out of our canoe. Thank God for Reynard and Michel, and François and everyone.*

He took a deep breath to steady himself, dug in his paddle and they were off, drawn into the current once more.

The river bent around rocky points, cascaded over rocky shoals, split into separate chutes that widened and then narrowed over small falls. *Where is it the deepest? The safest?*

André chose one and they shot through.

"Channel on the right."

"Faster around this bend—double-time."

"Left side hold."

"Paddle hard, both sides."

He took special care to avoid rocks and deadheads, lest they scrape. Where boulders loomed, André slowed, his shoulders tight.

Somehow the river doesn't seem as treacherous as before. Is the current slower, or the river wider—or am I imagining it? Maybe it's because we're more rested, having paddled over two days instead of the usual one.

❖ ❖ ❖

After what felt like hours, they saw the ruins of the fort and veered to the right into a winding channel which became a wide mouth into Lake Huron.

The lake appeared like a vast ocean after all the weeks they'd been hemmed in on both sides by trees. The open horizon awed them. Humbled them.

André, tense all day, breathed again and felt giddy. *The canoe held. I got us through—no, we got us through. How does Antoine stand this pressure?*

They hooted and yelled their relief. Baptiste tossed tobacco into the great lake ahead of them. "My heart, it was in my mouth these last two days. *Merci beaucoup*, Ste. Anne."

"We earned our pay on this river," Michel added. "Finally we'll have easier paddling."

"Nous sommes des voyageurs!" called Danny, feeling one with the crew.

For once Henry was not critical. "Good work."

Pretty Mouse led them in song after song as they paddled toward a grassy meadow along the shore—the traditional camping site of brigades. It felt eerily huge without other canoes.

❖ ❖ ❖

"The lake is so blue. Can we swim?" begged Danny.

Pretty Mouse looked doubtful.

"I'll go with you." Michel stripped off his shirt and moccasins and jumped in the water. Danny followed a moment later.

Two seconds later Danny screeched and ran back. "Yi-yi-yi-yi-yi! I can't stay in. Ow, my feet!"

They looked pale, bloodless. Michel left the lake as quickly, shivering as he rubbed his arms and shoulders.

"Water's always cold on the big lakes. Except you were in such a hurry, we could've told you," Baptiste said.

"Your feet, put them near the fire or they won't warm up until tomorrow," François predicted.

"And how do you know that?" Michel asked.

François laughed. "The same way you learned."

Most nights the crew retired early. Tonight André felt like celebrating their success. "Let's dance."

The others needed no more invitation.

André dug out the good tea. Pretty Mouse contributed maple sugar and Baptiste shared his high wines.

"Give me the spoon and the kettle and I'll keep time," Henry volunteered.

To the tunes of their favorite songs, they jigged and frolicked and promenaded.

When André showed them the demure steps of a French dance—and insisted Danny be his partner, bowing when André curtsied—they laughed until their sides ached.

"I used to be the best at leaping over the campfire. That's fun to try," François suggested, but glanced at Henry and thought better of it. "Over this bush instead?"

They did, each one, including Henry. Then they found a higher branch to test themselves, until only Reynard and André cleared it. Both knocked it down the next time so they declared the dancing and contests over.

They lay contentedly gazing at the evening stars and the sparkly band of Milky Way.

"See that group of stars. One star circles the pole," André said, pointing it out so Danny could find it.

"We used it to find our way on my first brigade. It's the *Grande Ourse*, the Great Bear," Baptiste said.

"We call it the Plow," Henry added.

Reynard said, "To my tribe, that's Fisher. The tail is the same and so is part of the body but Fisher's nose extends east, to there. And those are its front feet."

"Does Fisher have a story?" Danny asked hopefully.

"He does. In winter, Fisher and his friends liked to hunt but one winter lasted much longer and they guessed that wicked sky guardians kept the seasons from changing. When Fisher climbed the tallest tree, he found the opening in the sky and saw flowers blooming, bees buzzing and birds and butterflies everywhere. He called them to follow him through the opening so spring could reappear on earth. When they did, the sky's guardian ogres grew angry and chased Fisher down the tree. To trick them, Fisher ran back up the tree. They shot their arrows at him, pinning him forever in the sky."

"Fisher is a hero. Do you think I am as brave?" Danny said, gazing at the stars.

"When the time is right, you will be. But you have many years yet to prepare," Reynard said.

"Will you tell us another story?"

"Not tonight. On this big lake, we'll see more of the stars. On other nights, we'll show you them. But now we sleep."

Chapter 63

On the last brigade, as a new *gouvernail* on Lake Huron, André had found paddling the lake was not as easy as he'd expected. The canoe's round bottom slipped and slued and he could rarely keep it along the line he planned. He reddened at frequent zigzagging and the teasing from the brigade for forcing them to paddle extra—until he learned to maintain a straight path.

This year he discovered that their small canoe with almost no cargo handled more skittishly than the massive and heavily-loaded Montreal canoe. With no rudder or keel, it slithered. And steering from the bow was harder than from the stern. With every big wave, he struggled to keep them from swamping.

"François, I'm not comfortable so far out into the lake. Let's stay closer to shore," André said.

"We'll never get there if we don't cut across a few of the little bays," François shot back.

We're on the open waters—soon I should ask Reynard or Michel to steer but François won't give up being gouvernail, and I don't want to take orders from others as a milieu. I'd better stay as devant. It's hard to step back from being the leader.

◈ ◈ ◈

"Must be late July," André said at the men's first break to smoke. "Last night was chilly and the sun's setting earlier."

"Today is Wednesday, the seventh of August," Henry corrected.

What else does Henry keep track of, constantly writing in his secret locked desk?

"I will need to prepare things for Danny's departure and

for myself. How many more days do you estimate we will be traveling?" Henry asked.

"From the outlet of the French River, it's about three hundred miles to Fort St. Joseph. Express canoes can cross to Sault Ste. Marie in a week."

"A week is for experienced crews, but with our strength and skill, more like twelve days," François said.

"And don't forget about storms. Big lakes are notorious for surprise storms," Pretty Mouse added.

André's cheeks got hot—though it was true. He was irritated by Henry's knowledge of the calendar. *August is later than I realized. Cutting rations was the right decision before. Tonight I'll check the remaining food supplies to determine how much we need to complete the journey. If we have enough for two weeks, I won't need to change anything.*

Henry had his own concerns. "Now that we're off the rivers, Danny, we must begin lessons. Your father will expect you to read, write, do mathematics and understand some Latin. At the fort, he'll probably assign a tutor for your daily studies. We must begin to prepare."

Danny's face fell and Pretty Mouse stiffened.

"Obedience is required in military families, Danny."

"Yes, sir." He slumped, as Henry took out a Latin book and began reading aloud as they paddled. "Repeat after me: *Salve, Pater.* It means 'Greetings, Father.'"

Which Danny dutifully repeated several times—between the verses of the song Pretty Mouse had chosen—before Henry accepted his pronunciation. Danny learned several more Latin greetings and phrases.

Henry said, "Now we'll combine geography with some grammar. *Hic est aqua.* That means 'Here is the water.' Repeat."

Danny chanted the words.

"Say *Hic est lacus.* 'Here is a lake.' *Hic est flumen.* 'Here is a river.'"

Danny was briefly more interested, but soon he was bored, and tried paddling again.

"Let's try counting. Numbers are a useful skill. *Unum, duo, tres, quattuor, quinque.* One, two, three, four, five."

Danny perked up. "The numbers sounds like French."

"That's because much of French originated from Latin. As you learn more words, you'll notice other similarities. When you can remember the numbers in order, repeat them backwards."

As soon as Danny could recite whichever number Henry asked for, he again tried to sing Pretty Mouse's next song.

"That shows good progress, but we're not done yet. Let's return to grammar." Henry glanced at his book. "Say *Amo, amas, amat.* 'I love, you love, he loves.'"

Danny mumbled, he stilled his paddle but kept his eyes on the dancing waters.

"I can't hear you. Speak up," Henry said.

When Danny repeated the words, Henry added more, "*Amamus, amatis, amant.* 'We love, you love, they love.'"

Danny squared his shoulders. "How am I supposed to paddle if I don't sing?"

"Alas, my Dannee, practice your lessons," Pretty Mouse said in a dull voice. "We can paddle without singing."

But it turned out he was wrong—the men needed the rhythm of the songs to keep their paddles in unison on the big waters, so they returned to singing.

Danny sighed as Henry closed the book.

CHAPTER 64

Now on Lake Huron, the men paddled whole days without needing to portage or make *décharges*—a great change from the Ottawa and Mattawa rivers where they'd walked on land many times each day.

"Sorry Dannee," Pretty Mouse said, "but me, I cannot play with you. We are only stopping once or maybe two times during the day. We have yet many miles to go to find your father."

While Danny accepted Henry's daily lessons as fulfilling his father's expectations, his eyes roamed his surroundings. He begged to get out of the canoe to run and explore.

"It smells different, fresher," he said. "Why is that?"

"This breeze, it comes over the water, so it doesn't carry scents of campfire smoke or pine forest," Baptiste said.

"Or the earth smells of soil and green plants," Michel said.

Birds circled in wide arcs overhead.

"What are those?" Danny asked.

"Gulls," André said, and Danny studied their distinctive ways of swooping. He listened to their calls and began adding seabirds to his repertoire of hawks, finches, jays, doves and eagles.

Danny gazed into the crystal-clear waters, in awe at a monstrous form lurking sinuously below them. "That fish, it's bigger than I am. What is it?"

"I don't know, but don't lean so far over the canoe. We're never close to shore anymore," Henry answered, glancing at the land a quarter-mile away.

"Could be a lake sturgeon—they get as big as you," Baptiste said.

"Me, I didn't see it. Perhaps it is a *maskinongé*," François said. A muskellunge.

When various fish broke the surface leaping to capture insects, Danny learned to recognize them, as well as the whitefish and lake trout which Reynard occasionally speared.

"Dannee, now we come to *la Cloche*," Pretty Mouse said. "*La Cloche*, it's a big black rock sticking up in the middle of the water. To me it looks like a bell and sounds like one too. Throw these pebbles and you will hear why we call it the 'bell.'"

When they paddled past it, Danny and Henry pitched their pebbles, one at a time, listening for its ring.

"Me, I thought it would be more like a church bell," Danny said, trying to mask his disappointment.

CHAPTER 65

Whenever Henry had to limit schooling in the canoe, he picked it up that evening.

"Your father will expect you to act properly in polite society. We've become lax at mealtimes, so tonight we will practice table manners. First, when you're introduced to new people, you bow, placing your leg like so. Now you do it—and again. Here is how to offer your arm to a lady."

Danny reddened as he mimicked what Henry had demonstrated. He peered longingly at Pretty Mouse, hoping for a rescue from the barrage of etiquette, but Pretty Mouse thrashed at his kettle. The men disappeared as the lessons in manners proceeded, biting their lips in amusement and shared suffering.

Henry continued. "For meals—oh dear. First we had better scrub your fingers and shape your nails."

What's wrong with Pretty Mouse, today he was silent and now he's banging the kettle? Usually he's full of stories for Danny. You'd think he'd be glad for time to himself. I'm ready for quiet—and the chance to make our own plans.

❖ ❖ ❖

"What good is Latin? No one here understands," Danny complained.

"I remember saying the same thing," André said. "My teacher said that all the animals and plants have Latin names."

That he had such knowldege surprised Henry. "*Merci beaucoup*, Andre. Or, perhaps I should say *Gratias tibi*."

Danny didn't care. "*Monsieur Souris* says a bear is '*l'ours*' and Reynard says '*makwa.*' When we saw a moose,

Reynard called it *'naabe-mooz'* and *Monsieur Souris* says *'l'orignal.'* Why do I need to learn another word?"

"My teacher said their names show which animals are related to each other," André said. "When you describe one using its Latin name, people in other places understand which creature you're speaking of."

At that Danny brightened. "Will we get to that today?"

Henry shook his head. "Not this week."

Danny sighed.

Too bad I never got that far with Father Goiffon.

❖ ❖ ❖

"Will it rain today?" Henry asked, taking a break from having Danny practice his alphabet.

André glanced at the gray clouds far across the lake. "Unlikely."

François gazed longer at the building and darkening clouds, and disagreed. "Oho, Henry, it will come by noon. Enough rain to spoil your books, unless you put them away."

Wishing he understood weather as well as François, André remembered racing to shore more than once, getting caught in crosscurrents as wind and rain beat on them. Once, a black snake-like waterspout dropped from almost-green clouds, sucking up fish, stones and branches and spewing them in other places. A young sailor at the *rendezvous* had called the waterspout a "tornado." André's stomach churned at the memory.

"Will it rain much?"

"Count on it," François said. "These clouds, they hold lots of water—they'll make us wet. But not so much wind today. On days when it blows over open water, it's not like being on the rivers. Waves, they roll in for miles, bigger than you expect. They'll toss us up and down. One wave, it could sink our feather-light canoe, just like that."

"We better paddle as long as we can. François, let's watch for a safe haven, in case we need to find one in a hurry."

"Oho, we'll need one, André, we will. Mark my words."

Rain came earlier than François had predicted. The darkening clouds produced occasional drips, then splats, then sheets. And finally even the wind that François didn't expect.

They headed to shore to wait it out in a small bay. When sitting under the canoe grew crowded for them all, the men hastily erected the tent for Danny and Henry.

Watching dark waves crest and crash on the rocks, André knew he didn't have the strength to handle that much raw power. With his lack of skill in steering and control, their light canoe would have spun around, and maybe sunk. Nor were the crew's endurance and strength up to it.

Henry maximized the time, taking out a slate and writing stone. "Now that you've learned the Latin numbers, you must learn to write them. Later you can practice your penmanship. Your father will want you to know both skills."

After an hour, Danny fled. "*Monsieur Souris*, let's look for dry kindling for the fire."

"Dannee, maybe you can show me how to write those numbers," Pretty Mouse said.

Much later, after the deluge ended, everything was wet so they spent the night there.

"Warm days, cool nights and now rain—I predict we will see fog tomorrow. Anyone want to bet?" François asked.

He was right. It was mid-morning before mist cleared enough to leave and he pocketed coins from Pretty Mouse and Michel.

CHAPTER 66

The next days they paddled along the northern shore of Lake Huron, buffeted by winds and crosscurrents. Surprisingly, following the shoreline took as much focus as making constant portages and *décharges* on the river. André felt exhausted and knew the others were too. *We're struggling, though no one says it out loud. How did it get harder?*

One evening, he said, "In a few days we'll say goodbye to Danny and Henry at the fort. That's when I'll pay you men. What happens next is up to you. Those who want to return to Lower Canada can inquire about ships. I'll ask about posts in the interior where others could work if they want. Both Sault Ste. Marie and Michilimackinac are a long paddle so we should know who's going where. Each man should decide. Talk amongst yourselves —tell me before we arrive at the fort."

No one answered. Baptiste and Gabriel wandered into the forest, Michel whittled on a carving, François inspected seams and stitch holes on the canoe that might require reinforcements of gum and Reynard focused on the patterns in the water. Henry explained dinner etiquette to Danny—how to open his napkin before dinner, how to converse with his neighbor on the right for the first half of the dinner and the person on his left for the rest.

Now that I'll be looking for work again, I'll think carefully about what I promise, instead of grabbing the first opportunity. After depositing our boys, I really hope to visit Michilimackinac after hearing all of Papa's stories. Too bad our brigade has to disperse—Reynard's tribe lives somewhere around there and he'll disappear. Gabriel and Baptiste will probably take passage back home on a ship. François will easily get hired on as a voyageur, though if news of Pretty Mouse faulting on his contract has spread, he might find it hard. And Michel—I wonder what he wants to do.

André felt grateful knowing the expedition was about to end, but entering a British military fort without the protection of Colonel Markham made him suddenly leery. Though Antoine's brigades had kept their distance from the enemy garrison, André had searched for the glint of guns pointed at them across the water.

Henry's lesson the next morning was on history. "You'll be living at Fort St. Joseph. It's a military post on Canadian soil, built in 1796 to replace an old fur trade post, Michilimackinac, which was ceded to the Americans after the war. The Americans now control the southern region, though the king believes it all should be British. Now let's discuss the war. Your father will lead many soldiers."

André was surprised to learn what Henry knew about Michilimackinac.

War? Native, American, British, French, Canadian—all have fought each other. Who will end up the winner? My loyalty is with the French, but we lost to the British. Then the British lost to the colonies—that's why Grand Portage got moved to Fort Kaministiquia. I didn't realize it was so intertwined. I don't really like the British, but Colonel Markham was decent. And I never thought about the Americans—that they control it here, not the tribes. How does Reynard feel about that, when it's his land?

Chapter 67

Finally one afternoon, François announced, "Oho, that campsite looks familiar. If I remember right, we're one day from Fort St. Joseph. We can cross the bay tomorrow morning, follow the other shore for some hours and get to the fort in time to trade and eat supper. How about we stop here for the night?"

André was startled. "We paddled faster than I thought. Good idea. Let's eat and then talk about our plans. I've heard stories about Michilimackinac from my foster father, so I want to go there afterwards. And the rest of you?"

"Me, I better clean up first," Gabriel said.

After sprucing up, Gabriel and Baptiste disappeared into the woods on an old portage path.

Michel patched his least-stained shirt. "A lost cause."

"Take mine." Reynard offered a shirt which looked almost new—most days he'd only worn his breech cloth.

They heard Henry in the tent. "Danny, these are your good clothes. They will make the best impression."

When Danny appeared, several inches of ankle showed below too-short pants and as much wrist was exposed by the sleeves of a ruffled white shirt. He squirmed in discomfort.

"They're too small. Why can't I wear my everyday clothes?" he muttered.

"Your father should be proud of you when he introduces you to others. Sit still while I work on the tangles in your hair."

Henry sighed. No comb would undo the snarls—Danny needed a haircut, but they didn't have the right tools.

"Just tie it, so I look like *Monsieur Souris*. If I wear that shirt, people will laugh at me."

Henry released Danny, who promptly changed into his favorite shirt and leggings.

Later, when Henry pulled on his own best clothes, saved for this occasion, he was dismayed that he'd also outgrown them.

❖ ❖ ❖

Pretty Mouse discovered that his ostrich feather, the badge of a winterer, was so bent that it couldn't be smoothed. He jammed it in his *tuque* anyway. "Dannee, so busy you have been with your studies. Let us walk and talk."

They ambled towards a marsh. Across it was a path, made with dozens of thick tree limbs laid parallel to each other. Murky water covered a few sections. Reeds and low brush grew through others.

"Oho, *Monsieur Souris*, what is that?"

"Looks like a floating bridge. Probably *voyageurs* lined up those branches years ago as a shortcut instead of going around it."

"Let's cross on it—what fun." Without waiting, Danny leaped across, easily hopping over the puddles.

Pretty Mouse followed but, under his weight, a few waterlogged branches cracked. He sank and mud oozed over his toes up to his ankles. "For a man, it's not so easy. But wait yonder, by that boulder, Dannee. Me, I will take the long way around."

François took pains to trim his beard and mustache. He tied back his hair with a leather strip. Then he dressed in his cleanest shirt and pants and his best moccasins. He fluffed his ostrich plume, still clean and white and unbent, and slid it into his *tuque*.

He too wandered along the old portage path. When he neared the swamp at the floating bridge, he hesitated, looking for sections strong enough to carry his weight, took a deep breath and stepped lively, keeping his moccasins as clean as possible.

François was halfway across when one foot slipped between rotted branches. He plunged to his knee in the muck.

That foot hit something. It buckled and he fell.

"Yeow. It hurts, bad." He howled, his face contorted.

He put his other foot down to balance. When François attempted to pull himself out, he broke hip-deep through another soft section.

"*Aide-moi!* Help! My foot—something's wrong with it," François panted in pain, thrashing in the muddy slough.

Mouse leapt up, followed by Danny. "We're coming."

Seconds later, Gabriel and Baptiste appeared.

After testing for solid branches they could stand on, they grabbed under his arms and yanked. They couldn't hoist him.

"*Non, non.* You're making it worse—something's holding my sore foot. Wait—I'll try to move it," François said.

They stood on the oozing rickety bridge. After François was ready, they resumed pulling. To no avail.

"We need stronger men," Baptiste said.

"I'll get the others," Gabriel said.

When André, Reynard and Michel arrived, they attempted to raise François.

"If we yank hard enough, these rotting branches, won't they break?" Pretty Mouse asked.

"If that's what is holding him down, I hope they break. Lift on the count of three—*un, deux, trois*," André said, and they heaved upward with all their strength.

They heard fabric ripping, a popping, a different snap.

"Owww, stop, stop, stop!" François yelled, his face pale, his eyes squeezed shut.

But he was no longer trapped.

They released him onto a sturdier section of bridge. Slowly he lifted his hurt leg—blood and mire streaked down. A sharp branch had torn his trousers and gashed his calf. A root twined around his ankle.

"Sorry about your trousers," Michel said, removing the root, scraping away some mire.

François tried flexing his ankle. He winced. "My foot ... it ... it ... it ... won't bend ... ."

"I'll rinse it off. Then we can see what's wrong," Reynard said, sloshing swamp water over the leg. "Dark bruises and scrapes—what I expected. But it's starting to swell."

When Reynard touched him, François yelped.

Danny covered his eyes and cried.

"Here's a task, little boy—have Henry fetch clean water and gather some cloths," Gabriel said. "And remember those yellow flowers I showed you? Pick many. You can do it, *oui*?"

Danny nodded and ran.

"My foster mother sent willow bark and trillium for pain. They're in my pack. Do you want them?" André asked.

"*Oui,* but I'll also need goldenrod for a poultice. It's blooming now and the boy knows it. François, he'll need your willow bark soon."

"My ankle, it hurts like blazes, worse than it ever has," François said, grunting. "Usually walking on it makes it right—I'll be fine after I take a few steps."

But when they hoisted him to standing on both legs, he shrieked and crumpled. It was some minutes before he could talk. His ankle was puffy and misshapen.

"I ... bet I landed on a rock," he wheezed. "Make me a crutch—I need to walk."

André cut a Y-shaped branch to support his weight.

They tried to raise him, but François couldn't remain upright without pain.

"If he can't stand, how can he walk?" Baptiste asked.

"Especially across this broken-down path," Gabriel said.

"Make a chair with our arms?" Mouse suggested.

The precarious bridge made their balance worse.

"How about we carry him on a frame of branches?" André said. "Cut stout sticks longer than this crutch."

While they hefted him onto the carrying litter and hauled him along the narrow path, François' lips pursed in a tight line, his face pale. In addition to its purplish bruises, his ankle had mushroomed to twice its normal size.

Chapter 68

At the campsite, Henry had piled cloths and placed the full teakettle on the fire. "Come, Danny, you must pack your rock collections for tomorrow. It won't take long."

Danny looked torn.

"Before you go, I need the yellow flowers." Gabriel held out a pot full of green plants and water.

After Danny dropped them in, Gabriel heated the mixture.

Reynard washed as much blood and muck off the bruises and gashes as he could, but François flinched at the lightest touch to his puffed-up ankle. "Yeow! Not so hard."

"High wine might be faster than willow," Gabriel said.

Baptiste produced a small bottle which Gabriel passed to François. "This is all we have left. We were going to trade for more tomorrow."

François said, "I have a flask by my blanket."

André retrieved it and the willow bark, giving both to François, and began smoothing the crutch. After a night's rest, François would need it.

Many minutes later, after François had relaxed, Gabriel spooned the steaming poultice onto the wounded leg.

François gasped at the heat.

Which caused Danny to return. "*Monsieur Souris*, what's that stuff he's putting on François?"

"It sucks out dirt from the scrape and stops the ankle from getting bigger," Gabriel answered. "André's foster mother showed me." He began tying strips of cloth to hold the poultice in place.

Gabriel finished by wrapping a bandage from knee to toe, using old shirts.

François was eager to stand. "Gimme the crutch."

"Wait, wait. Not yet. Give it time," Gabriel said, trying to hold him back. "The willow bark is slow to take effect."

But André had already given the rough crutch to François, who planted it and took an awkward step.

He was upright for less than a second.

"What's wrong? I thought you fixed it."

Gabriel was angry. "I told you not to stand on it. You made it worse. Reynard, what do you think? A sprain? Broken?"

Reynard lightly probed it, causing François to gasp. He paused to consider.

"I'm not sure. I have an idea, but François, you won't like it. You'll have to sleep right here all night—no walking until tomorrow." Reynard assigned tasks. "Mouse, find a stone as big as your head. André, bring the small rope. The rest of you, gather a heap of branches high enough to raise his leg. Henry, if you'd wash these cloths, we'll need them again."

"I can find sticks," Danny said.

Reynard placed François' leg on the great pile of branches they'd collected and gently looped the rope around his foot. Once he'd secured the heavy stone to the other end of the rope, he dropped the weight over a low branch to provide traction.

As he did, François felt the pull on his ankle and shouted. "What did you do? That hurts."

Reynard didn't apologize. "I want the stone to pull your ankle back in line. But if you broke something or bones are out of place, it won't work. We'll look at it again in the morning."

"So I'm to sleep like this, with my leg in the air tied to a stone?"

Reynard nodded. "Your injury—it's worse than I can fix."

"Our maid, she sang to me when I got hurt. I could sing. Would you like that?" Danny offered.

"Good idea, my Dannee. When we paddle, singing takes our minds off how sore we are," Pretty Mouse said.

"We could stay here an extra day if it would make a difference in his healing?" André offered.

They were silent, wondering what might soothe him.

Henry spoke up. "Fort St. Joseph ought to have a medical man. He should know what to do."

All eyes rested on Henry. Hurrying to the fort seemed like a wise course of action.

"Chew on this pulverized willow bark. Tell me when you need more," Gabriel said, giving François some.

François moaned.

"There's willow near the swamp. We'll cut some," Pretty Mouse offered.

"Before we can leave tomorrow, we'll decide about your foot. Maybe you'll be ready to walk and paddle. But maybe not," Reynard said.

"What if we wrapped some slats outside the bandage to strengthen his ankle? Then he could stand longer," André said.

Gabriel nodded.

Michel asked, "How long should the slats be?"

"An elbow's length, and as flat as you can make them."

We worked together to sort out this crisis. I'm grateful for their skills and ideas.

Chapter 69

The next morning, François looked listless. His eyes had none of their usual sparkle. "I didn't sleep a wink—it throbbed all night. But I think I can paddle on today."

Gabriel removed the poultice. "Your skin that got scraped, now it looks clean. But over here it's still hot and red—I'll make another poultice."

Reynard untied the stone. "Your ankle seems less swollen, so the weight of the stone did its work. Michel and André, did you finish those slats to keep his foot from bending when he stands or paddles?"

After they treated his wounds, they immobilized his ankle, wrapping it tightly and gave him more willow bark.

When they finished, François looked at his ankle. "It looks silly but I'm ready for that crutch."

As others reloaded the canoe, François tried walking. But when he put weight on his ankle, he gasped in agony and slumped against a tree for support, steeling his face to cover the pain. "*Mon Dieu*, how can I steer if I can't stand?"

"And in the canoe, it'll be worse when the waves shift us," Baptiste said. "How will you balance?"

André was stunned. He had not considered that he'd be without a steersman. "Pretty Mouse, will you paddle *gouvernail*? Just for one day?"

"*Non*. I am sorry, André, truly I am, but my eyes, they are not sharp like they used to be, before I fell. My head, it still aches."

"Reynard?"

"I don't know what François knows, but I'll help."

"I bet I could paddle *milieu* if I kneel next to Michel," François said.

Even that proved too much for him. He bumped his swollen ankle getting in the canoe. With the first few twisting strokes, pain shot through his leg and blood seeped from his wounds. While François exploded in frustration and anger. Gabriel tightened the bandage.

"I understand that it hurts, but keep your language appropriate," Henry said.

"Back to shore, men," André said. "This makes no sense, François. Just rest today—the rest of us will paddle."

"And ride, like the fancy fur trade partners do?"

"Have you never wondered what it felt like to be a rich partner on your way to the *rendezvous*?" André grinned.

François didn't argue.

"If I paddled next to Pretty Mouse, and Gabriel moved back by Baptiste, François could stretch his legs out," Michel suggested.

When André nodded, they made the switch.

Steering with Reynard proved easy.

On the water again, Henry began lessons. "Danny, let's review all your studies, starting with Latin. How will you greet your father?"

"*Salve, Pater.*"

"Describe the geography of the area."

"*Hic est aqua.* 'Here is the water.' *Hic est lacus.* 'Here is a lake.' *Hic est flumen.* 'Here is a river,'" Danny mumbled.

Before Henry could continue, Danny begged to stop. "Henry, I know all that, but without François, the men need me to paddle more than ever. And I need to sing to keep my paddling in time. Oh, Henry, pleeease? It's my last day in the canoe No more lessons today?"

Henry relented.

The crew, augmented by Danny who used Reynard's

milieu paddle, worked with focused energy all morning and into the early afternoon, but without François' strength and speed.

❖ ❖ ❖

André recalled his grandiose daydreams of being honored by reuniting father and son. *Even if wanting glorious rewards and public commendations was foolish, that moment when the two see each other again is important. What will happen is a grateful Captain Ashton will greet Danny with a hug, exclaim at how tall he is and shake my hand to express his thanks. I will introduce the crew who contributed to our success. The boys will leave. I will have proved—to myself and Colonel Markham—that I did what he asked. It's enough of a reward.*

❖ ❖ ❖

Finally Danny shouted, "Smoke! I see smoke! Up there."

"Must be nearing the fort—with smoke coming out their chimneys," said Baptiste.

That news cheered them on—except Pretty Mouse. Everyone's paddle dug deeper—except his. But they didn't spot the corner watchtower or the pier until an hour later.

"Is there a special song when coming to a fort?"

"*Alouette,* it's always good," Gabriel said.

And so they sang it, Baptiste adding his own verses, to Danny's laughter.

Danny arranged his packs, deciding which rocks, shells, driftwood and feathers to show his father. The snakeskin was first.

"I wonder what Papa will say about me."

"He'll be right proud of you, Danny," Michel said.

"I'm called Giant, remember?" Danny grinned. "And I've learned so many things. I'm going to be a *voyageur.*"

"That will surprise your father," Henry said.

The others discussed what they hoped to do while there.

"Anyone hungry for *rubaboo*? I'll ask about *pemmican* and dried corn at the fort's trading post," Pretty Mouse said.

"We're out of high wines," Baptiste said.

Chapter 70

Near the fort, they were struck by the bustle of activity—and the noise—after so many weeks of natural silence.

An impressive fort rose high on a steep bank with cannons thrust outward, manned by British soldiers in crisp red uniforms and clean white breeches.

Instinctively, André slowed, suddenly remembering his first fear of being inside one of their forts. The British, whom he'd once considered his enemies, were not exactly friends, but had become something between. He patted his sash where he'd placed the letters of introduction from Colonel Markham, which would ease some of his tasks.

A sailing ship was moored at the main wharf, its timbers creaking and groaning with each wave and swell. A half-dozen workers carried heavy bales and boxes up a gangplank that dipped with their every step. From deep inside the ship's hold, they heard someone bellowing directions for stowage.

André looked up at its mast and British flag fluttering in the light breeze.

This ship is bigger than the one at Fort Kaministiquia. It carried mostly buffalo pelts because they were so heavy to portage. If these men are loading cargo, it might be preparing to leave. Gabriel and Baptiste may have to hurry.

They steered their canoe to a smaller pier next to the main wharf. Though André had been eager to be in a town again, he felt suddenly nervous about meeting Danny's father.

"I'll look for the commanding officer—I hope Captain

Ashton can meet us here to show us where the boys will live. Henry, can you help collect all your baggage? While I'm gone, Baptiste, you should check about the cost of passage to Montreal," André said.

"No, first ask about their medical man—tell him about François. Danny and I can wait a bit," Henry interrupted.

André bit his tongue. *I was so eager to complete the job with Danny that I put it ahead of medical attention for François. As a crew, we didn't talk about the future and what everyone plans after today—and don't have much time before we divide up.*

"Lots of steps to the top. François, do you need help?" Gabriel offered.

François brushed him off, but after one step on the swaying pier, he fell—in front of the men carrying cargo into the ship. He didn't moan or yell—perhaps the willow bark was working or perhaps it was the presence of other men.

The fall startled the soldier in charge who beckoned for his work team to drop their cargo. "Move him out of our way."

Then, with a second glance at François' foot, he changed the order: "Carry him up the hill."

When André nodded his thanks, the soldier said, "None needed. He blocked our path while we're loading—and we are ordered to finish by tonight."

Pretty Mouse and Michel volunteered to stay with the boys and the canoe. Baptiste planned to find the trader. Reynard gestured toward a small wigwam village in the distance and disappeared.

André dashed away to locate the commander's office.

When André showed his letters, a sentry guarding the fort gate pointed to the office in the far corner of the fort. André hurried there and announced his errand to the clerk at the door—but was told to wait.

I expected to be admitted immediately but not so, since I still look like a rough voyageur. Though he'd cleaned up again that morning, making himself as presentable as possible, André's clothes were threadbare next to the soldiers' bright uniforms.

The fort's high walls made him feel closed-in. The air filled with the smell of gunpowder. While waiting, he watched soldiers march in formation to drum cadences, turning at right angles, dropping to their knees to aim and fire their weapons. Then they rose and marched until signaled to pivot and charge with their bayonets. In another corner of the enclosed field, teams manhandled cannons and fired them. Each unit obeyed orders with precision. They were well-trained for war, André noted.

Being at the fort reminded him of being branded a collaborator but meeting Colonel Markham had dissipated that fear. And since assisting Danny, the son of a military man, and Henry, André understood the British better. *Stay calm—after all, today your task ends. And remember to speak your best English.*

❖❖❖

Finally his turn came and a clerk ushered André into an inner office where a short man sat writing at a nearly-bare desk. The gold embroidery of his uniform epaulets caught the sun and glittered. The man seemed irritated.

The clerk introduced André. "Lieutenant Colonel Wilkins, sir, this ... this ... this *voyageur* says he carries letters—from Colonel Markham in Montreal. Wouldn't he have used official channels? Could this be a ruse?"

"Noted. Dismissed."

As the clerk disappeared, the commander glanced out a window at the men drilling in the yard. He looked at André with distaste, took a scented lace handkerchief from his desk drawer and breathed into it. Then he continued writing.

It felt to André like clouds swept over the sky and the temperature dropped a dozen degrees. He waited, awkwardly.

Finally the commander capped the ink bottle, wiped the quill and spoke. "I will now see your letters from Markham."

"Here, sir." André answered, removing the letters from the oiled cloth packet. "But first, one of my men needs your physician. He hurt his leg last night and needs medical attention."

The lieutenant colonel rang a bell and called to the outer room. "Call for the blacksmith."

"Blacksmith?" That alarmed André.

"Is your man on the *voyageurs*' pier?"

"He's at the top of the stairs."

"Better, so we don't have to fetch him up the steps. Our surgeon is away, so the blacksmith takes over. Higgens sets a lot of bones. He'll take care of your man."

"Yes, sir."

The clerk relayed the orders, followed by a bustle of activity.

Lieutenant Colonel Wilkins took his time to open the letters and scanned them. "Oh."

He reread the the first one slowly, frowning.

"I wasn't informed about the death of Captain Ashton's wife and child. I must properly extend my sympathies—yet another letter to write at the end of my day. There should have been an official notice. Why was it not sent?"

André kept silent.

The question consumed the commander who then turned toward a row of mail slots on the wall, found one with several letters and rifled through them.

"Yes, one is from the Colonel, which Ashton hasn't received yet. But Markham didn't inform me." He voice dropped to a mutter. "And they've brought the son? Here? By canoe? When he might have gone by ship? Very confusing. And unprofessional, I should say."

André said, "Danny Ashton is at the *voyageurs*' pier. He's about seven years old. Where should we deliver his trunks? May I speak with his father?"

The commanding officer gazed out the window for several moments, pinching the bridge of his nose.

Finally he turned to André. "It is most unfortunate but Captain Ashton has left on a special assignment regarding developments among the tribes. He's been gone some weeks."

André swayed in shock. His men had struggled for two months to deliver Danny, but now Captain Ashton was gone. This father didn't know about the changes in his family. He hadn't prepared a new home for his child.

André's head spun. "When ... when will he return?"

"We never know. In the interior, anything can happen—bad weather, the canoe, the men, the Indians. A person like you, a *voyageur*, should realize that," the commander said.

"What should I do with Danny? Where will he stay?" André blurted. Then he realized the answer made no difference—his responsibility was to deliver the son to the father, not leave him where the father might have been. And especially not at a fort that felt so unwelcoming. His shoulders sagged.

"This is a military garrison for training troops. Surely you can see that the lad cannot stay here while Captain Ashton is away. Even when his father returns, it will be difficult. A few Indian families camp nearby, and we employ some, but no one can tend to a small boy. A pity that he was sent out here and not to England."

André felt defeated. "We must leave his larger trunks here. How are we to find the captain?"

The officer folded Colonel Markham's letters and handed them to André. He was silent for some minutes, deciding what information was safe to give this too-young *voyageur*. Finally, resigned to getting rid of the intruder, he said, "The trunks may be stored here. I'll grant permission for our sutler to resupply you and to let you study a chart of the area as necessary. Captain Ashton should return on the Fox River through Green Bay—you will have to meet him, and hope he accepts this complicating addition to his work responsibilities. Be on your way tomorrow at the earliest possible hour. Good day."

The commander had performed his job. This interview was complete. He breathed once more into the handkerchief, opened the ink well and dipped his quill as he called for the clerk to escort André out of his office.

Chapter 71

André left the commander's office discouraged and confused. *How will I tell Danny that we have to track down his father somewhere? Will Henry be as disappointed? Gabriel and Baptiste might have returned to Lachine after today—but now those two can't leave, regardless of their exhaustion. We need them to paddle. How long? Where? I hope François will be better after his treatment today.*

Dizzy with the changes, André hurried back to the pier where Pretty Mouse and Baptiste had secured the canoe and piled the boys' trunks and Danny's collections on shore.

Henry, practicing handwriting with Danny, stopped the lesson.

Danny spoke first. "When is Father coming? Do you know where we are to live? I have so many things to show him—do you think there will be room for all of them?"

A second later, Baptiste said, "A big man came for François so Gabriel and Michel went with him. I know where."

"*Merci,* Baptiste. I'll go see him, but first, I have such strange news I hardly know where to start. Danny, your father is away from the fort on a special assignment. He left before Colonel Markham's letter arrived so he didn't know he should make accommodations for you. The commander doesn't want you to stay here by yourself—we must locate your father en route."

"Lucky for me," Danny chirped. "I can be a *voyageur* longer. I won't need etiquette this week."

Henry rolled his eyes and tucked away the slate.

Pretty Mouse beamed. "So we go on? Until we find him?"

André nodded.

Baptiste shrugged. "But maybe the boys could leave their big trunks and rocks here?"

"That's fine for Danny, but I'll keep all my baggage with me," Henry said.

"Mouse, can you find a place for all of us to camp tonight? Take turns going to the trading post," André said as he turned back toward the fort.

"Francois, he's at the cabin near the forge," Baptiste called.

François lay on a table in the middle of a dark log cabin, lit by open windows. He looked sleepy. In a wooden bucket near him were the poultice and bloody bandages. His leg had large purple bruises, many raw, rough scrapes, speckled with dried black blood, and a deep oozy gash. And a very swollen ankle.

The sight of it made André queasy.

The room smelled strongly of sweat and blood as well as exotic pungent herbs. Gabriel gazed with curiosity at a shelf of glass bottles with colored liquids—clear, pinkish, grassy green, oily yellow, thick and brown—while Michel wondered at labels on pottery jars, labels he couldn't read.

A man with a smoke-blackened leather apron was grinding herbs with a pestle and a stone bowl. After he mixed them with steaming water from his hearth, he looked up.

"I'm Higgens. You're the leader? And what is this man's name?" he said in English, pointing to François.

"François. Will he be able to paddle tomorrow?"

"Not likely."

Higgens wrinkled his nose as he examined the wounds. "Not a bad poultice. But something reeks, so he'll need another."

André translated, pointing to Gabriel. "This man made the poultice."

"Ah, did you now? High wines have slowed him down so he's nearly ready. And so am I."

André glanced at François, who lightly snored. "Last night

we tied a stone to pull his foot back to right. It looked better this morning."

"A stone, eh? I may try that sometime. But I expect he stood on it, so then it got worse?"

The blacksmith studied the ankle, turned it, flexed it, prodded it. He rubbed his finger along the bones until he found what he was looking for. Today François barely reacted—the blacksmith's high wines must be potent.

Finally Higgens nodded. "Put this here stick in his mouth."

"A stick?"

"He'll bite down. Because of the pain."

Gabriel frowned at the stick, so André translated.

"You, the leader, hold his good leg, keep him from kicking. The others, take a firm grip on his arms. When I pull, he won't like it."

When they appeared ready, the bone setter grasped François' right foot and pulled hard.

"YEOWWW!" François jerked with the sudden pain.

Pieces of shattered stick burst from his mouth.

André's knees wavered as a surge of nausea rushed over him. *I can do this only if I close my eyes.*

"Don't go soft on us now, man. Bear up. This next time should do it. Here's another stick."

They grasped François' limbs. Once again the blacksmith yanked and François yelled. His left foot shot out, nearly smashing André's jaw.

André took a deep breath and gritted his teeth—anything to keep from vomiting.

"Hold him still, I said. I'm going to pull, one more time. Now."

They pulled and held. This time the blacksmith twisted François' ankle a little at the same moment.

François relaxed.

Higgens slid his thumb along the bones and grinned.

Satisfied, he spooned the poultice he'd mixed onto the

wound and bandaged it. Then he tied the stiff slats on each side of his foot and wrapped it tightly, thigh to ankle, encasing the leg so it looked like a great pillow.

When he finished, he rubbed his thumb against his fingers for payment and took two coins from André.

"This one, François, you said? He got a good deal today—our medical man charges more. Let him rest another hour or so, until the liquor wears off. But he won't walk without a crutch, not before the snow flies."

"Winter? Not tomorrow? He can't paddle with us tomorrow?" André was stunned.

"Not tomorrow. He can paddle again but he'll never carry as much as he used to. He should stay off that foot for a month or two. That's what I think, not that he'll listen to me."

The three hurried out the door.

"I'm glad to be out of there," Michel said.

"I almost threw up. I figured the bone setter would give him some awful medicine to drink," André said. "But I never expected him to wrench his foot like that."

On the path to the pier, André translated Higgens' last comments.

"Months? He can't stay here that long. What will happen to him?" Gabriel asked.

"He has to paddle again. What else can he do?" Michel asked.

André had major complications to solve.

Chapter 72

Near the *voyageurs'* pier, they found a camping area where the others had moved the canoe and set up the tent. Henry had Danny practicing mathematics on the slate while Mouse stirred their pea soup. André reported on François.

"*Monsieur* François, can he walk now?" Danny asked.

"*Non*, his foot will take a month—or more—to heal, so he can't go with us. But he won't be able to stay at a British military fort. At the same time we must find your father. All these problems—I don't know what to do."

"I visited those wigwams," Reynard said, gesturing to a small native village near the forest. "An elder will let François live there. We can take him tonight."

André was amazed. "*Miigwetch*. That was thoughtful of you, Reynard, and generous of the elder. Here's more confusing news—Danny's father isn't at this fort. He was sent elsewhere. Danny can't live here until his father returns—the commander wants us to meet his father around Green Bay."

"Green Bay—my people are only a few days away."

"It means we can't disband yet. Baptiste, did you request passage to sail back to Montreal?"

"*Non*, we didn't."

Gabriel seemed cross. "If Baptiste's nephew is out here somewhere, why would we go back there?"

"I need you both to paddle. I'll pay for the extra time."

"How many days to Green Bay?" Baptiste asked.

Henry's head rose, curious about the answer.

Reynard counted it on his fingers. "To the strait, two days. Crossing the strait, one day. To Green Bay, five more. But without François, maybe ten days all together."

Pretty Mouse relaxed. The others digested the news.

"I can cross the strait with you, but will leave before Green Bay." Reynard added.

"We need you as long as you can paddle. You've navigated these waters—what can you tell us about them?"

"Often the currents and winds oppose each other. We begin early, before the wind rises. And each of us must be at our best."

"Can we leave by tomorrow morning?" Henry asked.

"Don't you want to visit the settlement where you'll be living?" André was surprised.

"I have no interest in looking around. The sooner we leave, the better," Henry said abruptly.

His sharp edge rankled André.

"What do you say, men?"

"I can be ready," Michel said.

The others shrugged.

"If you'd pay us a little now, we could visit the trader," Gabriel said.

"Perhaps you can trade for better food," Henry said.

"I'll arrange our provisioning tonight. Afterwards, I'll study their chart. That way we could paddle tomorrow. Will that work, Reynard?"

"The wind is what tells us when to leave, not our plans. We should see to François after we eat."

"Mind if I look at the chart with you?" Michel asked. "Then I want to trade for a few things."

"And find out where we stow Danny's trunks," Baptiste added.

CHAPTER 73

After arranging with the sutler for provisions, André and Michel stood around a table covered by a large parchment map, its curling corners held down by heavy stones.

"So this is a map. Where are we?" Michel said.

André traced out the locations. "Here's where we started. the Ottawa River, the French River, Lake Huron, Fort St. Joseph."

"That line doesn't seem like any river. How can you tell?" Michel gazed at the map, trying to make sense of the route.

"By reading these words. A few years ago at the *rendezvous,* I studied their map—and it looked different from where we'd paddled."

"Reynard said it's two days to the strait. Where is that?"

"Here. See those barrier islands—they'll confuse us, trying to find the best way through. Then we follow this shore to the mission. After that, we round this point and cross the strait."

"Can we cross with only six of us to paddle?"

"We have to—there's no one else to hire. Natives are at their summer camps and *voyageurs* aren't back yet from the *rendezvous*. Fortunately we're in good shape, you especially."

The sutler directed their attention outside. He spoke to them in English. "Those waves are slate blue today but winds whip up white caps in a trice. When they're gray, you won't much like them. At the strait, where Huron and Michigan meet, it's like two great inland seas fighting. Crosswinds and tricky currents will buffet you all day. The weather changes quickly."

"Lake Superior was like that," André recalled.

At the forge, the blacksmith pointed to a groggy François sitting on a bench.

"Look at this fat foot—Higgens won't give me my crutch. But tomorrow I should be ready."

"François, he said every time you put weight on it makes it worse, that you shouldn't walk for a couple of months."

"Months, he said, not days?" François looked defeated.

"While you think about that, we have news about Danny's father," André said. "He isn't here. The commander wants us to meet him near Green Bay," André said.

"His father didn't know Danny was coming," Michel added, "so he didn't arrange a place for him to stay and someone to watch over him. We can't stay either. We leave tomorrow."

"François, we have to go on without you. I wish it weren't so—we need you," André said.

"Go on? Without me? What am I supposed to do, with all these soldiers saying 'Yes, sir' and drums and cannons and all?"

"An old friend of my uncle lives near here," Reynard said, gesturing with his chin at the almost-deserted native village. "I spoke with him. You can live with him until you can walk again."

François gazed at the lake for a long time, absorbing the messages.

"When you're ready, we will meet this elder." Reynard's voice was quiet.

François glanced at their faces and became gruff. "How am I to get there if I can't walk?"

Michel and André made a chair of their arms and Reynard hoisted François onto it. They carted him through a side gate in the palisade wall, pausing outside.

"I'll bring the others to you," Reynard said.

"And my blankets and pack?" François asked.

Reynard nodded and trotted toward the canoe.

André counted out a large pile of coins. "Here are your wages, and more for steering, plus more for a few months of living here. Colonel Markham gave me extra, for unforeseen problems. François, I'm sorry it took me so long to learn from you. I'll miss you. You've been a godsend with all the ways you helped us."

François marveled at the coins, more than he'd expected. "André, I've never been in a brigade like yours. You let everybody help, not just decreeing rules because you were the head man—though sometimes you had to, like cutting our rations. You tried my shortcut at *Grand Calumet*. And such fun we had at the baptism. This brigade, it was better for me, maybe for all of us. If you lead another group, I'm your man."

"I carved you a puzzle," Michel said, handing him what looked like a mass of twisted roots. "Thank you for teaching me how to whittle and tie knots, for baptizing me, even for testing me —and accepting me. I wasn't sure about you when we left Lachine, but I'd paddle with you again."

Reynard returned leading the others who carried his blanket and pack.

Gabriel and Baptiste offered small vials—medicine and high wines.

Pretty Mouse was gruff as he shook hands. "You're a better *gouvernail* than I ever was—and you got us through more than one rapids that I hate. Perhaps we will meet again. *Au revoir.*"

They brought him to one of the bark-covered wigwams.

Danny, wide-eyed, absorbed as much as he could in the village. "I like this place. May I visit you when I come back?"

As they left, François rummaged through his pack for a small silver thimble and tobacco to offer as gifts to his host.

Chapter 74

The sutler, who had sent men to retrieve the boy's trunks, provisioned them amply. "Commander said to charge it against Captain Ashton's account so I gave you three weeks' worth. Probably won't need that much. Good luck. Tomorrow's not a day I'd want to be on the water, even if it is the end of August."

The next morning the lake was more gray than blue, its waves topped with froth. Their canoe seemed empty without François' presence and brash comments. André missed his strength as they followed the ragged shoreline.

Finding a way between the barrier islands baffled them.

By late afternoon, André saw how tired they were. "We've paddled long enough today and need a break. Look for a campsite in a protected bay."

When they found one, Danny leapt out. "*Monsieur Souris,* Henry said I don't have to study any more Latin today!"

Henry said, "You could say *Gratias tibi*, the words for 'Thank you.'"

Pretty Mouse said, "I traded for *pemmican* and dried corn at the fort so tonight we're cooking *rubaboo*. You'll like it, Dannee. Now watch carefully."

"Without François, it was lots harder to paddle. At least this trader had some good salve for my poor joints," Gabriel said, rubbing his shoulder. "Today I almost wished we'd taken the ship. How think you, Baptiste?"

"The same. But without François, André needs us all the more. We stay the course."

At daylight, when they set off again, the winds were blustery and the skies cloudy, and the rain held until late in the afternoon when they reached the mission. Pretty Mouse and Danny stirred another batch of *rubaboo* for supper, while Michel concentrated on his carving. Reynard seemed quieter than usual.

"That, my old friend, is Michilimackinac," Baptiste said, pointing to the distant island. "My nephew and I, once we went to their big *rendezvous*. Quite the place it is."

Gabriel squinted for the fort's gray log walls. "No one's there now, that I can see."

André bit his lip. *Not only have we missed the summer gathering but we can't even stop to visit with the traders, not with our boys still with us. How will we find Captain Ashton? What if he's not headed back on the same river? Or if he has another special assignment? What if he can't take Danny with him?*

The wind worsened during the night. At dawn, Reynard tested its direction and strength and studied the waves that beat the shore. He watched the clouds and smelled the air. Finally he opened his hand to release the tobacco, which swirled away, along with his prayers.

Danny copied as much of it as he understood.

"The winds are growing—a big storm is coming, maybe it won't hit until tomorrow. Current's not that strong, but this wind complicates it. We should cross now, before it gets worse," Reynard said. "Expect to paddle a long day—we can't stop for breaks until we're well past the strait."

"Do you want to paddle *devant* instead?" André asked.

Reynard shook his head.

"I'll help paddle. You too, Henry?" Danny said.

André accepted the offer though their efforts added little to the power needed. With white knuckles, they all dug their paddles hard into the water. Singing kept their minds off the crosscurrents that often stymied their forward progress.

Hours later, after they'd finally rounded the point and turned westward into Lake Michigan, a blast of relentless wind funneled toward them.

"It's trying to push us back into Lake Huron. I'm wearing out—how much longer?" Gabriel asked.

"No pipe break yet," André called. He glanced toward the old Michilimackinac post on the mainland, nearly four miles away. With the gusts, he couldn't spare more than a look.

After another hour of toil, Reynard estimated they were far enough from the strait for a short rest. They pulled off, ate and contemplated the enormity of what they'd paddled through and what was ahead—the bay seemed vast and unending. When they started again, Danny and Henry slept, freed from paddling.

The men watched the clouds blacken, the temperature drop and the wind intensify. They found a camping site early and hunkered down—relieved to have survived their first battle.

That night a furious storm broke, the worst since they'd left Lachine. Winds screamed. Lightning pierced the black sky. Thunder boomed overhead. The men rigged their largest canvas over the canoe and crawled beneath. Danny and Henry yelped every time rain dripped through their tent, but nothing could be done about it.

The storm released its grip by morning, though the waves stayed rough and the wind kept beating at them. Reynard had predicted the weather correctly. By noon, the wind subsided enough for them to leave.

For two more days they hugged the shoreline warily, not so near that waves would smash them into rocky cliffs, not so far away from safety on shore. Without the muscle of François, they needed longer each night to recover.

"These last days were hard, I know. But sometimes when a wind comes from the south, the waves have rolled a long ways and get big," Reynard said, pointing that direction. "If that happens, we'll have to wait it out. Many days."

But they were fortunate. The wind didn't shift. The skies gradually cleared, bringing cool weather.

CHAPTER 75

They settled into a quiet routine of paddling.

On a few mornings, frost glittered on the ground, and later yellow leaves swirled in the air and flocks of birds collected and wheeled, flying noisily overhead. Only Danny commented on the changing colors of trees on the distant shore, the ripe autumn scents.

For the others, the days seemed empty without François.

André expected Captain Ashton to emerge around every bend, scanning the horizon for red uniforms. He mentioned it often.

"I think that's a pair of canoes—can it be them?"

"Look at the point of land—something red there?"

"Maybe they were held up by that storm and stayed an extra day in Green Bay."

"Enough, André. Stop." Michel said. "We'll see him when he comes. We won't know when."

It surprised the others to hear Michel gently chide him.

André nodded, accepting that his frequent comments wouldn't bring Danny's father to them more quickly.

When they saw native encampments along the shore, their thoughts turned to Reynard, wondering how much longer he would be with them.

One morning after more than a week on Lake Michigan, Reynard said, "Tonight, after the moon rises, I leave you. The night will be clear so stars will guide me back to my people."

André dreaded the announcement. *First François. Now*

it's our last day with Reynard. What a good person he's been for us—rescuing Danny from the bear, teaching him to read animal signs, rebuilding the canoe, aligning François' broken foot and finding an elder—all done without fanfare.

That afternoon as they crossed a wide bay, Reynard gestured toward an inlet. "My people fish this river. If we camp here tonight, tomorrow you can keep following the shore to Green Bay. In a few more days you'll arrive, the same night that I'll see my people again."

After supper, André prepared to pay Reynard his wages. "Instead of extra coins for steering, would trade goods be more useful to you or your people?" Pleased, Reynard selected metal tools, blankets and several pairs of silver earbobs.

Baptiste and Gabriel came to shake his hand.

Michel gave him a small owl that he'd whittled. "You saw so many things we didn't notice. I learned every time you showed Danny something. *Miigwetch.* I'll miss your wisdom."

Danny needed a prod from Henry. "You saved my life and I am grateful. At first I needed that net to catch bad dreams, but you showed me how to be at home in the forest. *Merci.* I mean, *Miigwetch.*"

Reynard smiled. "May the Great Spirit watch over you."

Henry extended his hand. "I too appreciate your quiet knowledge and kindness, beginning with the fish our first day."

Pretty Mouse gave him a small packet of food supplies. "You forage in the wilds better than any of us, but this will help you travel faster."

"André, at the fort you spoke of a drawing with rivers and big lakes," Reynard said. "Can you show me, here on the sand? I want to tell my people of those places."

Henry said, "I have a map. Do you want to see it?"

André was speechless. *Henry carries a map but didn't share it, while we've been traveling without any charts, just using our collective memory.*

Henry unlocked his desk, turned to the back page of a book and unfolded a crisp parchment map.

Together they examined it closely, Henry tracing the route along with saying the printed words, which Reynard repeated.

"Where I am pointing, that is a great salty ocean, far from here. We started near Montreal. Look along this line—it's the Ottawa River. Here it feeds into Lake Huron and there is Lake Superior. The fort where we left François—that is here, and then the strait. The lake we are paddling is called Lake Michigan, and there is Green Bay. What else do you wish to see?"

Reynard slowly pored over the paper. Finally he asked about lands south and west. "What is this? And this?"

Henry squinted to read the faded letters. "The Wisconsin River. The Mississippi River, which flows very far to St. Louis, where it meets another great river, the Missouri—but that's not on this map."

Reynard pronounced the words. "Now I can tell my tribe about those places."

"Would you like me to make you a copy?"

"No, I will remember."

CHAPTER 76

The moon rose late that evening and everyone was asleep when Reynard nudged André. "Let us speak alone."

Reynard led him to an open area away from the others. "It was my fortune to travel with you, through the lands of some of my enemies. You're a good friend and a good leader. *Miigwetch*."

André felt honored by Reynard's words.

"That first night you came to my house—that was when I believed we could make this voyage," André answered. "You made it work, especially in bad times—when Danny almost drowned, repairing the canoe, finding a place for François, navigating us through the strait. You helped each of us."

"I did my part when it was needed, as each of us did."

"How can we finish with only five left to paddle? It's too much for Gabriel and Baptiste—they're tired."

"We rise to the occasion when we face a problem. I didn't know I could speak to the moose or the bear, or fix the canoe. It helps to share what we know. You too have learned. You're at your best when you hear what others offer. You'll find the Fox River is gentle, not like the Ottawa—and Michel is ready."

André hesitated, but his friend glanced at the moon.

"If our paths cross again, my tribe would welcome you."

Then Reynard slipped away.

A great loss washed over André. Without Reynard, he felt alone and more than a little scared. *Maybe we should quit and be done with the expedition. Maybe we should stop at Green Bay and wait there for Captain Ashton.*

The next day was difficult for all of them.

"Reynard showed me how to read tracks but I couldn't even find his footprints," Danny said.

"I miss Reynard's quiet as much as François' bluster. It feels strange," Michel said.

"This canoe, it's too big," Pretty Mouse complained, again paddling as *gouvernail*. "We ride too high in the water. One big wind, it will blow us out into the lake. When can Michel start steering? You know my eyes aren't seeing right?"

"As soon as we get into more protected waters," André answered. "Because we're short two men, it's hard for me to keep the canoe in line."

"Maybe you can trade for a smaller one in Green Bay?"

Why haven't we met up with Captain Ashton? Did something happen to him? If we don't find him, should we take Danny and Henry back to Fort St. Joseph? How will we all find winter work? Gabriel and Baptiste—they can't do much more.

With fewer men, everyone had to paddle harder. Gabriel and Baptiste struggled, exhausted at each day's end, and rued not stopping longer to rest at Fort St. Joseph. Pretty Mouse seemed close-lipped, not his ebullient self. Steering took its toll on him.

They talked about how François might be faring, when he might walk again.

Where they saw Indians along rivers, they wondered about Reynard.

"He'd wave if he saw us," Danny said.

Once they stopped at a large gathering of wigwams, and gazed with longing at the ripening apples and squashes.

Pretty Mouse traded for them, and for wild rice and onions that would improve their *rubaboo*.

On they paddled, staying close to the shore, needing respite, eager for their journey would end, eager to meet Captain Ashton.

But his brigade did not appear.

CHAPTER 77

Several days after Reynard had left, the land on both sides narrowed toward the mouth of a river. As they neared, they felt the Fox River's current pushing toward them.

"My Papa, he will be here?"

He must be. He has to be.

In the distance, cabins appeared here and there. Behind each was a strip of cleared field where a crop had been planted and harvested.

They perked up, excited to arrive at their destination, and sang to announce themselves, though no people waved back.

"Look—it's like a village," Danny said, counting the cabins in French.

"Now count them in Latin," Henry urged.

As they neared the main settlement, they saw small gardens surrounded by low fences woven from thin sticks to keep rabbits from eating the plants. A few chickens clucked and picked at seeds. Two cows, no longer harnessed to a nearby grinding stone, looked up from grazing.

Smoke rose from a small outdoor oven. The aroma of baking made their mouths water.

"It looks like home," Gabriel said.

Finally, by mid-afternoon, they saw a few overturned small canoes and boats on a grassy incline. They eagerly pulled their canoe up on a pebbly shore.

No one came to meet them.

No soldiers in red uniforms waited on shore.

André was dismayed—he'd counted on Danny's father being there. It was like a punch in his gut. "I was sure Captain Ashton and his soldiers would be here, with two big canoes."

"Maybe he's over there," Baptiste said, pointing to buildings up a small hill.

"Wouldn't he have better canoes than these?" Michel asked.

"Or assign men to stay with them?" Baptiste said.

Pretty Mouse nodded. "These don't look official. Bet they belong to locals."

They looked around, trying to decide what to do.

"Danny, I don't think he's here. But I'll ask at the fur trade post up that hill. The traders should know about Captain Ashton," André said, putting hope he didn't feel into his voice.

"You go—I'll stay with the canoe," Michel said.

The traders were chatty, sharing what little news they had, curious for more.

"Your lad's a little young for being a *voyageur*, ain't he?"

"You going to sign on with a brigade when you sprout up a bit like your papa?"

Danny glowed. "*Oui*, like *Monsieur Souris*."

André was about to clarify the relationship when Pretty Mouse dropped his pipe.

"Lucky for me it didn't break. But that reminds me, I'm nearly out of tobacco. I should trade for twist." When Mouse picked it up, he caught André's eye.

André clammed up while Pretty Mouse bargained for tobacco.

Danny soon bored of the traders' ramblings. "Can we look around? Maybe we can trade for some of their bread." Danny dragged at Pretty Mouse's arm and they headed out.

When they'd left, André asked whether a British brigade had stopped.

"That was weeks ago. Bound for Prairie du Chien, they was. Hired a local guide and *voyageurs*, though they shouldn't have needed anyone that direction. But they were in a hurry."

"Yessiree, some 'important personage' they wanted to see, coming up from St. Louis. The leader, he wouldn't say who—he was as tight-lipped as they come. Fortunately one of his paddlers spilled a few beans before he left."

"How many did he travel with?" André asked.

"Can't rightly say. Only the big man himself came up here. Down at the landing is where he hired paddlers."

"So if I need to hire a couple of men?"

"Outta luck—if you want good paddlers."

"You don't know when they're returning?"

"Their wives have been asking us the same thing. They need their wood cut and game put up for the winter."

Now what? Do we wait? Do we get a smaller canoe?

When André asked who built canoes, they extolled the virtues of Claude and gave directions to find him.

"I watched you come in," Claude said. "Your canoe, it's too big for the Fox—almost like an ark. This late in the summer, the river's shallow and bendy and narrow. You're like to hit every boulder and dead tree, patching it twice a day."

"We started with seven men and no cargo to speak of. Since I can't hire here, I'm looking for a canoe that holds five paddlers and two passengers. What have you got to trade?"

"I'll have to make a new one, and that could take me most of a week. You do know it's not a good season for getting bark off the trees?" Claude said. "Or you could trade for my family's canoe. It's smaller—take a look."

André inspected the canoe but shook his head. "*Non*, too crowded for us. I'll talk to you later."

He was discouraged. *Our canoe is too big for five paddlers—I know that. If we hit rocks we don't have Reynard to repair it. A whole week to get a new one? Too many problems for one day. I'm over my head—again.*

When he arrived back at the canoe landing, only Michel sat, whittling. "I figured we'd be here for the night so I set up the tent for Henry. He's inside. Others are gone. What's the news?"

André vented his frustration. "No sign of Ashton. Who knows when he'll appear? He hired the best paddlers, so we can't replace François and Reynard. The canoe builder could make a smaller one, but not for a week. I don't know what to do—wait here for a new canoe or go on. Do you have any ideas?"

"If we wait the week, Captain Ashton might arrive. But you don't like waiting around—you'd rather paddle the Fox River to find him. Sleep on it—decide in the morning."

Michel made sense.

"I'm not surprised Danny and Mouse are still wandering, but where are Baptiste and Gabriel?"

Michel pointed to a small inn upstream. "Replenishing their supply of rum and swapping for new stories?"

They hadn't returned by supper time, which surprised Pretty Mouse. "They're always first in line with their bowls. You wouldn't think they'd buy a meal at a tavern when this is free?"

"Maybe their story about François or the shortcut at Grand Calumet is earning them something?" Michel suggested.

Chapter 78

After the meal, Pretty Mouse and Danny played checkers, using acorns and rocks on a grid scratched in the sand. Too soon, the sun began to set and small lights twinkled in one or two of the nearest cottages.

"Baptiste and Gabriel, they've been gone too long. I'm going to find them," André said.

"I'll go with. I'd like to see the village." Michel rose.

At the closest tavern, a patron, well into his cups, gestured farther up the hill. They weren't at the second place, but a few local farmers recalled seeing newcomers having the best time. They gave directions to follow the trail along the lake's edge.

"Uh oh. Betting on some game? But they don't have much money to lose," Michel said as they hurried on a twisty path through the woods.

When they heard shouts and loud laughing—familiar voices—André groaned. "Too much high wine. I hope Gabriel and Baptiste can walk."

"And paddle tomorrow."

Both Gabriel and Baptiste sat on a bench outside a small cabin, holding wooden mugs and looking very pleased. A young man sat between them, a piglet on his lap.

When Baptiste saw them, he stood, wobbling a bit. "Oho, look who's here. André, meet my nephew, Jean-Baptiste. I've told you about him. He's my sister's oldest—she named him after me. And, can you believe it, he lives here, here in Green Bay. Jean-Baptiste, he built this cottage and has a brand-new pig. We found him—isn't that the best news you've heard? Jean-Baptiste, this is André, our leader. The other young fellow, that's Michel."

Jean-Baptiste shifted the piglet and stood to shake hands. "Glad to make your acquaintance." He looked remarkably like his uncle—short and barrel-chested, a head of wiry black hair, a full beard and mustache and a cheery sparkle in his eyes.

"We had this feeling he was out here somewhere," Gabriel said. "So it's good we didn't take that ship."

"I tell you, André, we've been worried about what to do," Baptiste said. "The two of us, we didn't want to go back to Lachine. Now we won't have to. My nephew, he said we can live with him. What good fortune! What do you think of that?"

"But our task isn't done yet," André said. "We have to find Danny's father."

"Pfft—smart as you are, that's nothing. You'll meet him in no time. Gabriel and me, we're worn out, truth be told, but we stuck it out this far, being loyal to you, getting you through the straits. You've hardly needed us for the last days. Besides, his father must be close."

"We promised Jean-Baptiste here our wages so he can buy chickens and a plow," Gabriel said. "I like chickens."

The nephew grinned. "Never thought I'd see my old uncle again in this lifetime. But today he turns up, out of the blue. And I get two uncles in the bargain, willing to share my work."

Gabriel looked surprised at the mention of work.

"Well, we know a thing or two. Living with Jean-Baptiste, it'll be a godsend," Baptiste said.

Their news deflated André.

Gabriel added a half-hearted, "Slow as we are, I thought you'd be glad to have us off your hands. But luck like this, it doesn't come around twice."

The last thing André expected had happened—his oldsters found their own place to settle. He knew they wouldn't change their minds. "I'll pay you in the morning."

"Let's do it now. We can fetch your blankets and packs," the nephew said.

The three chattered amiably about the new arrangements as they walked back to the canoe. André and Michel were silent.

André counted out more than enough *livres* and added food rations and a few tools. "There's extra—especially for working so hard through the straits. You've helped as you were able, not just in the canoe. *Merci.*"

"Mighty good of you. See? I told you he'd do us right."

After they left, André was conflicted. He didn't depend on them like he had François and Reynard, but without them it changed everything. Somehow the glue was disappearing and he felt adrift. "I'm angry they left us alone to deliver Danny, but what could I say?"

"They worried about this nephew every single day, though maybe you didn't hear them," Michel said.

"True. Baptiste mentioned him when they first asked to join the venture but I brushed it off as impossible."

"Today is the first time they've looked happy," Michel said after a long silence.

André said, "They looked after us, in their own way. I'll miss them." The depth of his emotion surprised him.

"Me too. The old guys did what they could. More than fair to increase their wages."

"They've lived so close to the bone for years that it didn't take much to make their lives easier. Tonight it made me feel good to share with them. Like it did when I paid off François and Reynard. The colonel included extra money for unusual circumstances, of which we've had plenty—François for the bone setter, medicine and not being able to work for so many months. Reynard preferred trade goods. Having that bag of coins, sure it made me feel important. For a while I hoped to set myself up in a trading post, but this was a much better use for his money."

Chapter 79

Still, André stewed much of the night.

Half my crew has disappeared. I understand why, but now what? Is Gabriel right, that three of us can handle the next part of the journey? New people—if we could find any—would have to get used to Danny and Henry. It's taken me this whole trip to understand them.

Well, thank God Pretty Mouse tends to Danny. He'll be glad to be relieved of that responsibility. Tomorrow Michel starts steering. I'll have to be as patient as Antoine was when I began.

What if we don't find Danny's father? Does it make sense to proceed on the route? It would be easier to wait here.

The next morning, he still felt unsettled.

"Have you decided?" Michel asked.

"*Oui*, a little. Assuming we can trade our canoe for the small one the builder has, we'll start with the three of us. If that's too hard, we'll look for a paddler or two. I counted our coins—we have enough to hire new *voyageurs*. But it doesn't feel right. Yesterday afternoon started with a single decision about a smaller canoe. It became more complicated once Baptiste found his nephew. And no Captain Ashton. This is all strange."

"Too many changes all at once," Michel said. "How about I go to meet the canoe builder?"

"Me too?" Danny glanced at Henry, who opened the history book, about to start a lesson.

"If Henry agrees."

Henry closed the book.

Claude met them on their way to the canoe works. "You didn't order a new one, and the best trees for a canoe are a half-day's walk. So, me, I came to find you." He stepped back to scan them. "Is this all of you? Didn't you tell me five paddlers and two passengers?"

André shrugged. "Only three paddlers now, plus our passengers—yesterday two men found a nephew here."

"Oho, that'd be Jean-Baptiste then? Word's out already."

"Any men around here we could hire?"

"*Non*. Most aren't yet home from the *rendezvous*. They'll be back before the snow flies, if you wait that long. But the river's so tame, my boy could handle it—even this little guy. Let me look at your canoe before I make the trade."

Danny chatted brightly as they walked back to the landing where Henry was napping in the tent.

Claude examined Reynard's patch, pressing it, testing it. "Well done, but it's not an even trade—my canoe, she isn't this banged up."

They hiked to Claude's cabin to get the new canoe, and André produced more *livres*.

"Oh—you painted a fox on the bow," Danny grinned.

"That's for the Fox River. You like it?" Claude said.

"What's the river like this time of year?" Michel asked.

"Slow. Shallow. Winding. More deadheads than usual, after last week's storm."

"What do we need to know about the route?"

"Not far from here, you come to the big lake—for this crew, in about two days," Claude said. "The inlet you want, it's on the west side—watch where the river flows in. After that it meanders, and the current all but disappears this late in the season. Expect a portage or a *décharge* or three. After a few more days of winding, you'll come to the long portage over to the Wisconsin River and that'll take you to Prairie du Chien."

CHAPTER 80

"Michel, today you steer from the stern and I'll take the bow. I always meant you to start before, but tricky waters and crosswinds prevented me," André said. It was mostly true. "Tomorrow I'll paddle *milieu* and Mouse, you'll be our *devant*."

Pretty Mouse was relieved for the day of respite.

"I'll help too," Danny volunteered.

They left Green Bay quietly. Gabriel and Baptiste didn't come to see them off—they were already helping the nephew.

André let Michel experiment, and only called out the most critical alerts. He gritted his teeth to keep from blurting out suggestions, grimacing when the new canoe scraped deadheads or submerged rocks. *Still this place is ideal for Michel to take over. My first day of steering wasn't better—I had to learn too.*

As a new steersman, Michel struggled, unable to keep them in a straight line. The canoe fishtailed from bank to bank, which embarrassed and frustrated them all.

By the time they stopped for lunch, Michel understood—mostly—how to move the little canoe where he wanted it to go. Determining the best passage would take longer.

They paddled through attractive country, with low banks fed by streams. Yellow and orange leaves whirled down on a golden afternoon. In the distance, dense woods hid the land.

When they passed a native village, Danny looked longingly at the children climbing trees, shooting arrows, running along the banks among racks of drying fish.

"They have friends their own age to play with," he sighed.

Henry watched women sewing skins into clothing. "Maybe we left the fort or Green Bay too quickly. My shirts are threadbare. Will the tribes have cotton or muslin to share?"

André considered his own stained and patched clothing. "*Non*. We missed our opportunity. We might find a trader with bolts of cloth and pay someone to sew clothing."

Now that winter was coming, their clothing would be insufficient.

The next day Pretty Mouse groused but took the bow. André sat in the middle, not directing anything. It was dull without the energy of François, the quiet awareness of Reynard and the small surprises of Gabriel and Baptiste.

André felt off-kilter. Watching Michel and Pretty Mouse navigate irritated him and he swallowed his flippant remarks.

I hate not being in charge. Too bad I felt so insecure—I could've learned more from François and Reynard, even from Gabriel and Baptiste.

His stomach was in a knot. While he'd made the best choice, he didn't feel at ease. Wait-and-see wasn't a reasonable plan. Having staked his hopes on Captain Ashton being at the fort or in Green Bay, now he feared they might never complete their task. His end goal had disappeared.

Autumn's darkness descended on him personally. The weight of leadership, a nearly impossible assignment, the rapid changes in his crew, the season's coolness—all wore him down.

Oddly, he no longer cared to hurry—they would either meet Danny's father on the river or they would paddle to Prairie du Chien. He'd given up hope of finding winter work, and had no other ideas. Nights were worse, when worries filled his brain and prevented him from sleep.

Thanks to the fort's sutler charging their provisions to Captain Ashton's account, they had enough *rubaboo*. They stopped at Indian encampments to trade for whatever food the tribes might share. But there were no fur trading posts for Henry or the others to get warmer clothing.

The river entered the large lake the canoe maker had mentioned and, by late afternoon, Mouse and Michel had located the tributary to the west.

"Why doesn't that hill have any trees?" Danny asked.

"A burial mound? Like that one Reynard saw, where we traded with Hurons?" Michel guessed.

Danny shivered. "A lot of people must have died. Why?"

"Maybe warriors attacked because other braves hunted on their grounds," Pretty Mouse said. "If warriors from one band died, their friends might take revenge against their enemies."

"Are they still fighting?" Danny looked panicked

"No, Danny," André answered. "It was made years ago, many, many years. Think how long it would take to carry all that dirt."

"Which tribes live around here?" Henry asked.

"Reynard said Menominee, Winnebago, Ojibwe and Fox."

"Will my father fight them? Or Americans?"

"I hope he will try to keep peace instead. Would you like to read history?" But Henry didn't reach for a book.

Though their conversation ended, each person recalled comments they'd heard about war between the French and British, the Americans and natives. It was a somber evening.

What if Captain Ashton returns on different rivers—will we ever find him if he doesn't realize we're searching for him? If we arrive at Prairie du Chien without seeing him, I suppose I'll need to write letters to Colonel Markham and Captain Ashton, and maybe the commander at Fort St. Joseph.

I keep wanting Danny to reunite with his father, that it'll be a wonderful reunion, but what do I know about how families act? My own brother Denis left for France shortly after I reconnected with him. Michel's uncle dismissed him. Mouse never talked about his family. Is that why our crew of misfits has become its own family?

Chapter 81

The days became chilly and gray, with a mist that threatened drizzle. Henry gave up being a zealous teacher. They didn't sing, and they didn't talk much.

The Fox River, once wide and flowing, now snaked back and forth through reeds and brush that clogged its flow.

They saw no other paddlers along the river and few tribes camped on the banks—and they missed those conversations with others to enliven their quiet. Sometimes the only sound was the twitter and honk of migrating birds.

When Michel steered as *gouvernail*, Pretty Mouse and André rotated guiding from the bow, navigating twisty turns on the river, avoiding submerged roots and branches obstructing the narrowed current.

"This must be where the canoe maker warned us about. What a mess. Dead tree roots in the water and sticking up all around," Pretty Mouse said.

"These last miles remind me of the water meadows on the Mattawa. It took forever to wind through that," Michel said. "Here I can hardly decide where the river is or what is land."

"Nor can I," Pretty Mouse conceded. "It was easier when we followed that little open stream—maybe because hundreds of *voyageur* canoes had deepened the route before us."

"Will we ever get to that long portage the canoe builder told us about?" Michel worried.

"Let's hope someone knows about Captain Ashton's soldiers. If not, we continue to Prairie du Chien," André said.

"And that's a few more days?" Michel asked.

"*Oui.*"

Henry abruptly lifted his head from his book.

"André, will you paddle *devant* the rest of today? This watching hurts my head," Pretty Mouse asked.

"*Non.* Michel decides when he wants a break. If not, you and I will trade off each day."

❖ ❖ ❖

André knew he could have made it easier for Pretty Mouse. Paddling *milieu* was dull—it only required his back and arms. He had more time to ponder, and fell into a daze.

The trip had changed for him somehow—it no longer gave him pleasure to plan, to lead. And what might be coming made little sense to him.

Neither Mouse nor Michel have talked about the future, though I've asked. Wish I knew what they are thinking. What if some prospect comes up quickly and I have to make a fast decision without their ideas?

What would I like? Being a voyageur or brigade leader hasn't been what I'm good at. All I do is stand in the bow, watching for errant tree roots and rocks and making decisions for people. I thought I liked exploring, but I'm uncomfortable in new places. I don't speak Indian languages well enough to be an interpreter. I don't know enough of the waterways to guide. Trader at a post? At Bear Tooth Rapids, I chatted up the trappers during the days and totaled figures at night. There's more to life that that. So what else interests me? The priesthood? Military? Medicine? Law? A business? What do I know of those pursuits? What am I supposed to do with my life if I go back to the village? Will I have to go to France, if Papa and Mama have left the cottage in someone else's care?

However, musing brought no clear answers.

Chapter 82

André felt bound by his agreement with Colonel Markham, yet thwarted, because it wasn't working out like the plan. Since he didn't have anyone to express his frustration to, and to keep it from boiling over, he began separating himself from the others. Torn up inside, he no longer slept deeply.

So one gray afternoon when he was paddling *milieu*, he'd slid his paddle along the gunwale in a narrow section of river, waiting for Pretty Mouse to direct them again. Not needed for the while, he slumped down—and dozed off.

Pretty Mouse, guiding the canoe, didn't notice. Nor did the boys, sitting behind Mouse, both napping as well.

Michel, in the stern, said nothing. As lowest man in the group, it wasn't his place to speak up. Michel sensed the weight André shouldered—his friend needed rest.

So they snaked through the vast marsh, reeds higher than their heads, struggling to find the best waterway.

After a time, Pretty Mouse spoke softly. "Michel, does this place look familiar?"

"*Non.* All these rushes and reeds, they look the same to me. Are we lost?"

"We ... uh ... might be circling. I can't tell if we're making headway."

"Let's mark something. Then if we come upon it again, we'll recognize it."

Pretty Mouse steered along the edge of a bed of reeds and Michel used a few rushes to tie a cluster together.

They set out again, more energized, as they watched for anything to clarify their location.

Until they came upon the reeds they'd bound together.

They stopped.

"We're going the wrong way. How could that happen?" Mouse said, ashamed of his error.

"I could get out and stand on something? Maybe I could see where we're headed."

"If there were any bit of land to stand on in this marsh."

Michel sighed. "I'll try anyway, see what I can tell you."

He clambered out and sloshed up to his knees. With rushes reaching over his head, getting enough height was impossible.

"Stand on my shoulders," Pretty Mouse directed.

Pretty Mouse anchored the canoe into some rushes and planted his feet—up to his knee—in the water. Michel climbed atop, but had only a brief view before losing his balance and plummeting down.

The cold splash jolted André.

"What happened?" he shouted, groggy.

After a few seconds, Michel answered. "We might be going in circles. See those weeds in that bundle? We tied them like that and paddled a while. Now we've reached them again. I got on Mouse's shoulders to get our bearings."

"How could you be lost? This is a river—there aren't islands to confuse us." André's voice was angrier than he meant, but it covered his guilt at awakening.

"You're the one who fell asleep while we kept paddling."

"You were sleeping? In the canoe?" Pretty Mouse was incensed. "You're supposed to know where we are."

"How do I know where we are or how far to go?" André yelled, now fully awake. "I've never been here before."

At the boys' shocked faces in witnessing an outburst, he knew he should apologize, but he couldn't right then. With nowhere for them to go, he would have to find a solution—the right solution—immediately.

He gave himself a moment to breathe.

"New territory or not, we can figure this out," André said. "Your marking reeds—that was smart thinking. Since these are tied, let's paddle for 500 strokes, and see what happens. If we come to any junctions, we'll tie reeds, but with different knots. Henry, you have a map. Can we see it?"

"Yes, but the distances are wrong. It's hard to understand how far apart places are."

They pored over the map Henry produced, but it didn't look enough like the one Michel and André had studied at the fort to assist them. Danny tossed his bits of grass to determine the current's direction and they set out, cautious but suspicious.

When Danny announced the count of 500, they hadn't come upon any marked reeds—a minor success. But they felt anxious. Maybe they weren't lost, but they still didn't know where they were.

At several confluences, André bound other sets of reeds together. He knew by the set of their shoulders they were angry for good reason. He hung his head. He had no excuses.

Chapter 83

After what felt like several hours of trying to determine where the waterway was, Pretty Mouse said, "Night comes early these days—we'd better get a campsite firm enough for the tent."

"Fine. Michel, you stand on both of our shoulders—that will be more stable than on one person."

André and Pretty Mouse braced themselves while Michel looked uncertainly for a place to plant his feet. He decided on their hips and reached around André's neck to pull while boosting himself up. When he felt secure, he put his knees on their shoulders. He still wasn't high enough, or balanced.

"Danny, hand us the steering paddle so Michel can steady himself."

Michel grabbed it, glancing around. "Over there I see trees. And one … "

When he lifted his hand to point the way, he lost his balance, let go of the paddle and splatted into the water.

After he rose, he pointed. "I saw plenty of trees in that direction. But one tree was odd."

"How can a tree be odd? We've seen hundreds around here, all alike." Henry was dismissive.

"It had a tuft on top. But I only saw it for a second."

Pretty Mouse nodded. "Long ago my town had a tree with a growth on top. When they cut it down, grapevine or holly had made a great knot on its crest."

"At least there are trees. Let's head that way. Is it far?"

Michel shrugged.

As they paddled, a bit refreshed, they mused on such a tree. In the next miles, they didn't come upon either more of their marked reeds or the strange tree. Finally Pretty Mouse pointed the canoe toward an almost-solid bit of raised ground with enough space for the tent, the canoe and a campfire.

Discouraged and needing solitude, needing space to keep from blaming others, André hurried away.

Danny's chirpy voice carried. "Are we lost? How will my father find us if we're lost?"

Henry answered quietly. "They'll sort it out."

Pretty Mouse muttered as he got the fire going and started the *rubaboo*. "As usual, leaving me to do this while you … " He stopped and looked around for Danny. "Now that supper is cooking, Danny, how about you boys skip stones? I have something to do."

Danny was elated. "Yippee, we haven't done that since before François got hurt. Come on, Henry."

Pretty Mouse grabbed Michel to join him and they pushed their way through the bushes. "We can't fight in front of the youngsters. We have to work this out. Where are you, André?"

They found him by an overgrown shrub.

Pretty Mouse was ferociously angry. He roared, "After I fell, my eyes make two pictures of everything so I can hardly tell which one is real. Michel—this is his first trip, he's learning. We rely on you to do this right. It's time to be the leader."

Michel felt uncomfortable with their tension. "Soldiers—or someone—will come by if we wait here."

André snorted. "And rescue us? Danny's father will scorn us for being lost. We can't just stay here. I don't know what to do —I need more time to think."

"But if we keep moving, how will they find us?"

"Dannee, he deserves better. You can't fall asleep again. You have to …"

"A little more time."

Pretty Mouse huffed away in disgust. "It's like we're all talking different languages."

After Michel followed, André conceded. *Neither of them trust me any more. I don't trust myself. Colonel Markham was foolish to give me this assignment.*

Next morning dawned cloudy, again, without a sunrise to tell them which direction was east.

Danny tossed bits of grass into the current which they studied for many minutes.

After André suggested the direction of travel, they concurred, sullenly.

They zigzagged all morning through the walls of reeds, seeing only a few yards ahead of them.

But this day was in a new part of the marsh—they didn't come upon any of their marked areas. And the ground was subtly different. They saw an occasional tree. When they stopped to eat, they found solid earth.

"I heard something," Danny said.

André asked, "Geese or ducks?"

Danny was irritated. "No. I know what they sound like."

They listened intently. Nobody else heard sounds.

"Danny, climb on me and Michel. Maybe you'll see something," André said

Pretty Mouse boosted Danny to their shoulders where he held tightly to a steering paddle. He stood for several seconds, looking around, and climbed back down. "I saw lots of trees. But one is different. What's the name of that tree with needles and a pointy top—a spruce? Anyway, the top is there, but no branches below, only the trunk."

"Branches are missing? The lower branches? A tree disease?" André was mystified.

"Hit by lightning? Eaten by porcupines?" Pretty Mouse suggested.

"It could be the same one I saw," Michel said.

"A tree with top branches but no bottom ones?" Pretty Mouse said slowly, bringing back a memory he'd long forgotten. "Could it be a lopstick?"

"What's a lopstick?" Danny said.

"Once on an island far north, we saw an odd tree like that. It marked a waterway that was hard to find, like a message to use that passage. That's what a lopstick is. We saw it from miles away. *Voyageurs* made them by lopping off the bottom branches and leaving the top."

"What would a lopstick mark here?"

"The right passage through this swamp?" Michel said.

Pretty Mouse frowned. "Antoine, he once told me their *bourgeois* wanted to honor the Montreal partner who was coming through in the next canoe, so his brigade was ordered to strip the lower branches off the tree, like a maypole, and carve the partner's name. Then the partner had to share high wines, to repay them."

"Reynard wouldn't like that," Michel said.

Danny interrupted. "I heard something again."

They stood quietly, trying to hear what he heard.

"Blackbirds? Jays?"

"No."

"Animals? A brush wolf?"

"No. Not like that."

"A tree falling? A rapids?"

"People?"

"*Non*, well, maybe ducks. But I can't hear it anymore." Danny was disappointed. "Doesn't any one else hear them?"

They were quiet for some moments but shook their heads, wondering. It perplexed them. A strange lopped tree and the mystery sounds became beacons calling them.

"The lopped tree—we aim in that direction. Let's try to find it," André said.

They were with him again. They set out.

CHAPTER 84

As they readied to depart, Danny halted, suddenly alert "I hear those sounds again. Loud ones."

Though they listened resolutely, they heard no sounds. Loud noises were rare in the wild.

Quickly they began paddling, moving toward where they thought the lopped tree was and where Danny's mystery sound might have come from.

Concentrating hard, they wound their way through the high reeds, swamp grasses and dead branches, but Danny didn't hear any more sounds. Nor did they come upon the tree. Their excitement—and hope—dwindled.

"We don't have to stop to eat," Danny said. He feared he'd lost face.

"If you're not hungry, let's keep going," André said.

After they'd rounded the hundredth wide bend, André's eye caught a movement in the far distance, screened by reeds and dead trees that clogged the stream.

He slowed, squinting his eyes to discern shapes—moving shapes—for a second, until they were again hidden.

"People! People on the bank—you're right, Danny. But red uniforms should stand out. I didn't see any."

Disappointed, they slogged through the swampy reeds.

"At least we can find out who they are, how long they've been on the river. Maybe they'll have seen Captain Ashton's soldiers," André said. But it was hard to glimpse them again for longer than a moment.

After hundreds of strokes and several more junctions, Pretty Mouse asked, "Are you sure we're going the right direction? Dannee, can you hear anything?"

Danny couldn't.

Their sight lines were almost constantly blocked.

Then Michel shouted, "That's the tree I saw, a lopstick."

"I see it too," Danny added.

Finally they could discern an open campsite where they could distinguish several men standing around a canoe turned upside down. They drifted closer, curious about their fellow travelers.

"Canoe repair. They're applying gum to the seams. They're *voyageurs*." André felt an instant camaraderie.

"And one of these roots punched a hole in their hull," Michel said.

"Friends!" Pretty Mouse said.

"With news to share," André said.

Blankets, a barrel of provisions and a pack of trade goods were heaped, blocking the canoe landing. Behind them, a few men tidied a heap of spruce branches and another one carved on a bare tree trunk, the lopstick. Others milled around, busy, unaware of the oncoming canoe.

"Traders visiting the tribes after the *rendezvous*?" Michel guessed.

"But they didn't bring much to trade," Pretty Mouse said. "I count only one pack of goods."

One man came into view, pacing in the only open stretch, clearly upset. Dressed in a tall top hat, green waistcoat, black breeches and white ruffled shirt and stockings, he looked like an important North West Company owner or partner. Having completed one loop, he pivoted, marching away from them.

"Fancy clothes. Is that what owners wear at the *rendezvous*?" It was new to Michel.

André nodded. "Maybe bound for Michilimackinac. He could be a good man to know—he might know of work for us for this winter."

They heard a sharp squeal.

"*Papa, c'est moi. Ici. C'est moi,*" Danny shrieked. Papa, it's me. Here. It's me.

He started crawling over their packs, trying to get out of the canoe.

"Easy now, Dannee," Mouse said. "Wait until we find some place for us to land—they left their gear all over."

Henry handed him the little paddle. "Danny, wave this when you call them."

"*Papa, es tu? Papa, regardes-moi,*" Danny panted and frantically brandished the paddle. Papa, is it you? Look at me.

His piercing shouts alerted a few men on land. They stopped repairing, smoking, carving on a tree, to size up the people in the oncoming canoe.

Intent on his own concerns, the well-dressed man ignored them.

"In English, Danny. Say it in English," Henry said.

Danny looked surprised—French had become his daily language. He rephrased it in English. "Father, it's me, over here. I'm here. Father, is it you? Why don't you look at me?"

At that, the citified man broke his stride. Rooted to the ground, he stared at the canoe, shook his head and rubbed his eyes.

Unable to wait for André to land their canoe, Danny leapt out and dog-paddled the remaining yards to the shore. Sopping wet, he scrambled up the bank and ran toward the man, jumping up and down and tugging at his hand.

Danny sobbed and laughed and words tumbled out of his mouth, now in a combination of French and English. "It's me, Papa. And look, I am a real *voyageur* and I saw a big moose up close and almost a mama bear. And that *milieu*, he is Pretty Mouse, but it's not his real name. He's my best friend. And now I have my own knife and I know lots of animals and birds. To prove it here is my knot string. Aren't you glad to see me, Papa?"

Barely comprehending Danny's babble, the man shook his head as he watched André and the others land their canoe.

He bent down. "Daniel? Why are you dressed like that? Why are you here?"

"I'm a *voyageur*, like they are. Because Mamma's baby got all these red spots and the doctor said they were measles that made her sick. And then Mamma got spots too and she was hot and slept a lot. But I wasn't sick. So that's why I came to you."

Captain Ashton turned abruptly, gesturing to the excited boy to follow him for a private reunion. "Son, let us walk over here. We have much to talk about."

Pretty Mouse looked crestfallen as he carried Danny's blanket, pack and bags with his newest rock collections and laid them carefully on shore. He sat, head in his hands, while Michel brought the tent. Henry added the slate and books from his desk.

Michel nudged into the circle of men by the upturned canoe, curious about the problem and its repair.

André rummaged through his pack to find the papers that Colonel Markham had sent. His head spun. *That's his father? Why aren't they wearing uniforms? We're supposed to transfer Danny and Henry to them, but it doesn't feel right.*

When Henry pulled out a small oiled packet from his desk, André choked. *After all this time, Henry is going to report on us—I thought he'd forgotten our infractions. I hope I can explain it all to Captain Ashton.*

CHAPTER 85

A short time later, Captain Ashton returned, with Danny holding his hand and chattering at top speed. "Daniel, be a good boy and sit quietly by that tree. Next I must speak to your leader."

Danny separated dutifully, his eyes beginning to water. Pretty Mouse scooped him up and sent him off to gather firewood and directed Michel to fill the big kettle. Mouse kindled a fire and began frying *pemmican* he'd dug out of their pack.

Captain Ashton watched for a minute before turning his attention to André, who held out the letters he'd carried. First he broke the seal of Colonel Markham's long letter. It required a second reading to grasp the deaths of his wife and an infant child he'd never seen. His eyes glistened and he glanced around, stiffening his face until he could regain control of his emotions.

Then he read the short one. "I see. But of course. You've a small crew to carry out such a task," Captain Ashton said. "You've apparently done your job well—the boy looks quite healthy, even purposeful. Unfortunately, due to the clumsiness of my men—or was it a ruse to make that foolish lopstick and get high wines—we are stuck here until the canoe is repaired. I expect we shall be off before long. What baggage does Daniel have?"

"We left several trunks at Fort St. Joseph, sir," André answered, "so it's just his blanket and tent—and some rocks he's found since then. And Henry's things."

The captain considered pile of the items. "Shift them over. We'll make room. But—who is Henry?"

Henry stepped close and thrust his letters toward the captain. "I am, sir. If you please, would you read this first? Perhaps over there, where we can speak without others listening."

Irritated, Captain Ashton strode along the bank before breaking the letter's seal, muttering, "So many interruptions on a day we should have traveled quickly. What next?"

◈ ◈ ◈

He read Henry's letter once and peered at him questioningly, and then reread the other letters more slowly. "I will consider this," he said abruptly and walked away.

"Is that all the things we did wrong?" André wondered why Henry's desk and trunks had not been taken out of their canoe to go along with Danny's.

"No. This doesn't concern you," Henry answered flatly.

They waited, regarding each other as foes.

Pretty Mouse had Danny add wild onions to the meaty *rubaboo*. The aroma penetrated the area and the *voyageurs* commented enthusiastically on Danny's participation.

◈ ◈ ◈

Finally Captain Ashton called Henry to join him. They sat. André couldn't hear, but saw the tension as they discussed a problem. After long minutes, the captain handed Henry's letters back to him. Henry nodded.

Captain Ashton was about to speak again when they heard hoots and huzzahs. Several *voyageurs* stood in the river with the repaired canoe, having checked it for leaks—it had passed their test for sea-worthiness.

"Finally we can leave," Captain Ashton said, checking for the whereabouts of his son, who was stirring the steaming pot of stew, guided by Pretty Mouse's hand. "We shall be taking off immediately, Daniel. Come."

"But Father, we've made this *rubaboo* for you. You must stay and eat it, Father. Please?" Danny's voice wavered.

"Son, you heard me. It's time to go. Hurry—no time to waste. I must report to Fort St. Joseph as soon as possible. This repair has cost me more than a day, and a keg of high wines in repayment for that tree."

Danny tried not to whimper as he handed the spoon to Michel, but when Pretty Mouse hugged him and swung him up in the air, he sobbed.

Though used to commanding soldiers, Captain Ashton faced a situation he'd never dealt with—instilling military discipline in a child, his child, whose mother had recently died, and in front of those soldiers who lived by his command.

Everyone was silent.

Pretty Mouse opened his arms and Danny slowly trudged to his father's canoe, sniffling, his head down.

Captain Ashton wavered. This was not the way it should be. Mere minutes ago, the boy had been bright and eager.

"We made plenty for all your men, sir," Michel called, holding up the serving spoon. "If you eat now, you can paddle longer tonight without having to stop."

The captain sighed. "Men, get your cups."

After Danny brought the first bowl of stew to his father, the canoemen elbowed for places around the kettle.

André grinned gratefully at Michel. "Brilliant."

Michel watched Pretty Mouse's bereft face.

Chapter 86

Having completed the meal, Captain Ashton began the formalities of leaving. "André Didier, I commend you for delivering my son safely."

"It was my honor, sir." André remembered his fantasy of receiving accolades in front of an appreciative audience—and shook his head. *Better than the money or hollow honors, I've gained in wisdom. While I'm relieved that we located his father, I am sad to see the boys go.*

"Daniel, thank your leader," his father said.

Danny stood stiffly, trying to obey. He extended his hand to André. "*Merci beaucoup, Monsieur* André. Thank you for bringing me to find my father. You were good to me and I shall always remember you."

"*Adieu.* Goodbye and good fortune. When I saw the river through your eyes, I remembered my first voyage," André said, shaking his outstretched hand.

Michel tucked a small whistle into Danny's hand. "I made this for you."

Danny turned it over in his fingers, a smile breaking through. He tried the whistle, tootling a little.

But Pretty Mouse hunched under the lobbed tree, his head bowed in his arms, shaking. Danny ran to hold him, bawling without restraint. They formed a tight ball of wailing sorrow. "I can't leave you, *Monsieur Souris*. You're my best friend ever."

After several moments, Henry touched his arm. "Come now, Danny. Time for you to go."

Danny and Pretty Mouse did not release their holds.

Captain Ashton cleared his throat.

"*Non, non*, not without *Monsieur Souris*."

The soldiers and canoemen quietly loaded the canoes, alert to their captain's inability to command his son's obedience.

"*Monsieur Souris*, I can't leave you."

Danny's howling was painful to everyone. But no one knew how to end it.

Henry tapped Captain Ashton's sleeve, pulling him aside. "If you please, sir, I have a suggestion."

André stood next to Pretty Mouse. "Mouse, stop this. Get a grip on yourself."

Pretty Mouse glared at him. "A moment, Dannee." He unwound his arms, daubed at Danny's wet eyes with his sash and sent the boy to help the *voyageurs* load. He rose angrily.

"Surely you realize Danny must go with his father," André said. "Besides, it's early. We could paddle more miles today. And we never did talk about where to look for work. We could head back to either Michilimackinac or Sault Ste. Marie. I've got a good record, even if yours ... ."

Pretty Mouse squared his shoulders and leaned toward André, his jutting jaw inches from André's. "I'm not going with you. I quit."

"Quit? You can't quit."

"I can. We delivered Dannee to his father. That was the deal. I'm done. Pay me."

"But ... what are you going to do?"

Their voices were loud and strident. André sensed that others were listening.

"Me, I'll figure it out. You talked about what you'll do afterwards, but did you ask me? *Non*. You assumed I'd go wherever you said. You expected to decide for me what I should do. I'm tired of it. I won't take it any more."

André's anger surged. "But I depend on you."

"Depend—hah! You used me—flattering me into being *devant* so I couldn't say *non*. But steering wasn't good for me.

I'm a singer and cook. You pressed me into guiding. I never asked for that."

"I let you become our *gouvernail*. You liked being in charge, being important."

"Let me? That's a joke. You paid off my contract. What else could I say?"

"I thought you'd be honored to steer."

"I was. But you nagged at my every mistake. You watched me like a hawk every time I took a sip of high wines."

Both were yelling now, too furious to care that they'd become a spectacle.

"Too much high wine is what caused your problem."

"But not this problem. You never noticed when I refused a taste. *Non*. A lot you know about other people's problems, what makes them scared or hurt. Don't smother me with your rules."

André looked stricken. "I meant it for the best. I didn't mean to lord any rules over you."

"Oh, but you did. Every day. Me, I can deal with rules, but worse, you didn't pay attention to Dannee. I'm a man—I know what to do. You ignored the boy because you were busy being the important leader. That shows me who you are deep down."

"Me ignore him? That's a lie."

"Starting our first day, who showed him Ste. Anne's shrine? Who found him maple sugar or dried meat to eat when he was hungry? Who walked with him so he'd be comfortable in the woods? Who held him when he was sad—did you ever notice that? Who taught him cooking, singing, trading, everything? Who watched over him on portages? Not big André. You were too busy being in command to notice what he needed."

"That's over now. He's going to his father."

"He doesn't know anyone there. You remember what that military fort felt like? How will a little boy survive there, with his father working long hours? You don't care."

André had no answer. He hadn't thought much about Danny like Pretty Mouse had. What he said was true.

"So I quit. Pay me."

"But I need you, Mouse. You've been my friend all these years."

"*Oui*, you saved me from that scum Basile Roche. You took him on at the height of his powers when you were but a kid. Me, I was grateful and I loved you for it. But now I'm only your puppet. How have you returned friendship? On this trip you've become Basile—or worse."

"How could I be Basile? He's dead. I'm sure of that."

"The way Roche had to be the big man. He controlled things and used people to get what he wanted—that part you've kept."

André took a step back. Bitter words rose, but he shut his mouth. Memories of the rivalry with Roche rushed through André. *Basile was cruel, manipulating, power-hungry, uncaring of the pain he inflicted on others. That's how Mouse sees me. Am I like that—wanting to be so important that I didn't take time for people, like Danny? Could I have become someone I despised? How do I untangle this?*

He looked at the ground, the trees, the sky, the river, any place but at Pretty Mouse. His eyes began to prickle with tears and he couldn't breathe. He scrunched his lips to stem the pain.

He swallowed and briefly raised his eyes to Pretty Mouse.

"Oh." André hung his head.

Chapter 87

Henry's voice broke in. "The soldiers have made a space for Pretty Mouse to paddle. They are waiting to leave."

Both spun around. Danny was holding his father's hand, his eyes still wet. He reached for Pretty Mouse. "Oh, *Monsieur Souris*. Henry has arranged it. You can live with us at the fort."

Captain Ashton nodded. "If you would, it would help Daniel to settle in. It may be some time before we can find a permanent housekeeper."

The news sank in.

"Mouse, I'm sorry." André extended his hand. "I wish I'd done this better. I don't like what you said, but it's true."

Pretty Mouse grabbed it and they held for a moment. Then their other arms swung around and they bear-hugged.

André poured out a heap of coins for Mouse. "*Devant, gouvernail*, singer, cook, teacher to Danny—and friend to me. It's still not enough."

The *voyageurs* and soldiers cheered. Some clapped each other on the shoulders while others paid off bets.

Michel carried Mouse's paddle, pack and blanket to the soldiers' canoes.

Pretty Mouse swung Danny up in the air, whirled him into the canoe and climbed alongside, paddle at the ready.

"*Adieu*, Pretty Mouse. You're the best mate I ever could have had." André felt hollow, unready for Mouse to leave.

"*Au revoir*—we'll meet again. You know how to find me. Write a letter to Dannee—he can read it to me."

They watched the canoes speed away, Danny singing with high-pitched glee, until they could no longer hear the song.

"Let's go." André's order was halfhearted. Pretty Mouse's truths and his desertion made sense, but they hurt.

"*Non*, André. We have to talk," Michel said. "Everything has changed."

When André turned, he saw Henry and his baggage still on the riverbank.

"I suppose I have you to thank for Mouse leaving. As Danny's companion, why aren't you with him?" André didn't veil his sarcasm.

"The boy needed a friend—but it was not me," Henry answered. "So I explained to Captain Ashton how Pretty Mouse could tend to Danny. You told us the fort had no one to care for him—who could be better than Pretty Mouse? And, as Michel said, things have changed. We have decisions to make."

"We? You're deciding things now? You weren't even willing to paddle before." Raw from his set-to with Pretty Mouse, André lashed out.

"Yes, I am deciding. We'll head to Prairie du Chien, but we need a plan."

André bristled at Henry's imperious announcement.

"Henry is right that we need a plan. Since we're clearing the air, I have a few things to say," Michel said.

"You, too?"

"With only two of us to paddle, I've suddenly become an equal partner. You don't have a choice."

"Michel, did Pretty Mouse speak the truth?"

Michel fidgeted, and finally let out a long, slow breath. Then he raised his head and looked squarely into André's eyes.

"*Oui*. You asked me, so I will say it. *Oui*. I was grateful to be included, so I kept quiet. But this whole journey you made sure everyone knew I was new, untried. I ate last, carried the heaviest packs, stood longest in the water, slept where no one else wanted to sleep. I watched and learned, I offered help whenever I could, I supported you—but you didn't notice. You kept your distance, like I wasn't as smart as you, because you'd been asked to organize this. You're not the André I thought I knew."

André hid his face to mask his pain. He could barely breathe.

"You used to be friendly, kind, not superior though your family could pay for schooling and the rest of ours couldn't. But you're not much of a friend."

Like Basile? Superior? Distant? Not friendly?

"I'm not going to quit," Michel said. "For one thing, I can't paddle this by myself. For two, there's Henry. For three, I like this country. I'm not going back to the village—this life suits me. Gabriel and Baptiste and Pretty Mouse found new lives. Here I can make something of myself that I couldn't back east."

André couldn't meet Michel's eyes. He took short hiccuping breaths.

Michel noticed. "You're all bottled up, André—you need to move. Check out the portage. Climb that lopstick. Yell. Cool your head in the water. Whatever time it takes won't make any difference. When you return, we'll talk. I have more to say."

◊ ◊ ◊

Relieved to disappear, André spun around and disappeared on the portage trail. He plowed through thick rushes and branches that snapped in his face, until dense foliage made it difficult to move. Furious at their betrayals, he swore, yelled, dug for rocks to pelt. Panting, he dropped onto the ground and lay there.

I've been so focused on my own wants that I forgot about others. All my life I've been taken care of—Michel hasn't. Danny's mother just died, not mine. Mouse is alone—was. Now he has a place. And they told me I don't have friends. Michel and Pretty Mouse took a risk to tell me. How do I make it right?

◊ ◊ ◊

When he returned, André saw Michel standing by the lopstick tree, fingering the marks carved into its trunk.

André felt sheepish breaking the silence, but he took the initiative. "Thanks for being honest. I didn't like hearing what you said but I understand better. Can we still make it work?"

"Maybe. Who is Basile Roche?" Michel asked.

"A distant relative who was jealous of my family. He hid and pounced on my brother Denis and almost killed us both. But he got his due, I saw to that."

"You killed someone?" Henry backed away, startled.

"*Non*, I didn't kill him—he set traps for us. My brother and I got caught in more than one. A year ago he intended to drop a tree on me but it twisted and fell on him instead. That's how he died. It took most of a day to bury him."

Michel and Henry didn't move.

André looked from one to the other. "You think I could kill a person?"

"I had to ask about Roche, whoever he is," Michel said. "I need to know who you are. I'm not blindly following anyone."

"What do I need to do to prove myself?"

"Listen to my ideas, my questions. I want a friend who values me. If you can't do that, I leave the first opportunity I get."

It was the lifeline André needed. He met Michel's gaze. "I've been an idiot—but I'm lucky for this second chance. Before we left, my foster father said to trust my mates. Instead I kept trying to do this all myself. You'll tell me when I get too puffed up?"

"That I will. It's been quite the day. Now we're burning daylight, partner. Let's go."

"Not so fast. I too have things to say." Henry stood, his arms folded, his chin jutted out.

Chapter 88

"Why are you still here?" André was embarrassed that Henry had witnessed their outburst.

"Because Captain Ashton agreed I should go to Prairie du Chien. They'll have better transportation."

"Aren't you supposed to teach Danny about Latin and etiquette?" Michel was scornful.

"I taught him what I'd been taught, but Pretty Mouse's lessons were better. When his father hires a tutor, it won't be me."

"You didn't answer—why are you still here?" Michel and André stood shoulder-to-shoulder, like a wall.

"Danny's father said it would be best to travel on."

They waited.

"I don't like this any more than you do," Henry said.

"Something's fishy. You're not telling us everything," Michel accused.

"True," André added. "You gave him secret letters. What did they say?"

"It's not for you to know." Henry twitched anxiously.

"You sound like a spy. We tried to treat you fairly—at least at the beginning—but all you did is make life miserable. And now you expect us to obey you—I won't do it. André and I, we were honest with each other. If you don't own up, we won't help you." Michel turned his back in a huff.

André watched Henry. Something didn't add up.

"I ... I ... I apologize." It was hard for Henry to speak.

They waited but Henry was silent.

"I don't accept it. They're just words—you have no remorse." Michel was angry.

Henry added, "I was awful. That took a toll on everyone and I am sorry." He hung his head.

Michel turned around. He and André waited.

"Once you called me names—thistle, black fly, wolverine. They hurt but I deserved every one, every despicable thought you had. I was intentionally mean and hateful." Henry looked up.

This was a new Henry. They listened intently.

"Thank you for all you did to make this trip a success for Danny. And for Pretty Mouse, François, Reynard, Gabriel and Baptiste—you did your best for each of them. Now I ask your continued help. I have to do one more thing—and I need you."

"Back up. Why did you have to be mean?" André asked. "What possible reason could you have? We all feel mean sometimes but we don't act that way, especially to people we depend on."

Henry struggled. He examined a fingernail, frowned, rested his forehead in his hand. shook his head.

They waited.

He scrunched his face, shifted from from one leg to another, studied the earth by his feet, closed his eyes and exhaled.

Henry took a deep breath—he had made a decision.

"You don't know much about me. I've kept it secret and now I have to trust you. But it's hard."

He found a clean piece of sleeve to wipe dirt from his face. His eyes seemed bigger.

Taking off his over-sized *tuque*, he untied the band tightly wrapping back his hair. Long brown hair fell out, fluffed out.

He peeled off the top shirt he always wore. That left at least one shirt and trousers, which stayed on.

Beneath the streaks of dirt, freckles and rough hands, thick layers of clothes—and cloak of meanness—Henry looked like a girl, a girl who had hidden herself among them.

Michel gasped.

André was thunderstruck.

"I acted cross—mean—to keep you from getting close to me. I couldn't risk you learning I wasn't who you thought I was."

André said, "At the beginning, we thought maybe your family lost their income and became poor."

"People took pity on you and offered you this job," Michel added. "But who … who … are you?"

"Colonel Markham is my uncle. My name is Venetia Markham."

André stopped. "Your uncle is the colonel who hired me?"

Michel said, "You're not Henry Leonard?"

"To make sure you wouldn't guess, I sniped every time you tried to be kind or helpful. I do apologize."

Both André and Michel turned her words over.

"Why would a girl want to come out here?"

"Exactly. But Uncle couldn't find the right companion for Danny. At the same time, he had received letters that alarmed him —about problems arising here in the west. He needed to send word, but how? A courier by express canoe would be noted, and might not even arrive to deliver the message. It had to go with someone who wouldn't be suspected."

"I understand. To find Denis, I 'hid' in plain sight, among a brigade of Antoine's top *voyageurs*." The bitterness began to seep out of André.

She met his eyes. "Uncle had nobody else. Soldiers from the garrison couldn't carry this message—they're needed where they are. Uncle believed Danny's father—or the commander there—could solve this. Though you were already engaged to go to Fort St. Joseph, you couldn't deliver that kind of letter. So I volunteered and, of course, he refused. He was set against my coming—not safe, not suitable for a young woman. I insisted. I cut my hair, created a disguise and became a different person. That convinced him I could manage it. He suggested that I keep my distance so no one would guess. To be certain, I took it farther, and was downright harsh. The ruse did work—none of you saw the truth. But I am sorry, truly, that I made things so unpleasant." Venetia reddened in embarrassment.

"Henry always criticizing, pointing out our deficiencies—there was a reason."

Michel and André looked at each other. It made sense. Certainly, a girl traveling with a brigade would be noticed, and in danger. Her biting comments kept them at bay. Suddenly all that criticism was not their fault—it had been to protect herself.

"I knew you wondered about me. Every day it got harder to keep the secret. I was so tired of this double life I nearly gave it away more than once. So to cover myself, I snapped back with a vengeance. I made enemies of you all."

"That's why you always stayed in the tent."

"And didn't sing or paddle."

"And wouldn't carry at portages."

"And never came out in the native villages."

"And wouldn't visit Fort St. Joseph."

"And didn't learn to swim."

"I wanted to swim the day you taught Danny, but at least I can skip rocks, identify birds, animal tracks—things girls never get to do. Michel, you like this country—I do too. This is my only chance to see it because soon I'll be sent to live in England."

"Why to England?"

"Before I am to be married off, and girls of my class must be taught embroidery, singing and painting."

"Embroidery and painting?"

"Married? But you're too young."

"Yes, married. Likely within the year, or as soon as I complete what is called finishing school. Uncle has been writing letters on my behalf." Venetia grimaced.

It gave Michel and André pause.

"Thank you for baptizing me as a *voyageur*. Michel, you earned your spot in the brotherhood, and it couldn't have pleased Danny more. But you also accepted me, not realizing I ... wasn't a brother. I can't tell you how much I appreciated that."

"Venetia," André said quietly. "I accept your apology."

Chapter 89

"André can accept, but I don't. You have to prove it by your actions," Michel said.

André's face flushed with a flood of memories. Had he proved his apology to Michel by his actions?

Such stupid grandiose dreams I had of being honored for my heroism, cleverness, attention to duty. I imagined accolades, bags of coins thrust at me in gratitude and the respect of the British military. Empty gestures, all of them. Instead I wanted Denis to acknowledge me an equal adult, though I'm not, at least yet. To affirm Father Goiffon's recommending me. To show my foster parents how I'd followed in the ways they'd raised me.

"On this journey, I tried to prove I could make a success of it so Colonel Markham would see that I'd done his task well, that I deserved his confidence."

"Uncle would be pleased—you provided the adventure of Danny's life, connected him to his father and gave him a friend in Pretty Mouse."

"I was lucky. This crew helped in a hundred ways."

"True. You often balked at accepting help, but Uncle would have approved, mostly," Venetia said. "He believed you could rethink poor decisions and change your plans. It's a quality he prizes and the reason he took a chance on you, though he worried you were too young to undertake such a responsibility."

André started to puff up. "Too young? I ..."

She interrupted. "Early on, it was a battle of wills between you and any other good idea. But you did catch on. After François convinced you to try the Muskrat River instead of the *Grand Calumet*, you listened better."

"At first I assumed François was always bragging, but he was a godsend. And so was Reynard's quiet confidence," André said. "Even Baptiste and Gabriel knew a thing or two at the right time. But Michel, you were the best pick. From the very first day you had my back."

Michel grinned.

"I never thought that 'Henry' might need our kindness," André said. "It irritated me when you were right so often. I felt foolish being corrected. I wanted to be important. Fear of looking stupid got in my way."

She waited. "I'm listening."

"Venetia, I apologize," André began haltingly. He hadn't realized how hard begging forgiveness was. "I felt so threatened that … I wasn't a good leader. You had a secret to keep, but I didn't have to be the way I was."

Michel interrupted. "André, you focused on being the leader and didn't pay attention to the rest of us. But you weren't mean and we didn't need babying. You had our goal in mind."

"Did your uncle say what he was worried about?" André probed.

"No, Uncle said it was safer if I didn't know."

"Can you guess what was in the message?" Michel asked.

"I'm not at liberty to say."

"That's not fair!" Michel snapped.

"It's not like you think." She bit her lip, pondering."You two became equal partners. Am I also one?"

"But this forces us to collaborate with you," Michel said.

"We already are, collaborating, and equal partners," André said. "I used to think collaborating was when you told a dirty secret about someone to get better treatment. Maybe it's just working together for the best."

"*Merci*," Venetia said slowly. "War. Another war is what Uncle fears most. England is very anxious about the colonies. Americans went to war about what they felt were high-handed taxes from the Mother Country. Natives feel the tension—and these last weeks I've learned how our settlements have created problems. All that could start a war."

André gazed the empty river where toward Captain Ashton's men had departed. "True, we've heard rumors. Fears that Indians might rise up and side with the British or Americans instead of the French. Which sides are allies now? Would it affect this country, here?"

"We might be called to serve as soldiers," Michel said.

"More than anyone, Danny will champion the cause of peace to his father," Venetia said. "If there is hope of lasting peace between our countries, it will come through people like him who can understand all sides."

The thought of war troubled them.

"Unfortunately, Uncle didn't realize how slowly we would travel when transporting a child. Captain Ashton said the letter came too late. He'd already uncovered the same information—that an American expedition was sent to survey the Mississippi River. It's why he left Fort St. Joseph before we arrived."

"And needed to return quickly, to pass information to his superiors. He learned something," André guessed.

"Uncle said the United States has been busy organizing expeditions. More than a year ago, many men were sent to explore new territory all the way to the far ocean. They haven't returned—maybe they won't, nobody knows. A second group, led by a Zebulon Pike, is to find the source of the Mississippi."

"So Captain Ashton wanted to observe them."

"Which is why they were dressed like *voyageurs* and the captain like a merchant," André added.

"Like Venetia dressing as Henry—they could gather more information by not being who they really were."

"Captain Ashton left Prairie du Chien shortly after Pike's expedition continued northward. Though we're too late to observe this Pike, we might learn something useful. I will write to Uncle about what I've seen."

"What's at Prairie du Chien?" Michel asked.

"I don't know. Probably a North West Company trading post, maybe a military post," André said.

"Here's another problem," Venetia said. "Since the treaty, it's on American land, not British. But North West Company is British-owned, and the French-Canadians run it."

"Does that make a difference?" Michel asked.

"It's the reason the *rendezvous* moved from Grand Portage to the New Fort on the Kaministiquia River. Things are changing, with or without war."

They pondered the consequences for some time.

Finally Venetia broke the silence. "The entire journey I've wondered how to undo this secret identity. My original plan was to tell you about myself at Fort St. Joseph, but after François hurt his leg, that would no longer work. Since then, I've struggled with when and how to become a girl again. That day at the Fort, I saw a girl wearing a dress, perhaps she was a *voyageur*'s daughter. Starting tomorrow I'll become someone like her."

"You have a dress?"

She nodded. "It's one reason I never let you see what all I carried in my trunks."

"Why did Captain Ashton mean about having better transportation at Prairie du Chien? To where?" André asked.

"To St. Louis, because I must arrange passage to New Orleans, and then to Montreal, hopefully before winter sets in. If it doesn't feel safe to travel to St. Louis, would you please consider accompanying me? I have enough money to hire you."

André and Michel looked at each other. "We'll help you figure it out when we get there. Does that seem reasonable? You too, Michel?"

"What did they carve on this tree?" Michel asked.

Venetia pointed to "Captain Ashton" and "Sept. 1805" while Michel traced the letters in wonder.

"Michel, we could teach you to read, if Venetia still has some of her books. If you want to, that is," André said.

Michel fought the tears that filled the corners of his eyes. "More than you know, I want to read. Would you?"

André reached out his hand to shake Venetia's.

She smiled.

"*Merci*," Michel said. "All three of us are partners?"

André glanced at the sun. "It's getting late. Let's camp here tonight, make a new start in the morning."

"What about supper—is there anything left in the kettle?"

"*Non*. Those soldiers, they ate it all."

They looked at Venetia.

"Danny learned to make pea soup but I didn't. I was trained like André, Latin and history, geography and mathematics. Cooking—no."

"Another place to be equal partners," André said. "My turn tonight."

About *voyageurs* and the fur trade

Each spring, beginning in the mid-1600s, hundreds of French-Canadian *voyageurs*, having signed contracts as *engagés* for up to five-year terms, paddled birch bark canoes into the great wilderness, called the *pays d'en haut*.

The owners of the fur trade, the *bourgeois*, determined at which fur trade post each *voyageur* would work and for what wages. Contracts also identified a canoe position: most paddlers were middle or *milieu* (plural *milieux*), the least skilled. The *devant*, the most skilled man, steered from the front or bow while the second in command, the *gouvernail*, steered from the rear.

Voyageurs paddled whenever possible, but in shallow or rocky areas with dangerous current, they needed to *décharge*, towing the canoe upstream using ropes, or to *portage*, carrying a canoe and all its cargo on their backs across rough trails.

The company furnished meals of pea soup each day on the trip from Lachine, so when they reached the interior, *voyageurs* looked forward to *rubaboo*, a stew made from foods that natives produced—dried corn and *pemmican*, which was made from dried bison meat.

Voyageurs hauled immense amounts of goods to trade over winter with indigenous tribes for their furs. To reach the tribesmen, voyageurs paddled river systems throughout Canada and the U.S. In mid-summer, *voyageurs* gathered at a *rendezvous* to resupply their trade goods and send back the furs, while the owners and partners, the *bourgeois*, planned for the upcoming year.

◆ ◆ ◆

Glossary of French-Canadian terms

Note: Although this book is written in English, try to imagine that all the voyageurs' conversations were in French. To hear how they sound, visit my website at www.nikkirajala.com.

une, deux, trois, quatre,	1, 2, 3, 4,
cinque, six, sept, huit, neuf	5, 6, 7, 8, 9,
dix, onze, douze, treize	10, 11, 12, 13
quatorze, quinze, seize	14, 15, 16
dix-sept, dix-huit ...	17, 18, ...
deux cents cinquante-six	256
deux cents quatre-vingts	280

Adieu.	Farewell.
aigle	eagle
Allons-y.	Let's go.
Au revoir.	Good bye (until we meet again).
Au secours!	Help!
beaucoup des framboises	many raspberries
bleuets	blueberries
Ce ne sont pas des bleuets.	They're not blueberries.
Ce sont des ...	They are ...
C'est lui.	It's/That's him.
C'est vrai.	It's true.
Comment?	How?
Comme ça.	Like this.
devant	lead paddler, in charge of the canoe
Encore une fois.	Again.
Et moi aussi.	And me too.
gouvernail	stern paddler, second in command
huards	loons
Ici.	Here.

J'ai seize ans.	I am 16 years old.
Je suis André.	I am André.
Je suis un voyageur.	I am a voyageur.
Là-bas	Over there.
loutres	otters
maskinongé	muskellunge
milieu (milieux)	middle paddler/s, the least skilled
Moi? Porquoi?	Me? Why?
Monsieur	Sir, Mr.
Mon suisse	My chipmunk
mouches noires	black flies
moustiques	mosquitoes
Nous sommes des voyageurs.	We are voyageurs.
orginal	moose
ourse	bear
petit serpent	little snake
poisson	fish
Regardes-moi.	Look at me.
renard	fox
ratons laveurs	raccoons
Réveillez-vous.	Get up.
S'il vous plait?	Please?
tortue	turtle
tuque	knitted cap worn by voyageurs

A few Ojibwe words

To hear native speakers say these words, visit the Ojibwe People's Dictionary at https://ojibwe.lib.umn.edu.

miigwetch	thank you
maang	loon
naabe-mooz	bull moose
pemmican	dried pulverized buffalo meat with fat and dried berries
wattap	spruce root used to stitch birch bark canoes
wiindigoo	an ogre

Other animals André's crew would have seen:

beaver	*amik*
bear	*makwa*
deer	*waawaashkeshi*
fox	*waagosh*
lynx	*bizhiw*
muskellunge	*masshkinoozhe*
mink	*zhaangweshi*
otter	*nigig*
raccoon	*esiban*
woodchuck	*akakojiish*

A few favorite books on the fur trade

"The Illustrated Voyageur: Paintings and Companion Stories" by Howard Sivertson. Lake Superior Port Cities, Inc. (Duluth, Minnesota, 1999).

"The Voyageur" by Grace Lee Nute. Minnesota Historical Society Press (St. Paul, Minnesota, 1987).

"Five Fur Traders of the Northwest" Charles M. Gates, ed., Minnesota Historical Society (St. Paul, Minnesota, 1965).

"Making the Voyageur World: Travelers and Traders in the North American Fur Trade" by Carolyn Podruchny. University of Nebraska Press (Lincoln, Nebraska, 2006).

"Where Two Worlds Meet: The Great Lakes Fur Trade" by Carolyn Gilman. Minnesota Historical Society Press (St. Paul, Minnesota, 1982).

See my website (www.nikkirajala.com) for additional resources.

THANK YOU

I appreciate so much:

the expertise of many who answered my questions on the fur trade and the historical resources which make this research fun;

supportive friends and family who encouraged me throughout;

my astute advance readers—Kathy Knudson-Mestnik, Jean Leiran, Charlotte Stephens and my sisters Mary Rajala and Kris Rajala;

Benedictine Sister Hélène Mercier for French-Canadian language comments, Mary Rajala for wilderness medical treatments, Patrick Mestnik for Latin;

Jenni Grandfield, for her photograph of Colin Pendziwol and friends at Fort William Historical Park;

Carol Jessen-Klixbull, for top-flight copy editing;

and Bill Vossler, my most exacting reader and best friend.

www.ingramcontent.com/pod-product-compliance
Lightning Source LLC
LaVergne TN
LVHW091631070526
838199LV00044B/1017